WITHOUT
a DOUBT

Other books by Kenneth Richard Samples

Prophets of the Apocalypse: David Koresh and Other American Messiahs
(with others)
The Cult of the Virgin: Catholic Mariology and the Apparitions of Mary
(with Elliot Miller)
*Lights in the Sky and Little Green Men: A Rational Christian Look at UFOs
and Extraterrestrials* (with Hugh Ross and Mark Clark)

Saved by grace (Eph. 2:8-9)

Regards,

Ken Samples

WITHOUT a DOUBT

ANSWERING THE 20 TOUGHEST FAITH QUESTIONS

KENNETH RICHARD SAMPLES

BakerBooks

Grand Rapids, Michigan

© 2004 by Kenneth Richard Samples

Published by Baker Books
a division of Baker Publishing Group
P.O. Box 6287, Grand Rapids, MI 49516-6287
www.bakerbooks.com

Second printing, November 2004

Printed in the United States of America

Library of Congress Cataloging-in-Publication Data
Samples, Kenneth R.
    Without a doubt : answering the 20 toughest faith questions / Kenneth Richard
  Samples.
         p.   cm.
    Includes bibliographical references and indexes.
    ISBN 0-8010-6469-4 (pbk.)
    1. Theology, Doctrinal—Popular works. 2. Apologetics. I. Title.
  BT77.S26 2004
  239—dc22   2004003422

To Joan Ann Samples:

My wife, my companion, my best friend, and the mother of our children.
This book would not have been written without your constant support
and loving encouragement.

CONTENTS

TABLES

FOREWORD

Writing a book is easy if a person overcomes three obstacles. The first of these is the first sentence. The second is the last sentence. And the third is everything in between. Ken Samples knows how to do that job. He has identified twenty questions which every Christian ought to be able to answer. And, he provides good, solid responses to them.

Without a Doubt crosses the boundaries of several disciplines: theology, apologetics, and philosophy, to mention only three. It presents a wealth of information regarding basic faith questions for a wide variety of readers. A long time ago when I served several churches as a pastor, having this book would have been a big help to me. The material in it could also have improved any number of sermons I've heard over the last fifty years.

When you've been around as long I've been, you know this information is somewhere. But where? Chances are a person can find what they are looking for in this resource. *Without a Doubt* can be helpful to laypeople who are looking for solid material to share with students. And speaking of students, I can easily think of several college and seminary courses that could be improved by using Samples' book as a text.

I trust by now I've made it clear that I have a high regard for this resource and its author. Ken Samples is a fine teacher and scholar who knows how to handle tough questions and lays their answers out in a way easy to absorb.

Dr. Ronald Nash
Southern Baptist Theological Seminary
Louisville, Kentucky

11

ACKNOWLEDGMENTS

Many people have helped me both in my life's journey and in the writing of this book. My parents assisted me in innumerable ways. My father's valor on the battlefields of Europe during World War II taught me the importance of courage, honor, and self-sacrifice. I have tried to shape my life around these important values. On the other hand my mother always modeled for me a simple and sincere Christian life of faith, hope, and love.

In terms of preparing this manuscript, my children Sarah, Jacqueline, and Michael were a big help. Sarah skillfully helped with some of the word processing tasks. Jacqueline kept me well supplied with iced cold drinks during my many hours of writing. And Michael retrieved books from my library and was an enthusiastic supporter. Thanks, kids, for your patience during my writing marathon. My love for my family is the *sine qua non* of my life.

Strong editorial support for this book came from a number of individuals. My friend and colleague Robert M. Bowman, Jr. edited the manuscript and significantly improved its quality both stylistically and in terms of its arguments. The Reasons To Believe (RTB) editorial staff also worked hard to improve its quality and readability. Warm thanks go especially to Patti Townley-Covert for her diligent editorial work. Special thanks as well go to Tani Trost, Marj Harman, and Joe Aguirre for proofreading and checking the manuscript and notes. In addition, Baker editor Paul J. Brinkerhoff provided insightful editorial counsel. Working with him has been an enormous pleasure. A special thanks goes to Baker's acquisitions editor Robert Hosack who strongly supported this project.

Thanks as well to my apologetics colleagues at Reasons To Believe who offered me helpful input and/or support on the project, including Dave Rogstad, Fuz Rana, Krista Bontrager, Bob Stuart, and Ken Hultgren. I also appreciated the helpful assistance of Sandra Dimas and Phillip Chien.

I'm especially grateful for Kathy Ross's enthusiastic support of this book project and for her keen editorial wisdom. And special thanks go to Reasons To Believe's president Hugh Ross, who graciously allows me to work for and with him in RTB's exciting apologetics endeavor.

To have Ronald Nash write the foreword to this book is truly an honor. He is one of the great Christian philosophers of our time, and I have significantly benefited from reading many of his outstanding books.

Little of the apologetic content of this book is actually original with me. I therefore owe a debt of gratitude to the many fine Christian apologists and scholars (both past and present) that I have quoted and/or referenced in this volume.

I appreciate my friends at Augustine Fellowship who have supported and encouraged me over the years, including: Dave Andrews, Wes Hoffmaster, Robert Dargatz, and Martin Schramm.

I would also like to acknowledge some of my friends at Christ Reformed Church in Anaheim, California, who have encouraged me, including Henry Nowakowski, Cliff Steele, Jeff Sikkema, Glen Bulthuis, Vince Martinez, Lloyd Cadle, Gino Lucero, and Winona Taylor. In addition, I am very grateful to the consistory of Christ Reformed Church along with its pastor Kim Riddlebarger for allowing me to teach our congregation many of the things in this book during my weekly Sunday school class. It is an honor to serve with them.

Much appreciation goes to my friends and colleagues at Cerritos College, in Norwalk, California, who have taught me much about philosophy over the years, including Douglas Wessell, and Joseph van de Mortal. And thanks to two of my former students (now friends) who have supported this writing project: David Aubuchon and Jose Villalobos.

To my friend and West Point graduate, Pete Pilet, "duty, honor, country."

With gratefulness and love to my dear wife Joan, to whom this book is dedicated.

Finally, praise and gratitude forever to the Triune God: Father, Son, and Holy Spirit.

Faith Seeking Understanding,
Kenneth Richard Samples

INTRODUCTION
Playing Twenty Questions with Life

Who am I? Why am I here? Does God exist?

Is there meaning to life? How should I live my life? Is there life after death? These "ultimate questions" have perplexed and challenged thinking people in all generations, including me.

Unaware of any significant and enduring meaning or purpose to life, I felt a deep sense of emptiness growing in me as a teen. Going from one activity to another I desperately hoped somehow to "find myself." In California where I grew up, I competed in baseball and basketball, listened to the Beatles and hung out with my friends. Some nights we'd sit around a campfire by the Seal Beach pier trying to figure out the answers to life's questions. And though I enjoyed these activities, they never really allowed me to escape the unsettling feelings of meaninglessness and boredom that at times seemed to stalk me.

The French thinker Blaise Pascal (1623–1662) said that much of human life is taken up with acts of diversion. In my case, the attempts didn't help and only left me with an inner sense of estrangement. My older brother's premature death intensified these rather desperate feelings.

This angst drove me to desire something deeper and more significant, and I continued contemplating the "big questions." During my first year in college, my older sister gave me a copy of *Mere Christianity* by C. S. Lewis. It sat on my shelf untouched for many months. One day, however, I picked it up and began to read. Lewis, an astute thinker, presented a clear case for Christianity. For the first time I understood the basic message of the gospel. I grasped who Jesus Christ is (the God-man) and what he came to Earth to accomplish (the redemption of lost sinners). Many of the arguments Lewis marshaled in defense of the Christian faith (particularly his moral reasoning) brought me fresh insight, moral conviction, and intellectual challenge.

Deciding to purchase a Bible for myself, I began reading the New Testament—something I'd never done before. Thoroughly engrossed, I studied Scripture for at least a couple of hours every day for months. On one occasion I read the entire book of Acts at a single sitting.

This pursuit of answers culminated on a warm summer evening when I knelt by my bed and confessed to almighty God that I was (and am) a sinner in need of his grace and mercy. I finally believed that Jesus Christ is the divine Son of God, the Lord and Savior of the world.

Although I was never confirmed, as a young child I had sporadically attended the local Catholic church, so now every weekday morning I got up early and went to church before heading on to my college classes. Hungry for spiritual truth I often attended two different services on Sunday mornings. My thinking, motives, intentions, goals, and behavior began to change drastically. My closest friend since first grade described the change in my life as "the difference between night and day."

But the courses I took in religion and philosophy still left nagging questions. No one seemed able to answer them. Skeptical philosophers' responses to Christian truth-claims especially bothered me. The local priest told me that if I read the Bible too much I would become "burned out." He said I shouldn't be so concerned with the "intellectual content" of my faith. (I learned later that his thinking did not reflect the historic Catholic view which has had a deep and abiding commitment to an intellectually satisfying faith.)

It was important to me to have my questions answered, especially as I learned more about the Christian faith. I needed both to assure my heart and to satisfy my mind. This meant the need for an integrated faith—my beliefs had to comport with the truths I was learning in school. However, at times I began to wonder whether Christianity could stand up to rigorous philosophical, scientific, and historical analysis. This intellectual insecurity created some serious tension in my life.

During my second year in college three people came into my life and offered me guidance. Walter R. Martin, a Christian scholar who hosted a popular call-in radio program called the "Bible Answer Man," had what seemed to be an encyclopedic mind. He answered questions over the radio for an hour each day. I listened to the show regularly and even called in several times and spoke with him. Hearing and writing down his answers helped me think carefully about my faith. Several years later I had the privilege of working closely with Walter as a research consultant for the organization he founded, Christian Research Institute (CRI). After his untimely death, I served as one of the regular cohosts of the "Bible Answer Man" program—ironically answering some of the same questions I'd asked myself only a few years earlier. The time I spent on the air underscored for me how important it is for people to have their questions answered.

John Warwick Montgomery, another radio-show personality, also challenged my thinking. A Christian theologian, historian, and attorney, Montgomery hosted a weekly call-in program, "Christianity On Trial," that dealt exclusively with apologetic questions—queries about the truth-claims of Christianity. Montgomery's wealth of knowledge, biting wit, and passion for defending the faith made the show not only educational but also entertaining. Reading his books and listening to his tapes and lectures, I began to realize that Christianity has nothing to fear from philosophic, scientific, or historic scrutiny. In fact, the more I learned, the more I began to understand that of all the world's religions, Christianity uniquely stands up to honest intellectual inspection.

Professor Douglas F. Wessell, then chairman of the philosophy department at Cerritos College in Norwalk, California, also taught me much. After class I'd follow this skilled teacher into his office and pester him with dozens of questions. A veritable fountain of knowledge in both philosophy and religion, he spent hours with me patiently explaining reasonable answers. Doug was deeply infected with the "disease" known as the "love of wisdom"—philosophy! I quickly contracted the same disease and for the past thirteen years have had the privilege of passing it on to my students at the very same college. Doug's passion for Reformation theology also profoundly influenced my own theological views. (Today, I am unswervingly committed to the truths of historic, Protestant confessional theology, the Reformed theological tradition in particular.)

One important truth Doug taught me transformed my Christian life and in part has led me to devote a good portion of my adult life to the Christian apologetics enterprise—teaching, writing, and debating. *God is pleased with us when we think* (see chap. 20). Using our God-given intellectual faculties honors the Creator. It is the scandal of our current church era that so many Christians actually believe being intelligent and well-educated is somehow unspiritual. In reality, the mind plays a critical role in theology, evangelism, apologetics (the defense of the faith), and even in one's everyday devotion to God.

A Question-and-Answer Book

Perhaps in coming full circle I now address many questions about the truth of the Christian faith. Whether asked over the radio, on television, during a debate, in class, or while instructing my own children—whatever the forum—these questions are important. And so are the replies. It is my humble prayer that God will use this question-and-answer primer to challenge readers to think through the Christian faith.

The book is written not only for the Christian, but also for the skeptic, the seeker, and any person considering the claims of Christianity and who wants satisfying responses to his or her questions. In it I have tackled real, tough questions—the kinds of questions thinking people ask. The topics are often framed in the form of an objection and they cover a broad range of subjects. Sometimes the reading may become challenging—but tough questions deserve thorough answers and at times philosophical details are important. If one topic seems more intriguing than another, a reader can feel free to read the chapters in any order.

The first part of this book answers questions that pertain to knowing God. The second section addresses questions regarding Jesus Christ. The final portion responds to analytic, scientific, and ethical objections to the historic Christian faith. In order to make information as accessible as possible (especially for those not familiar with the Bible) parenthetical lists of Scripture references have been included in the text. Reading the indicated verses will greatly enhance biblical understanding; so they have not been relegated to endnotes. It is my hope that the reader will turn the pages of this book with one hand and the pages of Scripture with the other. Discussion questions and suggested reading lists at the end of each chapter are intended to challenge the person who wants to explore a topic further.

For those who may wonder what methodological approach to apologetics I embrace, let me say I'm mildly eclectic. I've been exposed to various methodologies: historical evidentialism, classical apologetics, presuppositionalism, the new Reformed epistemology, and other integrated approaches. While I've learned from each distinctive apologetics method, I doubt that I fit neatly into any one particular camp. Some may think that I am inconsistent or unclear in my thinking because of this blend. However, the history of Christianity is very rich in providing apologetic material, and I am glad to have many tools at my disposal. The same need to constantly examine arguments in light of Scripture and sound reasoning exists for me as it does for anyone. If any label is applicable to my apologetic thinking, perhaps deeply Augustinian fits best. Augustine (AD 354–430) is widely considered the greatest theologian of the first one thousand years of Christian church history. In this author's opinion, Augustine anticipated many of the insights contributed by later apologetic schools.[1]

The twenty questions in this book are ones I've wrestled with for many years. They've also been asked of me often. Studying, pondering, and discussing them have brought assurance to my heart and satisfaction to my mind. May God grant you the same as you consider historic Christianity's tried and true perspectives.

Soli Deo Gloria,
Kenneth Richard Samples
Easter 2004

PART ONE

THINKING THROUGH QUESTIONS ABOUT FAITH IN GOD

1

How Can Anyone Know That God Exists?

I believe in Christianity as I believe that the sun has risen, not only because I see it, but because by it I see everything else.

——C. S. Lewis, *The Weight of Glory and Other Addresses*

Human beings are never neutral with regard to God. Either we worship God as Creator and Lord, or we turn away from God. Because the heart is directed either toward God or against him, theoretical thinking is never so pure or autonomous as many would like to think.

——Ronald H. Nash, *Worldviews in Conflict*

Does God exist? Did he create man or did man create him? The question of God's existence may be the ultimate of what philosophers call the "big questions of life." What people perceive as real, true, right, valuable, and meaningful is dramatically influenced by their view of whether God is real or not. Since this perspective forms the context of an overall worldview, the atheist and the Christian view all of reality in different ways. For the Christian, the God of the Bible defines the ultimate context for all life and thought (see chap. 16). Are there valid reasons to believe he exists?

A Meaningful Reality

A good hypothesis, be it scientific or philosophical, is accepted because it possesses real explanatory power. The God of the Bible (hereafter referred to as God) provides a solid and consistent metaphysical foundation for explaining the important realities and phenomena encountered in life in at least nine specific ways.[1]

God uniquely accounts for the physical universe's beginning.

Two powerful lines of scientific evidence lead to the conclusion that the universe had a beginning.[2] First, according to prevailing scientific theory, the universe had a singular beginning about 14 billion years ago. All matter, energy, time, and space came into existence and rapidly expanded from an infinitesimal volume. This hot big bang (which continues to expand in an extremely fine-tune fashion) gradually cooled and diffused sufficiently to allow for the formation of galaxies, stars, planets, and so forth. The basic big bang cosmological model, which is embraced by the vast majority of research scientists because of the accumulation of extensive astronomical evidence and successful testing,[3] demonstrates that the universe is not eternal, but had a specific beginning a finite period of time ago.

Second, the Law of Entropy (also referred to as the Second Law of Thermodynamics) provides further confirmation that the universe had a beginning. This well-established principle indicates that the energy in the universe is being dissipated gradually and equally in all places. Thus a time will come, if nature takes its course, when "thermal equilibrium" (all locations in the universe manifest the same temperature)[4] will inevitably result and all physical activity will cease. If the universe were eternal this halt would have already happened by necessity. Therefore, the principle of entropy supports the view that the universe has been in existence only a finite period of time.

In light of the compelling scientific evidence that the universe had a definite beginning, the question asked by German mathematician and philosopher Gottfried Leibniz (1646–1716) is all the more stimulating: "Why is there something rather than nothing?"[5] Why indeed? Knowing that the universe had a singular beginning a finite period of time ago makes it very difficult to sidestep the simple but compelling logic in the *Kalam* Cosmological Argument:

1. Whatever begins to exist has a cause for its coming into being.
2. The universe began to exist.
3. Therefore, the universe has a cause for its coming into being.[6]

Given the nature of the effect (the contingent universe), it is logical that the cause or Creator would have to be transcendent, uncaused, eternal, and immutable. (Any cause that did not have these characteristics would itself need a cause, for the very same reason this universe needs one.) Such a deity, by definition, matches the general description of the God of the Bible but not of most other religious conceptions of god.[7] And the biblical creation accounts comport well with the findings of modern science concerning cosmology (see specific details in chap. 14).

Are there possible explanations for the beginning of the universe that don't involve a divine Creator? Yes, and they are worth considering.

The first option is that the universe somehow caused or created itself. This conclusion, however, is irrational because in order to create itself the universe would have to exist before it existed—a clear absurdity. Something cannot both exist and not exist at the same time and in the same way.

The second option is that the universe popped into existence from nothing and by nothing (or from no one). This concept, however, is also irrational because something cannot be derived from absolute nothingness (no energy, no matter, no power, no mind, no reason, and so forth). An effect cannot be greater than its cause, and in this case the cause would be nothing. The old scientific and philosophical maxim *ex nihilo nihil fit* makes sense—"from nothing, nothing comes."[8] To conclude otherwise is to violate one of the foundational principles of the scientific enterprise: causality.

A third, and exotic, quasi-scientific option is to conclude that there are multiple universes (sometimes called multiverse[9]). This position suggests an eternal mechanism of physics may actually pop universes into existence one after the other. This provocative view, however, is not based on any direct observable data, but instead on theoretical speculation. As a highly speculative and nonfalsifiable hypothesis, this view offers no viable challenge to the notion that the universe had a beginning.

A fourth option is to consider the cosmologies of other religious traditions, specifically those of the East. However, the cosmologies of Eastern religion can be dismissed rather quickly for they are incoherent and do not comport with the best scientific evidence concerning the origin of the universe.[10] For example, strands of Hinduism deny the very existence of the physical universe.

To return to the option that God is the personal causal agent behind the universe, the scientific evidence for the beginning of the universe matches well with the teaching of the Bible. "In the beginning God created the heavens and the earth" (Gen. 1:1). The Christian doctrine of *creatio ex nihilo* teaches that there was nothing but God (an infinite, eternal, personal spirit), and that God by means of his incalculable wisdom and infinite power alone brought the universe (all matter, energy, time, and space) into existence from nothing (not from any preexistent physical reality such as matter) and sustains its existence moment by moment (Rom. 4:17; Col. 1:16–17; Heb. 11:3). The God of the Bible is therefore the transcendent Creator and the providential Sustainer of the universe. God is the necessary metaphysical explanation for the existence of a contingent (caused, dependent, unexplained) universe.

God uniquely accounts for the order, complexity, and design evident in the universe.

Even the staunchest atheist would admit that the universe exhibits amazing order, regularity, complexity, and intelligibility. However, the general acceptance of the anthropic principle (the view that nature's laws appear to be fine-tuned to ensure the emergence of human life) by the scientific community has heightened the intuition that the universe is the product of a cosmic Designer.[11] The astonishing intricacy, harmony, and organization of the cosmos in allowing for human life is evidenced from the fine-tuning of the fundamental constants of physics, to the "just-so" nature of the galaxy and solar system, to the information-laden building blocks known as the DNA code, to perhaps the crowning teleological (relating to design) achievement: the incredible and delicate complexity of the human brain-mind relationship.

If a person rejects the logical intuition that a cosmic Designer stands behind the universe, then he or she must conclude that all the order, complexity, and intelligibility contained in the universe ultimately results from chance and coincidence. Yet this naturalistic, evolutionary, atheistic option is so extremely improbable as to be inconceivable. The sheer statistical probability of the universe coming into existence by chance with the properties that would support life would be utterly staggering.[12]

But the improbability of the naturalistic, atheistic position isn't the only thing that makes it rationally untenable. Embracing the grand evolutionary view that the sensory organs and cognitive faculties of human beings are the result of random and purposeless natural process raises an issue of trust regarding that which is observed. Does one's observations and thoughts actually correspond with reality?[13] As a matter of reasonable practice, a person doesn't typically accept the idea that information, knowledge, and truth can come from a random, accidental source. How can such rational enterprises as logic, mathematics, and science be reasonably justified when the human brain and mind are the result of a nonrational, mindless accident? Naturalism, in effect, purports that life, the mind, personhood, and reason came from a source that lacked each of these profound faculties and qualities. This would certainly be an effect much greater than its cause!

In table 1.1 two explanatory models show the plausibility of the atheistic and biblical positions:

Table 1.1
Naturalistic and biblical models
for explaining life and the universe

Naturalistic atheistic model:	Biblical theistic model:
a. world created from nothing	a. world created by a Creator
b. life from nonlife	b. life from ultimate Life
c. persons from the impersonal	c. persons from the Superpersonal
d. minds from the mindless	d. minds from the ultimate Mind
e. order from the orderless	e. order from an Orderer
f. reason from the nonrational	f. reason from a rational Being
g. morality from the nonmoral	g. morality from a moral Person
h. information without a sender	h. information from a Sender
i. code from a nonprogrammer	i. code from a personal Programmer
j. truth from an accident	j. truth from ultimate Truth

God uniquely accounts for the reality of abstract, nonphysical realities.

Some of the most important and wondrous realities of life cannot be detected by the human senses. These abstract, intangible realities are conceptual in nature and consist of such things as numbers, propositions, sets, properties, the laws of logic, moral values, and universals. They are considered by many to be objective, universal, and invisible.[14] They clearly don't appear to be physical in nature nor are they readily reducible to, or explainable in terms of, physical matter and its processes. Materialism as a metaphysical theory faces some insurmountable logic problems.[15] These conceptual entities also don't appear to be the product of mere human convention (invention). Consider two brief examples.

First, the objective nature of numbers. The notion or idea of "nineness" (symbolized by the number 9) was discovered and certainly utilized by the human mind, but clearly wasn't invented by the human mind. The reality of nineness is demonstrated in such statements as "The nine planets in the solar system existed prior to the emergence of the first human mind." At least nine planets in the solar system existed prior to man's recognition of this fact (and even prior to man's existence). But if nineness existed prior to the first human mind, then it requires a conceptual foundation.

Christian thinker Augustine of Hippo (AD 354–430) argued that the human mind apprehends universal, objective, unchanging, and necessary truths superior to the human mind itself.[16] Since truth must reside in a mind, Augustine reasoned that these eternal truths are grounded in the eternal mind of God. Thus an eternal God exists to explain these eternal truths.

Second, the fundamental laws of logic (for example, the laws of non-contradiction, excluded middle, and identity) are not a product of human convention. The principle of noncontradiction (nothing can both be and not be at the same time and in the same way) is not only cognitively necessary and irrefutable, but it is ontologically true, that is, it defines the very nature of reality itself.[17] Logic also appears to need a foundation beyond the mind of man.

Since mathematics and logic (the foundations of science) have validity and provide human beings with real knowledge about the world, then these two conceptual disciplines couldn't be about merely subjective and man-made notions; they must be dealing with objective realities. But if these abstract entities are invisible, nonphysical, objective realities, then how can they be accounted for appropriately? Surely the naturalistic worldview—belief that the physical universe is all that exists—isn't adequate to account for them.

The Christian theistic worldview, however, grounds these conceptual realities in the mind of an infinite, eternal, and personal spiritual being. God is the Creator of both the visible and the invisible, the source of both the sensible and the intelligible (Ps. 148:2–5; Col. 1:16–17). In a Christian conceptual framework, God serves as the metaphysical foundation that adequately accounts for these critical conceptual and epistemological entities (independently existing realities).[18]

God uniquely accounts for the reality of objective ethical values.

Moral values are a fundamental part of human life, every bit as real as the law of gravity. And people are generally intuitively cognizant of their moral obligations. In the human heart, people readily experience the pull of real moral duty and obligation. This sense of moral oughtness is indeed prescriptive in nature, and transcends mere subjective feelings and individual considerations (see chap. 18 for a refutation of the claims of moral relativism). People may conveniently deny or attempt to rationalize or even violate their moral obligations (see chap. 11 on the doctrine of sin), but they are nonetheless a necessary part of human life. Basic moral intuitions such as "It is wrong to murder" or "It is right to be loving, truthful, courageous, and compassionate" testify to the truth of objective moral values. These values appear to stand as distinct from, and independent of, the human mind and will. In other words, they are discovered, not invented.

But what accounts for the existence of objective, universal, unchanging moral principles? What guarantees their validity? And what is their source and foundation?

Objective moral values are logically incompatible with all forms of ethical relativism, including naturalistic, atheistic, evolutionary theory. Ethical relativism is incoherent and cannot serve as an acceptable moral theory. In the absence of a morally perfect, personal God morality can only be conventional, arbitrary, and subjective in nature.

Objective ethical principles do exist, but they cannot exist in a metaphysical vacuum. What is morally good (ethical) cannot be separated from what is real (metaphysical) and what is true (epistemological). But atheism has no foundation upon which to ground man's conscious awareness of moral obligation. Without God, objective moral values have no metaphysical anchor and thus cannot be accounted for.

Unlike secular attempts to account for morality, the ethics of Christian theism are grounded in the morally perfect nature of God who has specifically revealed his will to mankind. God is therefore the source and foundation for objective moral values (see chap. 18 for an explanation of God's relationship to ethics). Absolute moral law extends from the cosmic moral Lawgiver. The God revealed in the Judeo-Christian Scriptures is the morally perfect person who stands behind the objective moral order discovered in the universe.[19]

God uniquely accounts for the meaning, purpose, and significance that human beings sense and yearn for.

If God doesn't exist and the universe is a mere product of blind, purposeless, natural processes, then there can be no objective meaning to life. Given that perspective, the fact that people exist is simply an amazing accident of evolution. Human beings live on this planet for a very short period of time and then cease to exist (permanent extinction). With this forlorn naturalistic outlook, the only meaning and purpose that humans could possibly enjoy is what they subjectively create for themselves. Yet in light of imminent personal death, along with the inevitable extinction of the human species and the death of the entire physical universe due to entropy (the loss of available energy to perform work), can there be any genuine meaning, purpose, significance, and value in life, even in a temporary way?

In light of this question, atheists tend to be divided into two camps, some optimistic and some pessimistic. Optimistic atheists tend to strongly emphasize the perceived benefits of atheistic belief (for example, personal autonomy). However, atheistic existential philosophers such as Jean-Paul Sartre (1905–1980) and Albert Camus (1913–1960) say that reflection upon this scenario (meaning and purpose) leads to philosophical angst, despair, and dread.[20] Man is, according to the atheistic existentialist, alone in the universe, and alone to face his cosmic existential predicament.

Yet three things in human beings conflict with this godless and nihilistic perspective. First, most human beings intuitively sense that their lives have real and objective meaning and purpose. Perhaps people simply lack serious philosophical reflection upon their condition in life, but even if they are not happy with the content of their individual lives, humanity in general lives with the sense that something meaningful is going on behind the scenes.

Second, people yearn for a meaning and purpose that extends beyond the grave. For most people, this desire for and pursuit of an ultimate meaning extends to a belief in life after death, usually involving belief in God. While human beings may possibly engage in a cosmic form of wishful thinking, anthropology and sociology reveal that humanity has always possessed a deep spiritual intuition of eternal significance—virtually from the first day of human existence. This intuition is unique to humanity and extremely difficult to explain in terms of Darwinian evolution. It is fair to say that the search for meaning and purpose is one of the defining characteristics of the species known as *Homo sapiens*. The American philosophical theologian Paul Tillich (1886–1965) has suggested that everyone, including atheists, seeks an ultimate concern in life.

Third, if the world is actually meaningless then human life is equally meaningless. But this concept creates a great dissonance in thought. How could people living in a meaningless world come to the amazingly meaningful recognition that the world has no meaning? As Christian thinker C. S. Lewis pointed out, meaningless creatures would never discover the truth of their own meaninglessness.[21] Is man's unique ability to reflect about the meaning of life a strong hint that there is indeed something deeper to life?

Man's deep sense of, and need for, meaning comports well with the Christian truth-claim that God created human beings in his image and that man's greatest need is to be reconciled to God and to enjoy fellowship with him forever (see chap. 11). The unique gospel of gracious redemption in Christ offers genuine meaning, purpose, and significance to sinners estranged from God, from each other, and from themselves.

God uniquely accounts for man's sense of the divine.

Scripture reveals that human beings at their core know there is a God. God created human beings in the expressed image of himself with a built-in awareness of the Creator (see chap. 3). He also created an environment for humans that triggers and supports this inner sense of God. This divine consciousness is therefore evident to people based upon powerful external and internal factors. Externally, God's existence, power, glory, and wisdom are evident to mankind, being manifest in the cosmic cathedral that surrounds him—namely the universe (Ps. 19:1–4). Internally, human beings are intimately aware of moral accountability to their Maker through their conscience (Rom. 2:14–15).

Though people see, understand, and know there is a God to whom they are directly morally accountable (based upon these external and internal factors), nevertheless man in his state of sin suppresses the truth of this awareness (Rom. 1:18). Sinful human beings thus suffer from an intellectual and spiritual tug-of-war, both desiring and resisting God at the same time. While made for the specific purpose of fellowshipping with his Creator, sinful man nonetheless refuses to acknowledge the true God or accept moral accountability before his Maker. God intends to judge unbelievers on the basis of this powerful external and internal revelation (Rom. 1:20). Man's greatest need, therefore, is redemption (to be reconciled to God).

This inherent and intuitive sense of the divine, if indeed rooted in truth, explains much about humanity. It accounts for mankind's deep-seated religious and moral impulse, as well as the universal phenomenon of religious experience. Some have referred to humans as *Homo religiosus* because of our basic religious tendencies and nature. In general, atheism appears to be quite contrary to basic human nature. The biblical view of mankind's sense of the divine matches well with human experience and behavior.

God uniquely accounts for the enigma of man.

An important criterion for accepting a religion as true is its ability to account for and explain the critical realities encountered in life. One of those chief realities is the enigma of man himself. Christian thinker Blaise Pascal (1623–1662) in his classic work, *Pensées*, described man as an unusual mixture of "greatness and wretchedness," being at the same time both the "glory and rubbish of the universe" (see chap. 6).

Human nature poses a puzzling paradox. While capable of great things in the areas of mathematics, science, technology, philosophy, the arts, humanitarian and charitable acts, and so forth, humanity is also equally capable of shameful and evil acts—rape, robbery, racism, slavery, and mass murder. Explaining human nature poses an extraordinary philosophical, psychological, and spiritual challenge.

Yet, the Bible holds the secret to unraveling the enigma of man.

The Christian theistic worldview asserts that man's greatness is a direct result of the *imago Dei*. As a creature made in the image and likeness of God, man reflects the glory of his Maker, thus he is God-like in many respects, especially when compared to the animals.

The wretchedness, on the other hand, can be traced to the first human beings' fall into sin (Genesis 3). Adam misused his freedom to rebel against God and as a result he suffered alienation from God and became pervasively sinful. Adam's sin, however, affected more than just himself. Biblical doctrine makes clear that the entire human race inherited guilt and moral corruption from the first man, Adam (Ps. 51:5; 58:3; Rom. 5:12, 18–19; 1 Cor. 15:22). In this present state of sin, man is capable of using his gifted qualities for evil purposes.

Neither the naturalistic worldview nor the alternative religions of the world do as good a job as the Bible of explaining the world's greatest riddle—mankind.

God uniquely accounts for the claims, character, and credentials of Jesus Christ.

According to the historically reliable documents of the New Testament (see chap. 7), Jesus of Nazareth made unparalleled claims to divine authority during his public ministry (see chap. 8). He equated himself with Yahweh (God). In fact, he made both direct and indirect claims to deity. For example, in the Gospel of John Jesus referred to himself several times as "I am," which (in the way he used it) is clearly one of the most sacred of divine expressions from the Old Testament and practically the same as claiming "I am God." (Compare Jesus' use of this expression in John 8:24, 28, and 58 with statements made by Yahweh in Isaiah 41:4; 43:10, 13, 25; 46:4; 48:12.)

The Jews at the time certainly understood this as a claim to deity because they attempted to stone Jesus for the sin of blasphemy (John 8:59). Similarly, in the Gospel of Mark, Jesus openly claimed to be the Messiah by stating that he possessed the privileges of deity (Mark 14:61–64). Jesus' indirect claims to deity are evidenced by his unique invoking of divine prerogatives (actions reserved for God alone). For example, he received worship (Matt. 4:10; 28:16–17), forgave sin (Mark 2:1–12), declared himself the final judge of humanity (John 5:22, 27), and even asserted his ability to raise the dead (John 5:21). These unprecedented claims to deity caused Jesus to be arrested, convicted, and crucified for the specific charge of blasphemy. He claimed to be God in human flesh. No other leader of the world's major religions ever claimed to be God. But are there good reasons for accepting Jesus' divine claim?

Jesus had excellent credentials to back up his claim to deity. Consider four brief points.

First, Jesus fulfilled dozens of very specific Old Testament prophecies concerning the identity, mission, and message of the coming Messiah.[22] These prophecies (written hundreds of years before Jesus' own birth) gave precise details concerning the birth, heritage, life, and death of the long awaited Messiah. Many of them were beyond Jesus' natural human ability to fulfill. The chance probability of all these prophecies' coming true in the life of Jesus is utterly staggering.

Second, according to the well-attested Gospel records, Jesus was a prolific miracle worker.[23] He healed incurable diseases, restored sight to the blind, multiplied small amounts of food to feed thousands of people, calmed storms, walked on water, and even raised the dead. And Jesus' enemies didn't question the authenticity of his miraculous acts. While an antisupernatural bias often keeps modern skeptics from carefully considering the life and actions of Jesus, such a bias shouldn't stand in the way of accepting remarkable events if those events are well established historically. It's reasonable to conclude that if God exists (certainly a rational viewpoint), then he would perform miracles if he came to Earth.

Third, Jesus exhibited a matchless moral character during his three-year public ministry that succeeded in changing the world forever. Family members, intimate friends, and staunch foes could not find any genuine moral fault with him. Not only did Jesus' teachings contain incredible ethical insight, but he fulfilled their lofty moral ideals. Jesus' pristine personal moral example and profound teachings succeeded in laying the foundation for much of the ethical theory embraced and practiced throughout Western civilization, even among non-Christians. A compelling reason for concluding that Jesus was indeed God incarnate is that he was so fundamentally different from every other person that ever walked on Earth. Even the world's great philosophers and religious leaders like Socrates, Siddhartha Gautama (the Buddha), Confucius, Moses, and Solomon pale in comparison to him. No one has impacted the world for good as Jesus of Nazareth did.

Fourth, the New Testament documents record in great detail firsthand testimony of Jesus' resurrection from the dead (see chap. 10). The apostles went to their graves (sometimes as martyrs) claiming to be eyewitnesses of Jesus' bodily resurrection. They specifically claimed to have seen, heard, and touched the risen Jesus on numerous occasions. The New Testament records a dozen such appearances.

Roman and Jewish authorities could not refute the resurrection. Support is also found in the empty tomb, Christ's many postcrucifixion appearances, the transformation of the apostles from cowards to zealots (even martyrs), the dramatic conversion of Saul of Tarsus into the apostle Paul, the historic emergence of the Christian church, the change in the official day of worship to Sunday to commemorate resurrection day, and the fact that all alternative naturalistic explanations for this event fail miserably (see chap. 10).

Jesus' credentials as the divine Messiah (Yeshua haMachiach) are indeed formidable: fulfillment of Old Testament prophecy, the performance of numerous miracles, matchless personal character, an incalculable influence upon history, and bodily resurrection from the dead. This evidence leads to one astounding conclusion: Jesus Christ is God. We do not have to doubt God's existence—he made himself known in Jesus of Nazareth. In fact, God came to Earth to be with us. Thus, the only genuinely reasonable explanation for the historical life, death, and resurrection of Jesus is that he was God in human flesh. In the historical person of Jesus Christ, God climactically and decisively made himself known to humanity.

God uniquely accounts for the meaningful realities of life.

All previously stated points compiled can be viewed as even stronger evidence for God's existence.

The meaningful and necessary realities require an adequate explanation. An acceptable worldview possesses genuine explanatory power and scope. One of the strongest evidences that Christian theism's truth-claims are correct is their ability to account for and justify the many, diverse, and undeniable realities of life as discussed above. Yet a final collective argument merits consideration.

A Cumulative Case

The arguments in this chapter appeal to the existence of the God of the Bible as a means of explaining reality (reasoning to the best explanatory hypothesis). These arguments can also be viewed as a cumulative case of compelling evidence for the God of the Bible. That is, while each individual argument has a certain logical or evidential force of its own, taken collectively the arguments have an ever increasing probative force in favor of the existence of God.

In light of the extraordinary realities present in the world and in human life, it makes very good sense to believe that the God of the Bible is the foundation for all reality and truth. For as the Scripture says:

> Anyone who comes to him [God] must believe that he exists and that he rewards those who earnestly seek him. (Heb. 11:6)

And yet, how can people believe in a God they can't see? This question is the topic of the next chapter.

Discussion Questions

1. How does belief in God provide a philosophical foundation for the meaningful realities of life?
2. Why does the universe require a causal agent to explain its existence?
3. Why couldn't the meaningful realities of life have come from a random, natural accident?
4. How does Christianity explain the human condition better than other worldviews?
5. On what basis can a person be convinced that Jesus Christ is God?

For Further Study

Boa, Kenneth D., and Robert M. Bowman Jr. *Faith Has Its Reasons: An Integrative Approach to Defending Christianity*. Colorado Springs: NavPress, 2001.

———. *20 Compelling Evidences that God Exists: Discover Why Believing in God Makes So Much Sense*. Tulsa, OK: River-Oak, 2002.

Evans, C. Stephen. *Why Believe? Reason and Mystery as Pointers to God*. Grand Rapids: Eerdmans, 1996.

Kreeft, Peter, and Ronald K. Tacelli. *Handbook of Christian Apologetics: Hundreds of Answers to Crucial Questions*. Downers Grove, IL: InterVarsity, 1994.

Miethe, Terry L., and Gary R. Habermas. *Why Believe? God Exists! Rethinking the Case for God and Christianity*. Joplin, MO: College Press, 1999.

Miller, Ed L. *God and Reason: An Invitation to Philosophical Theology*. 2nd ed. Upper Saddle River, NJ: Prentice Hall, 1994.

Moreland, J. P. *Scaling the Secular City: A Defense of Christianity*. Grand Rapids: Baker, 1987.

Moreland, J. P., and William Lane Craig. *Philosophical Foundations for a Christian Worldview*. Downers Grove, IL: InterVarsity, 2003.

Swinburne, Richard. *Is There a God?* Oxford: Oxford University Press, 1996.

2

How Can I Believe
in a God I Can't See?

Now faith is being sure of what we hope for and certain of what we do not see . . . By faith we understand that the universe was formed at God's command, so that what is seen was not made out of what was visible.

—Hebrews 11:1, 3

That which was from the beginning, which we have heard, which we have seen with our eyes, which we have looked at and our hands have touched—this we proclaim concerning the Word of life. The life appeared; we have seen it and testify to it, and we proclaim to you the eternal life, which was with the Father and has appeared to us.

—1 John 1:1–2

If God exists, why can't I see him? If he made an appearance and people could actually see him—or if I could see him do a miracle—then I'd believe. But otherwise, I can't believe in God. I only believe in what I see." This common concern raises questions about what is real (metaphysics) and how a person can know reality (epistemology). Two questions in particular come to mind: Is it reasonable to believe in anything a person can't see, especially an invisible God? And if God does exist, why didn't he make it obvious so everyone can believe in him? Tackling such questions about God's so-called lack of visibility actually underscores Christianity's distinctive doctrinal truth—that God has uniquely appeared in the world.

Reasonable Belief

The viewpoint reflected in the statement "I only believe in what I see" expresses a certain limited approach to the nature of reality. This metaphysical theory (view of reality) assumes that all reality can be reduced to, or explained by, physical matter—a crass form of materialism. In other words, for something to exist (be real), it must be visible. If visible to the eye, then it must be physical in nature.

This perspective also expresses how reality can be known. Christian philosopher J. P. Moreland calls this approach "crude empiricism."[1] *Empiricism* is the epistemological theory (view of knowledge) that knowledge comes exclusively through the five senses (seeing, hearing, smelling, tasting, touching).[2] *Seeing is believing* represents a crude form of empiricism because it is limited and unsophisticated in nature.

Consider the five following criticisms of this epistemological view:

1. "I only believe in what I see" is a self-contradictory statement.

A self-contradictory statement both affirms and denies its own basic meaning. Moreland points out that "the proposition 'I can believe in only what I can see' cannot itself be seen."[3] The underlying metaphysical and epistemological principle of "what is real is visible," is *not* visible! The statement, "I only believe what I see," expresses a conceptual principle distinct from the literal written sentence and is therefore neither visible to the eye nor detectable by the rest of the senses. Thus, to accept the statement "I only believe what I see" demands acceptance of a principle that cannot be seen. Put another way, if a person actually believed the declaration "I only believe what I see," then he or she would not believe the statement itself, because the belief cannot be seen. The statement "I only believe what I see" reduces to absurdity.

2. Many of life's most important realities cannot be seen.

A second major problem with claiming to believe only what a person sees is that many things that actually exist cannot be observed. A number of science-related entities cannot be seen but, nevertheless, are still considered a necessary part of reality. Magnetism, gravity, electricity, electrons, and neutrinos, to name just a few. Moral values such as justice and goodness exist, but they cannot be seen. People judge human actions to be evil or good, without actually seeing these values. The concept of truth is an undeniable invisible reality. Love, an indispensable reality of life, remains unseen. Feelings and emotions surely exist, but cannot be empirically observed in a direct manner.

Careful philosophical reflection shows that critical abstract entities such as numbers, sets, propositions, and properties cannot be seen. Yet they are real. These invisible realities need a metaphysical foundation. Christian philosopher Alvin Plantinga offers a provocative comment about the abstract nature of numbers:

> It seems plausible to think of numbers as dependent upon or even constituted by intellectual activity. But there are too many of them to arise as a result of human intellectual activity. We should therefore think of them as . . . the concepts of an unlimited mind: a divine mind.[4]

In contrast to the view that God doesn't exist because he can't be seen, many theistic philosophers reasonably presume his invisible existence as the necessary philosophical foundation for other undeniably real abstract entities. The Christian worldview asserts that what is visible actually depends upon what is not visible.

A central weakness of all forms of materialism, including its most simplistic form, is its inability to account for the transcendent components of life. This defect is uniquely true in relationship to cognitive or conceptual elements. We cannot see our thoughts, and although the brain is observable, the mind is not.[5] But we don't doubt the reality of either. For a person to deny the existence of the mind and thoughts because they are unobservable is considered irrational.

Are the formal laws of logic (laws of noncontradiction, excluded middle, and identity) physical, material, or visible? No. Yet these nonphysical, immaterial, invisible laws are realities[6]—the very anchors that make human rationality and the world's intelligibility possible.

Initially it may seem reasonable to believe in only those things that can be detected by the senses. However, upon serious reflection, this position lacks the explanatory power to account for even the most fundamental realities of life. This physicalist viewpoint is instead the height of irrationality.

3. The scientific enterprise depends upon things that cannot be directly observed.

Scientists committed to naturalism (nature is ultimate reality) often say, or imply, "I only believe in what can be observed empirically, or what can be inferred from what is empirically observed." This statement is also self-contradictory. Christian philosopher Greg L. Bahnsen echoes Moreland's earlier comment: "The proposition 'I only believe in what can be observed empirically, or what can be inferred from what is empirically observed' cannot itself be derived from empirical observation!"[7] The view that nature alone exists is not and cannot be derived from scientific inquiry. Rather, it is an unempirical presumption or dogma of secularism that too often interferes with scientific inquiry.[8]

Carl Sagan declared in the opening to his enormously popular PBS television series, *Cosmos*: "The cosmos is all that is, or ever was, or ever will be." Yet Sagan's bold naturalistic and atheistic assertion cannot be derived merely from the inductive scientific method which he so idolized.[9] In fact, a growing scientific consensus affirms that the careful study of the universe reveals a finely-tuned cosmos (big bang cosmology, the anthropic principle)—which necessitates an ultimate and intelligent causal agent beyond it.[10] The operation of science presupposes a number of foundational truths not wholly derived from science itself. In order for the scientific enterprise to work and thrive, certain nonempirical assumptions about the world must be true (see chap. 14).

4. "I can't believe in a God I can't see" commits a category error.

J. P. Moreland defines a category mistake and explains why insisting upon seeing the biblical God falls into that error:

> A category fallacy is the fallacy of assigning to something a property which applies only to objects of another category. For example, it is a category fallacy to state the color of the note C. Sounds are not colored. Similarly, it is a category fallacy to fault colors for not having a smell, universals for not being located at only one place, and God for not being an empirical entity. God, if he exists at all, is by definition (in orthodox Christianity) an infinite Spirit. It is not part of the nature of a spirit to be visible empirically as a material object would be. It is a category fallacy to ascribe sensory qualities to God or fault him for not being a visible object.[11]

Moreland notes the historic Christian position that God is an infinite eternal Spirit. If there is good reason to believe in the truth of Christian revelation (how God has revealed himself), then a person should be prepared to receive God on his terms. To insist that the Creator meet the creature's epistemological requirements may be presumptuous and spiritually misguided. Although intellectual testing, discernment, and logical reflection are perfectly appropriate in attempts to verify religious claims, the creature may want to exercise humility in recognizing that the Creator, if he exists, may be quite different in nature than his creation and may have his own sovereign plans for revealing himself.

5. Belief in God as an unseen explanation for the phenomena of the universe is justified.

Theoretical (unseen) realities are often postulated in order to explain what is seen. In science, theories are developed to explain a diversity of natural phenomena. The case is similar in the field of philosophy. The best explanatory theories (in science or philosophy) are balanced between complexity and simplicity, are coherent, correspond to the facts, avoid unwarranted presumptions, are testable, yield predictions, and thus possess true explanatory power. The existence of the biblical God (an infinite, eternal, and personal Creator and Redeemer) explains many things that, without belief in him, are very difficult to account for. Oxford philosopher Richard Swinburne argues for God's existence as an explanation for the complex phenomena found in the world.

> Scientists, historians, and detectives observe data and proceed thence to some theory about what best explains the occurrence of these data. . . . We find that the view that there is a God explains everything we observe, not just some narrow range of data. It explains the fact that there is a universe at all, that scientific laws operate within it, that it contains conscious animals and humans with very complex intricately organized bodies, that we have abundant opportunities for developing ourselves and the world, as well as the more particular data that humans report miracles and have religious experiences. . . . The very same criteria which scientists use to reach their own theories lead us to move beyond those theories to a creator God who sustains everything in existence.[12]

Belief in the God of Christian theism explains well the vast array of realities in human experience (see chap. 1 on God's existence). These realities extend to the universe (its existence, order, and uniformity), abstract entities (numbers, propositions, and the laws of logic), ethical principles (universal and objective moral values), human beings (their existence, consciousness, and rationality), and religious phenomena (the miraculous events of Christianity). Thus while God's essence can't actually be seen, his existence can be inferred as an explanation for the necessary realities of life. However, God's existence is not naively assumed as an explanation for human ignorance (a "god of the gaps" presumption), but rather as a genuine and valid explanatory theory for the nature of reality. Skeptical philosophies of life have real difficulties in explaining and justifying these realities.

The five points discussed show that to reject God's existence because God cannot be empirically observed is unreasonable. However, some still think that if God exists, he has failed to reveal himself sufficiently.

An Obvious Existence

Understanding the nature of revelation—the disclosure of something either previously unknown or not yet fully known—answers the complaint that God didn't make his existence obvious so that everyone would believe in him. Historic Christianity consists of the traditional beliefs and teachings of Christianity as found in the Judeo-Christian Scriptures and aptly summarized in the ancient historical creeds of Christendom (see chap. 4). As such, historic Christianity is a religion of revelation. In this sense, revelation refers to the self-disclosure of God. Christianity proclaims that God has revealed himself unmistakably and meaningfully to mankind in two distinct ways: in his general revelation in nature and conscience and in his special revelation in Scripture and ultimately in Jesus Christ (see chap. 3). God's general revelation alone states conclusively that "God's invisible qualities—his eternal power and divine nature—have been clearly seen, being understood from what has been made, so that men are without excuse" (Rom. 1:20).

So what about those who claim that the evidence for God's existence is insufficient? Some people argue that for those who are spiritually aware and open-minded there is ample evidence for belief in God's existence, but enough ambiguity remains that a spiritually insensitive and close-minded skeptic can, at least in his mind, justify unbelief. Biblically speaking, the noetic (cognitive and/or belief-forming faculty) effects of the Fall (Adam's rebellion) have blinded the minds of people to God's existence (Eph. 2:1–3; 4:17–19).

Without sin, God's existence would be overwhelmingly obvious to all. Nonbelievers fail to see that, from a biblical perspective, the hardness of their hearts (a spiritual and moral denseness) keeps them from believing in God. Their unbelief is rooted in rebellion and arrogance, which essentially is false worship (1 Sam. 15:22–23). Such evil produces idolatry and immorality. Though God has given powerful signs of his existence, the skeptic intentionally ignores and/or represses them (Psalm 14; 19; Romans 1). Nonrational human factors such as pride and a desire for autonomy often stand in the way of belief in God. Mere rejection of God does not prove that his existence is somehow insufficiently revealed.

Direct Contact with Humanity

People who say they would believe in God if he made an appearance might consider the uniqueness of Jesus Christ. Of all the world's religions, only Christianity makes the historically verifiable claim that God has entered the world of time and space. The doctrine of the incarnation (see chap. 9) teaches that Jesus Christ came into the world clothed in human flesh—the one and only *theanthrōpos* (God-man) (see John 1:1, 14; Phil. 2:6–8; Col. 2:9).

New Testament scholar Craig Blomberg comments on the historical nature of the incarnation: "Biblical faith is fundamentally commitment to a God who has intervened in the history of humanity in a way that exposes his activity to historical study."[13] The Gospels disclose the life of Jesus Christ and purport to reveal historical events (see chap. 7). While the apostles could not actually see Jesus' divine nature (for God in his essence is an infinite tri-personal Spirit), they nevertheless inferred his deity from his matchless personal character, fulfillment of messianic prophecy, and his miraculous works (especially his own resurrection; see chap. 10). They also claimed to encounter empirically the resurrected Christ. The apostle John writes that he saw, heard, and touched the risen Lord (1 John 1:1–3). The other apostles had similar experiences (Luke 24:36–43; John 20:24–31; Acts 9:1–9).

The great Christian thinker C. S. Lewis encourages reflection upon the reality of God's making an appearance in the world:

> The Second Person in God, the Son, became human himself, was born into the world as an actual man—a real man of a particular height, with hair of a particular color, speaking a particular language, weighing so many stone. The Eternal Being, who knows everything and who created the universe, became not only a man but (before that) a baby, and before that a fetus inside a Woman's body.[14]

(The purpose of his appearance is discussed further in chapter 9.)

Human eyes cannot see many critically important things that are undoubtedly true. Metaphysically speaking, the unseen lays the foundation for the seen. As an infinite, eternal spiritual Being, God's essence cannot be seen. However, that doesn't mean God didn't sufficiently reveal himself to humanity. Jesus' claim to Philip explains: "Anyone who has seen me has seen the Father" (John 14:9). Further clarification of how God has revealed himself is addressed in the next chapter.

Discussion Questions

1. Why is the statement "I only believe what I see" self-contradictory?
2. Why are abstract, nonempirical realities more compatible with Christian theism than with naturalism?
3. How is God's existence preferable to atheism as an explanation for the world and life?
4. How does the Christian view of revelation respond to the visibility objection to God's existence?
5. How does the doctrine of the incarnation make Christian revelation unique?

For Further Study

Erickson, Millard J. *The Word Became Flesh: A Contemporary Incarnational Christology*. Grand Rapids: Baker, 1991.

Montgomery, John Warwick. *History and Christianity*. Minneapolis: Bethany, 1965.

Moreland, J. P. *Scaling the Secular City: A Defense of Christianity*. Grand Rapids: Baker Book House, 1987.

Reymond, Robert L. *Jesus, Divine Messiah: The New Testament Witness*. Phillipsburg, NJ: Presbyterian and Reformed, 1990.

Swinburne, Richard. *Is There A God?* Oxford: Oxford University Press, 1996.

3

HOW HAS GOD
REVEALED HIMSELF?

We are bringing you good news, telling you to turn from these worthless things to the living God, who made heaven and earth and sea and everything in them. In the past, he let all nations go their own way. Yet he has not left himself without testimony: He has shown kindness by giving you rain from heaven and crops in their seasons; he provides you with plenty of food and fills your hearts with joy.

—Acts 14:15–17

Without special revelation, general revelation would be for sinful men incomplete and ineffective. . . . Without general revelation, special revelation would lack that basis in the fundamental knowledge of God as the mighty and wise, righteous and good, maker and ruler of all things.

—Benjamin Breckinridge Warfield,
The Inspiration and Authority of the Bible

How does a person know God exists? If he does actually exist, what can be known about his person, nature, and attributes? And how does God relate to the world?

The historic Christian answer to these questions is found in the doctrine of revelation. This teaching describes the disclosure of something either previously unknown or not fully known. The Christian faith proclaims that God took the initiative to dynamically and decisively reveal himself. Christianity is thus a belief system based on God's self-disclosure and teaches that revelation is necessary for an individual to genuinely know God. Evangelical theologian Millard J. Erickson explains why this revelation and subsequent relationship must be initiated by God: "Because humans are finite and God is infinite, if they are to know God it must come about by God's manifestation of himself."[1]

According to historic Christianity God has revealed himself in two distinct ways: through his world (general revelation—knowledge of God via the created order) and his Word (special revelation—knowledge of God via redemptive history). We can briefly explore the Christian concept of dual revelation by examining two important passages of Scripture and by considering how the two forms of revelation, God's world and his Word, relate to one another.

Christian Theology's Concept of Dual Revelation

Theologians have expressed a wide range of conflicting views over the centuries concerning the concept of a divine dual revelation. This diversity of opinions is especially pronounced when it comes to the nature, extent, and efficacy of general revelation.[2] At one end of the spectrum is Swiss theologian Karl Barth (1886–1968), who would not accept any revelation other than the "experience" of salvation in Christ (a virtual dismissal of all general or natural revelation). At the other end, Anglican theologian William Paley (1743–1805) constructed an expansive natural theology (the human interpretation of general revelation apart from the Bible). In spite of this broad scope of diversity, there has been and remains a general consensus among most Christian theologians that God has made himself known through general and special revelation.[3]

Revelation in Two Volumes

Orthodox Protestantism defines or classifies these two forms of God's self-disclosure in the following ways:

General Revelation

God's existence, power, wisdom, majesty, righteousness, and glory are manifested to all people at all times in all places (are generally available) through the created order, which includes nature, history, and the human conscience.[4]

This inclusive disclosure takes two distinct forms. First, *external* general revelation consists of the created order, or nature (which manifests God's work as the caring transcendent Creator of the world) and his providential ordering of history (which manifests God's work as the sovereign Sustainer of the world). Second, *internal* general revelation includes both an innate sense or consciousness of God and the moral law of conscience in the heart of the human person.

Internal general revelation is directly connected to the biblical teaching concerning the *imago Dei* (image of God: Gen. 1:26–27). As the crown of God's creation mankind uniquely displays the image of God by his rational capacities, moral volition, relational distinctives, unique spiritual qualities, and dominion over nature. As the only creature made in the image and likeness of God, humans reflect the splendor of their Maker, yet in finite expression. And after man's fall into sin this image certainly became tarnished.

Special Revelation

God's more specific and particular self-disclosure comes in and through his great redemptive actions, events, and words.[5] This form of revelation comes at special times and in special places. This detailed unveiling comes in two stages: First, God manifested himself through his covenant people such as the Hebrew patriarchs, prophets, and kings (as recorded and interpreted by the prophets in the Old Testament). Second, God's revelation culminated decisively in the incarnation of Jesus Christ, the God-man. The life, death, and resurrection of Jesus Christ (as recorded and interpreted by the apostles in the New Testament) chronicle God's climactic entrance into human history.[6]

Biblically speaking, the agent of all revelation is Jesus Christ—the divine Logos—the eternal Word and Son who "gives light to every man" (John 1:9). Evangelical theologian Carl F. H. Henry explains the christological focus of special revelation:

> The special revelation in sacred history is crowned by the incarnation of the living Word and the inscripturation of the spoken word. The gospel of redemption is therefore not merely a series of abstract theses unrelated to specific historical events; it is the dramatic news that God has acted in saving history, climaxed by the incarnate person and work of Christ (Heb. 1:2), for the salvation of lost humankind.[7]

This general/special revelation distinction, though theologically helpful and biblically derived, is not perfect and can be viewed as somewhat artificial. Ultimately God's revelation is a unity; so the distinction must not be drawn too sharply. The same God has unveiled himself in both a general and a special way.

Evangelical theologian Robert Saucy suggests that knowing God through his dual sources of revelation is roughly analogous to knowing a human artist.[8] While something significant of the artist can be known by viewing his or her work (general revelation), an expansive and more specific knowing comes through interpersonal communication (special revelation) with the artist.

Protestant theologians sometimes call this dual view of revelation the "two-books theory." God is the author of the figurative book of nature (God's world) and the literal book of Scripture (God's written Word). The Belgic Confession (a Reformed confession prepared in 1561) uses this two-books metaphor under the heading "The Means by Which We Know God":

> We know him by two means: First, by the creation, preservation, and government of the universe, since that universe is before our eyes like a beautiful book in which all creatures, great and small, are as letters to make us ponder the invisible things of God. . . . Second, he makes himself known to us more openly by his holy and divine Word, as much as we need in this life, for his glory and for the salvation of his own.[9]

The Biblical Basis for Dual Revelation

The Old Testament

The central text supporting this two-volume concept of revelation is Psalm 19:1–4, 7–11.

> The heavens declare the glory of God;
>   the skies proclaim the work of his hands.
> Day after day they pour forth speech;
>   night after night they display knowledge.
> There is no speech or language
>   where their voice is not heard.
> Their voice goes out into all the earth,
>   their words to the ends of the world. . . .
> The law of the LORD is perfect,
>   reviving the soul.
> The statutes of the LORD are trustworthy,
>   making wise the simple.
> The precepts of the LORD are right,
>   giving joy to the heart.
> The commands of the LORD are radiant,
>   giving light to the eyes.
> The fear of the LORD is pure,
>   enduring forever.

> The ordinances of the LORD are sure
>> and are altogether righteous.
> They are more precious than gold,
>> than much pure gold;
> they are sweeter than honey,
>> than honey from the comb.
> By them is your servant warned;
>> in keeping them there is great reward.

In verses 1–4 the inspired writer King David reflects upon the glory of God revealed in the created order. From these verses Christian theologian Bruce Demarest draws the following four points:[10]

Verse 1—Creation shows forth God's "divine 'glory' ([Hebrew]: *kābôd*)."[11] Nature clearly and powerfully manifests the Creator's existence, power, glory, and craftsmanship (handiwork).

Verse 2—God's self-disclosure in nature is "perpetual and uninterrupted."[12] The message ("speech" and "knowledge") about God's existence and attributes in creation continually and constantly bombards mankind's consciousness.

Verse 3—God's revelation in creation is "wordless and inaudible."[13] Nature's enduring and striking message about God is nevertheless nonpropositional. This nonverbal nature, however, does not detract from the natural realm's intelligibility though it illustrates the necessity for an actual, verbal message (special revelation).

Verse 4—God's manifestation through creation is "worldwide in scope."[14] The message ("voice") about the world's Creator is universal ("to the ends of the world"). God's revelation in the created order therefore should be understood as extending to all people, at all times, everywhere.

As the text transitions to verses 7–11, David reflects upon the perfection and power of God's written Law. He extols God's statutes, precepts, commands, and ordinances and the virtue that results from embracing and following them. God's written revelation nurtures the life of his people. Thus it is through the written Word that God uniquely revives and restores the soul. As the apostle Paul counseled his associate Timothy:

From infancy you have known the holy Scriptures, which are able to make you wise for salvation through faith in Christ Jesus. All Scripture is God-breathed and is useful for teaching, rebuking, correcting and training in righteousness, so that the man of God may be thoroughly equipped for every good work. (2 Tim. 3:15–17)

In this second book (the Bible) the infinite God condescends to make himself known personally and propositionally for the very purpose of salvation. This propositional revelation is, however, special—and is entrusted to a special people (Israel, then the Church) at special times and places.

The New Testament

The most important text relating to the question of general and special revelation is Romans 1:18–21.[15]

> The wrath of God is being revealed from heaven against all the godlessness and wickedness of men who suppress the truth by their wickedness, since what may be known about God is plain to them, because God has made it plain to them. For since the creation of the world God's invisible qualities—his eternal power and divine nature—have been clearly seen, being understood from what has been made, so that men are without excuse.
>
> For although they knew God, they neither glorified him as God nor gave thanks to him, but their thinking became futile and their foolish hearts were darkened.

The apostle Paul's language in this passage is abundantly clear. He asserts that all people "see" the glory of God reflected in the created order. They "understand" its divine implications, and thus "know" that the Creator exists (vv. 19–20).[16] Twice Paul reinforces a form of the Greek word *ginōskō* ("to know" by personal experience): in verse 19—"what may be known about God" (to *gnōston* tou theou), and again in verse 21—"For although they knew God" (*gnontes* ton theon). At least four times, in the broader context of verses 18–32, he mentions that human beings *know* God. These expressions in Greek convey the idea that all people have some authentic, objective, and accurate knowledge of God—though that understanding may be rudimentary in nature.

A careful exegesis of Paul's statements reveals that at least an elementary awareness of God is plain to all people, and this knowledge is neither vague nor ambiguous. God's "eternal power and divine nature" are clearly reflected in nature. Therefore, no one can legitimately claim the excuse, "I didn't know there was a God." God has not left himself without a witness (see also Acts 14:17; 17:24–31).

While Paul indicates that each person possesses a true knowledge of God by way of the created order, he also asserts that the natural predisposition of fallen man is to suppress this understanding. The Greek word for "suppress" (*katechō*) means to hold down or hinder illegally.[17] Man's state of sinful rebellion compels him to "suppress the truth." While human beings know there is a God, they seek to dodge their moral accountability to him.

Man's fallen condition of moral and spiritual obtuseness dulls his noetic (cognitive and/or belief-forming) faculties. Biblical scholars and apologists disagree as to the exact nature and extent of the noetic effects of the Fall on man. They ask such questions as these for example: Is the category of sinful effects a moral or cognitive one, or both? Is the extent (of the effects) partial or total? Millard Erickson offers this perspective:

> Sin's distortion of human understanding of the general revelation is greater the closer one gets to the relationship between God and humans. Thus, sin produces relatively little obscuring effect upon the understanding of matters of physics, but a great deal with respect to matters of psychology and sociology. Yet it is at those places where the potential for distortion is greatest that the most complete understanding is possible.[18]

In other words, while a person knows there is a God via general revelation, apart from the special grace of God working in his life he will choose not to believe (Rom. 3:10–12). Thus, anyone's response of faith results from the work of the Holy Spirit through the content of special revelation (the preaching of the gospel of redemption in Christ—see Rom. 10:17; Eph. 2:8–9; Titus 3:5). God's grace heals the fallen human will and illumines the mind while special revelation corrects a person's misperceptions and distortions of general revelation (Eph. 2:4–6; 4:17–24; Phil. 2:12–13).

The consensus among Protestant evangelical theologians is that general revelation by itself cannot save, though it can and will serve to condemn a person's unbelief (Rom. 1:20). Because of general revelation, the self-professed atheists of the world cannot justify their unbelief on the grounds that God provided insufficient evidence of his existence. In this way, special revelation reinforces the truth of general revelation, and general revelation supports the truth of special revelation. God's two types of revelation therefore complement each other.

Calvin's *Sensus Divinitatis*

Protestant reformer and biblical scholar John Calvin (1509–1564) wrote about man's possessing the *sensus divinitatis* (a sense of the divine). He said: "There is within the human mind, and indeed by natural instinct, an awareness of divinity. This we take to be beyond controversy. To prevent anyone from taking refuge in the pretense of ignorance, God himself has implanted in all men a certain understanding of his divine majesty."[19]

Historical theologian Richard Muller explains that Calvin used this term to refer to "a basic, intuitive perception of the divine existence; it is generated in all men through their encounter with the providential ordering of the world."[20] In light of the Pauline statements previously cited and Calvin's provocative interpretation of them, the following apologetic theory concerning the knowability of God emerges.[21]

Because God created human beings in his image, they were born with an innate knowledge or awareness of him. This knowledge is intuitive, not discursive (it is an immediate or instinctual awareness rather than a logical inference), though rational evidence in support of God's existence abounds. This innate intuition of the divine is triggered or becomes especially pronounced when humans observe the natural order, recognize the providential ordering of history, and reflect upon moral obligations of their conscience.

The Fall, however, has caused man's noetic equipment to malfunction (producing a distortion); therefore humans resist this powerful divine impulse. God's grace through the Holy Spirit is therefore mandatory for humans to embrace a correct, complete, and saving knowledge of God. The preaching of the gospel is the normative means by which this intuition normally becomes actualized as saving faith. Calvin described the Scriptures as a pair of "spectacles" that enable people to read the book of nature properly, that is, to draw the correct spiritual conclusions from it.

Theological Implications of the Dual Revelation

In light of Christian theology's dual revelation, many questions deserve careful reflection. Due to space limitations, only three of the more important questions are addressed in this chapter. The first has already been addressed in some detail and is summarized below. The second and third questions spring from it.

What is the relationship between the two sources of revelation?

The two forms of revelation from the same infinitely perfect God are equally inspired and mutually reinforce and complement one another. All truth is God's truth. Scripture instructs readers to take the message of general revelation seriously (Psalm 19; Romans 1). The created order illustrates the need for the specificity and completeness of special revelation's message. In other words, general revelation points toward special revelation, and general revelation provides a rational basis for accepting special revelation.

Ultimately divine revelation is a unity. Distinguishing between the two forms is appropriate, but they should never be separated. Exaggerating or diminishing the nature, extent, and efficacy of one or the other negatively impacts the proper balance between them.

What happens when the sources of revelation seem to conflict?

Properly understood, God's world (nature) and God's Word (Scripture), as two revelations (one physical, one verbal) from the same God, never contradict each other. The facts of nature do not conflict with the factual assertions of Scripture. However, human interpretation of these sources may indeed clash and when they do they stand in need of correction. Special revelation can and should offer correction to human misinterpretations of general revelation. And general revelation can help correct misinterpretations of special revelation (for example: archaeology, astronomy), though to a lesser extent because of Scripture's specificity and unique propositional nature (being expressed in the form of logical truth-claims; a verbal, factual revelation).[22] God's revelation in nature and in Scripture must be taken seriously. Interpretations of both need to be tested honestly. Being humble and wise enough to recognize differences between *opinions* of what the biblical text says and what the biblical text *actually* says leads to spiritual insight.[23] So does having the courage to follow truth wherever it leads, always knowing that God is the author of all truth (Ps. 33:4; 111:7–8; John 17:17).

How does the concept of dual revelation affect the principle of sola Scriptura?

Sola Scriptura[24] ("Scripture alone") is the Protestant precept acknowledging the Bible as the final and supreme written authority on truth. Certainly important truths of general revelation are not explicitly spelled out in special revelation (including many mathematical, logical, and scientific principles).[25] And it must be underscored that general revelation is every bit as inspired. However, in all matters that Scripture addresses, special revelation should be considered the final and supreme authority for the church and the individual Christian. On what basis? That of Scripture's specificity, its unique propositional nature,[26] and because of its self-authentication. God's verbal revelation speaks for itself in a way that general revelation does not. Scripture, through the work of the Holy Spirit, corrects man's idolatrous response to general revelation. In this way special revelation correlates and unifies the whole revelation of God.[27] Thus the full importance of general revelation can be affirmed while embracing the principle of *sola Scriptura*.

The Glorious Source of Christian Revelation

The author of the book of Hebrews provides an appropriate summation regarding God's self-disclosure:

In the past God spoke to our forefathers through the prophets at many times and in various ways, but in these last days he has spoken to us by his Son, whom he appointed heir of all things, and through whom he made the universe. The Son is the radiance of God's glory and the exact representation of his being, sustaining all things by his powerful word. After he had provided purification for sins, he sat down at the right hand of the Majesty in heaven. (Heb. 1:1–3)

God's dual revelation, his living word, and his creation have come through Jesus Christ. The truth-claims of Christianity emanate from Jesus' person and work. Exploring the way these are set forth in the historical creeds lends additional insight into the existence of God and how he relates to this world. The creeds are the topic of the next chapter.

Discussion Questions

1. Why is revelation such an important concept in historic Christianity?
2. What is the difference between general revelation and special revelation?
3. Why is it a problem either to exaggerate or to diminish general revelation?
4. How do general revelation and special revelation relate to each other?
5. How is Jesus Christ the ultimate revelation of God?

For Further Study

Erickson, Millard J. *Christian Theology*, 2nd ed. Grand Rapids: Baker, 1998. See pages 177–223.

Henry, Carl F. H. *God, Revelation and Authority*. Vols. 1–2. Waco, TX: Word, 1976.

Milne, Bruce. *Know The Truth*. Downers Grove, IL: InterVarsity, 1982. See pages 9–27.

Morris, Leon. *I Believe in Revelation*. London: Hodder & Stoughton, 1976.

Ramm, Bernard. *The Pattern of Authority*. Grand Rapids: Eerdmans, 1957.

Warfield, Benjamin B. *The Inspiration and Authority of the Bible*, ed. Samuel G. Craig. London: Marshall, Morgan & Scott, 1951.

4

Aren't the Creeds
a Thing of the Past?

Those who cannot remember the past are condemned to repeat it.

—George Santayana, *Reason in Common Sense*

In matters spiritual we owe a debt to the past which cannot be ignored.

—Gerald Bray, *Creeds, Councils and Christ*

The truth-claims of Christianity, which center upon the person and work of Jesus Christ, stand uniquely rooted in facts of history. The Jews refer to the God of the Bible as the God of history—a history that reveals the expanding Christian story of redemption.

Christendom's creeds are an integral part of that story. Not just a thing of the past, these creeds and the events that surrounded their formation can enrich lives today. Appropriate use of the creeds enhances Christian education, worship, and evangelism. An exploration of these ancient creeds—their origin, nature, development, and purpose—offers the strong biblical foundation that faith requires even in the twenty-first century.

Christianity's Creeds

The opening line of the Apostles' Creed in Latin reads *Credo in Deum*—"I believe in God." The term *creed* comes from the Latin *credo*, meaning "I believe." Many important English theological terms are derived from the Latin language because the ecclesiastical language of Western Christendom was exclusively Latin for more than one thousand years.[1]

Creeds are considered authoritative pronouncements that set forth in summary form the central articles, or tenets, of the historic Christian faith. Thus creeds usually start out as brief statements that attempt to capture the very essence of the Christian belief system. Four formal creeds have become known as the ecumenical creeds of Christendom. These creeds, which were formulated at various points in church history, include the Apostles' Creed, the Nicene Creed, the Athanasian Creed, and the Creed of Chalcedon.[2] These doctrinal statements can be found in their entirety at the end of this chapter.

The Creeds' Origins

Specific statements (recorded in Scripture) were used as creedal statements even in biblical times. For example, in the Old Testament the ancient Israelites used the *Shema*[3] as a creed. It emphasized their uncompromising commitment to monotheism, even though they lived amid a pagan, polytheistic world. The Israelites were the unique people of God, and their God (Yahweh) was "one." The *Shema*, which Jews continue to recite prayerfully even today, appears in Deuteronomy 6:4–9. *Shema* is Hebrew for "hear," and verse four appropriately begins as follows: "Hear, O Israel: The LORD our God, the LORD is one." This brief verse summarizes the essence of ancient Judaism. God's covenant people (Israel) worship and serve the one, true and living Lord God (Yahweh).

The earliest Christian creedal statement was most likely the simple yet profound New Testament proclamation "Jesus is Lord!" (Rom. 10:9; 1 Cor. 12:3; 2 Cor. 4:5; Phil. 2:11). Saying "Jesus is Lord" (Greek: *kyrios Iēsous*) was the New Testament Greek equivalent of saying "Jesus is Yahweh" (the Lord God).[4] This declaration of Jesus' Lordship as the Messiah and Savior set first-century Christians apart both from Judaism and from the Romans' worship of Caesar. Acknowledging Jesus as Lord lies at the heart of the Christian faith.

Another important New Testament passage that preserves a primitive creed from apostolic times is 1 Corinthians 15:3–4. The apostle Paul wrote, "For what I received I passed on to you as of first importance: that Christ died for our sins according to the Scriptures, that he was buried, that he was raised on the third day according to the Scriptures." This statement, which the apostle Paul received from Jesus' original followers, was likely composed as an early creed very soon after the time of Jesus' death and resurrection (ca. AD 30–33). Quoted in part in the Nicene Creed, this scriptural statement truly summarizes the christocentric saving message of Christianity. Capturing this doctrinal essence is an important function of a creed.

The use of creedal or protocreedal expressions, therefore, clearly has a biblical basis. The apostles and the earliest Christians saw great value in creeds and used them in critically important ways. These creeds summarized the early kerygma (proclamation) of the apostolic Christian church.

As Christianity grew in dominance in the Roman Empire, the need arose for a more detailed summary of Christian beliefs than just the brief passages previously cited. A more detailed creed could be used as a public profession of faith, especially before baptism. By the second century, Christians developed an early Latin version of the Apostles' Creed (known as the Old Roman Creed) that was intended as a summary of the main points concerning the gospel of Jesus Christ.[5] They saw this creed as a brief distillation of Christian truth, drawn from the doctrinal content of Scripture itself.

Creedal Authority

Because the creeds faithfully summarize biblical truth, they are considered authoritative. Many historic Christian churches recite creeds (especially the Apostles' Creed) as a means of professing their faith during their worship services. Creeds are also a useful tool in the formal, written and systematic study of Christian truth (catechism). However, for Protestants the authority of the creeds is not intrinsic, but rather derived from Scripture. According to the Protestant principle of *sola Scriptura* (see chap. 3), even the creeds are subject to the supreme authority—the written Word of God.[6] While creeds provide a valuable summary of universal Christian beliefs, they are not divinely inspired, as is the Bible. Creeds are at least conceivably open to correction, reform, or modification, but always in light of Scripture.

The Creeds' Major Purposes

Developed with a number of purposes in mind, the creeds have served several important functions through the centuries, including the following four:

1. The creeds helped formulate (provide definition and structure for) and still positively affirm essential Christian doctrine. For example, the creeds focus upon a fully formed Trinitarian theology. The Apostles' Creed, Nicene Creed, and Athanasian Creed identify the three divine Persons of the Trinity (Father, Son, and Holy Spirit), focusing on their unique roles in redemption. The creeds then concentrate in particular on the life, death, and resurrection of Jesus Christ, the very core of the gospel. As Oxford theologian Alister E. McGrath points out, the creeds "allow us to recognize and avoid inadequate or incomplete versions of Christianity."[7]

Because too many Christian churches today fail to focus adequately on the full triune nature of God, many Christians live as functional Unitarians with their attention fixed strongly or almost exclusively on only one of the divine persons (for example, Jesus or the Holy Spirit; see chap. 5). The creeds, which reflect a balanced trinitarianism, can serve as a helpful corrective to today's theological imbalances and lack of theological training.

2. The creeds draw attention to a common, historical Christian heritage. Reading and reciting the creeds reminds the Christian that to believe in Christ is to belong to a community, the historic Christian community. The creeds join today's believers with believers of the ancient past. The Apostles' Creed refers to this bond as the "communion of saints." This corporate confession of faith (an appropriate liturgical function) may also help correct the excessive individualism that exists in some quarters within evangelicalism. Lessons from Christian history can help solve contemporary problems among Jesus' followers.

3. The creeds can and do play a helpful role in catechetical instruction in Christian doctrine. They can help the believer to develop an organized, precise, and correct understanding of the faith. The creeds therefore give valuable aid as one learns the specific content of the Christian faith. In a time that seems to undervalue doctrinal content, the creeds provide a vital summary of biblical truth. The ability to summarize the essence of the Christian message increases a believer's preparedness to communicate that message to others (evangelism).

4. The creeds also have direct apologetic importance. All four of the creeds were written specifically to combat heresies that had arisen in the early centuries of the church. Even the precursor to the Apostles' Creed indirectly refuted early christological heresies (Ebionism, Gnosticism; see chap. 9). The church fathers formulated the Nicene Creed in large part to address the Arian heresy that denied the unqualified deity of Jesus Christ by making him a creature. Arianism is still seen today in the theology of Jehovah's Witnesses, Christadelphians, and *Iglesia ni Cristo*.

The Athanasian Creed sets forth the Christian doctrine of the Trinity (three in unity), rejecting both polytheism (belief in more than one god) and modalism (belief that the one God merely changes modes of expression). Polytheism is evident today in Mormonism, and modalism lives on in the United Pentecostal Church (Jesus only). The Creed of Chalcedon set forth the normative theological standard concerning the two natures of Jesus Christ (divine and human), thus rejecting various christological heresies (such as Monophysitism, the doctrine that there is only one nature in Christ, a belief still held by the Coptic Church). Theologically speaking, there is nothing new under the sun, and the creeds, in addressing ancient heresies, clearly speak to today's heretical sects (see chaps. 5 and 9 on the Trinity and the incarnation, respectively).

Today's apologists can therefore learn a great deal from the creeds and the events that surrounded their formulation (for example, how to defend such essential doctrines as the Trinity, the incarnation, and Christ's resurrection).

Creedal Opposition

Some Christians oppose the use of creeds altogether. The expressions "No creed but Christ" and "No book but the Bible" emerged among certain American Christian groups in the nineteenth and early twentieth centuries. Their concern was that creeds may somehow eclipse the biblical revelation of Christ. However, four brief points should be considered. First, the assertion that a person has no creed but Christ is itself a "creed," a personal creed. Creedal statements are hard to avoid. Second, creeds appear in Scripture and were used by the apostles. Third, creeds serve a very important function in identifying and clarifying beliefs. Fourth, having no formal and written statement of one's beliefs can be problematic. Groups can conveniently conceal deviant doctrinal views, and those unwritten beliefs can be open to unhealthy subjective interpretations of Scripture.

Christians from noncreedal or nonconfessional churches sometimes express the legitimate concern that recitation of creeds may become a replacement for dynamic, personal faith in Jesus Christ. Although creeds can be misused in this way, reciting memorized words, no matter how important, has no saving effect apart from a heart rooted in true faith and conviction. Alister E. McGrath addresses this concern cogently:

> A creed is not, and was never meant to be, a substitute for personal faith. It attempts to give substance to a personal faith that already exists. You do not become a Christian by reciting a creed. Rather the Creed provides a useful summary of the main points of your faith.[8]

Basic Creedal Descriptions

Apostles' Creed: The shortest and simplest of the four, the Apostles' Creed is the most widely accepted and most frequently used—both today and in the past. While not actually written by the apostles, in its earlier and briefer form (late-second century) it was called the "Old Roman Creed." This creed reached its present form by the eighth century AD. Trinitarian in focus, the creed has three sections acknowledging the three divine Persons' involvement in human redemption. Used by Catholics and Protestants alike, the Apostles' Creed often functions as a confessional affirmation during the Christian worship service.

Nicene Creed: While longer and possessing more theologically technical language than the Apostles' Creed, this creed has the same basic focus and contains the same doctrinal content. Though not derived directly from the Council of Nicaea (AD 325), the Nicene Creed does emphasize the Son's full equality with God the Father, thus repudiating the influential Arian heresy (which viewed Christ as a creature). Catholic, Orthodox, and Anglican churches make significant use of this classic statement of faith.

Athanasian Creed: Though not written by the fourth-century Greek church father Athanasius (whose name it bears), this creed emerged about the fifth century. It is the longest and most philosophical in content of all the creeds, with forty individual clauses. The Athanasian Creed explicitly and formally sets forth the orthodox doctrines of the Trinity and the incarnation. This creed is not accepted by the Eastern Orthodox churches.

Creed of Chalcedon: This technical theological statement, which laid down the theological parameters concerning orthodox Christology, was issued by the Council of Chalcedon in AD 451. The Creed of Chalcedon remains the definitive statement concerning the two natures of Jesus Christ (divine and human).

A Valuable Resource

The collective wisdom of Christian history, encapsulated in the ancient ecumenical creeds provides a rich and enduring resource for today, especially in theology and apologetics. Too often "chronological snobbery" (as coined by C. S. Lewis, the assumption that those who live in the present have greater insight than those of the past) blinds contemporary Christians from recognizing that many, or most, of Christianity's greatest theologians, philosophers, and apologists lived in the past.[9] Contrary to the message too often heard in churches today, doctrine and theology are critical to an individual's spiritual growth and can provide a much needed biblical foundation to stand on.

Discussion Questions

1. Why is a study of Christian history especially important?
2. What contemporary problems in the church might be helped by a serious study of the ancient Christian creeds?
3. What is the relationship of the historic creeds to Scripture?
4. How is the study of doctrine and theology critical to spiritual growth?
5. How can the study of the creeds aid in evangelism and in apologetics?

For Further Study

Bowman, Robert M. Jr. *Orthodoxy and Heresy*. Grand Rapids: Baker, 1992.

Bray, Gerald. *Creeds, Councils and Christ*. Ross-shire, UK: Mentor, 1984.

Brown, Harold O. J. *Heresies*. Garden City, NY: Doubleday, 1984.

Kelly, J. N. D. *Early Christian Creeds*. London: Harlow, 1972.

McGrath, Alister E. *I Believe: Understanding and Applying the Apostles' Creed*. Grand Rapids: Zondervan, 1991.

The Ecumenical Creeds of Christendom

Apostles' Creed

I believe in God, the Father almighty, creator of heaven and earth.

I believe in Jesus Christ, his only Son, our Lord, who was conceived by the Holy Spirit and born of the virgin Mary. He suffered under Pontius Pilate, was crucified, died, and was buried; he descended to hell. The third day he rose again from the dead.

He ascended into heaven and is seated at the right hand of God the Father almighty. From there he will come to judge the living and the dead.

I believe in the Holy Spirit, the holy catholic church, the communion of saints, the forgiveness of sins, the resurrection of the body, and the life everlasting. Amen.[10]

Nicene Creed

We believe in one God, the Father almighty, maker of heaven and earth, of all things visible and invisible.

And in one Lord Jesus Christ, the only Son of God, begotten from the Father before all ages, God from God, Light from Light, true God from true God, begotten, not made; of the same essence as the Father. Through him all things were made. For us and for our salvation he came down from heaven; he became incarnate by the Holy Spirit and the virgin Mary, and was made human. He was crucified for us under Pontius Pilate; he suffered and was buried. The third day he rose again, according to the Scriptures. He ascended to heaven and is seated at the right hand of the Father. He will come again with glory to judge the living and the dead. His kingdom will never end.

And we believe in the Holy Spirit, the Lord, the giver of life. He proceeds from the Father and the Son, and with the Father and the Son is worshiped and glorified. He spoke through the prophets. We believe in one holy catholic and apostolic church. We affirm one baptism for the forgiveness of sins. We look forward to the resurrection of the dead, and to life in the world to come. Amen.[11]

Athanasian Creed

Whoever desires to be saved should above all
hold to the catholic faith.
Anyone who does not keep it whole and unbroken
will doubtless perish eternally.

Now this is the catholic faith:

That we worship one God in trinity
and the trinity in unity,
neither blending their persons
nor dividing their essence.
For the person of the Father is a distinct person,
the person of the Son is another,
and that of the Holy Spirit still another.
But the divinity of the Father, Son, and Holy Spirit is one,
their glory equal, their majesty coeternal.

What quality the Father has, the Son has, and the Holy Spirit has.
The Father is uncreated,
the Son is uncreated,
the Holy Spirit is uncreated.
The Father is immeasurable,
the Son is immeasurable,
the Holy Spirit is immeasurable.
The Father is eternal,
the Son is eternal,
the Holy Spirit is eternal.

And yet there are not three eternal beings;
there is but one eternal being.
So too there are not three uncreated or immeasurable beings;
there is but one uncreated and immeasurable being.

Similarly, the Father is almighty,
the Son is almighty,
the Holy Spirit is almighty.
Yet there are not three almighty beings;
there is but one almighty being.

Thus the Father is God,
the Son is God,
the Holy Spirit is God.

Yet there are not three gods;
there is but one God.

Thus the Father is Lord,
the Son is Lord,
the Holy Spirit is Lord.
Yet there are not three lords;
there is but one Lord.

Just as Christian truth compels us
to confess each person individually
as both God and Lord,
so catholic religion forbids us
to say that there are three gods or lords.

The Father was neither made nor created nor begotten from anyone.
The Son was neither made nor created;
he was begotten from the Father alone.
The Holy Spirit was neither made nor created nor begotten;
he proceeds from the Father and the Son.

Accordingly there is one Father, not three fathers;
there is one Son, not three sons;
there is one Holy Spirit, not three holy spirits.

Nothing in this trinity is before or after,
nothing is greater or smaller;
in their entirety the three persons
are coeternal and coequal with each other.

So in everything, as was said earlier,
we must worship their trinity in their unity
and their unity in their trinity.

Anyone then who desires to be saved
should think thus about the trinity.

But it is necessary for eternal salvation
that one also believe in the incarnation
of our Lord Jesus Christ faithfully.

Now this is the true faith:

That we believe and confess
that our Lord Jesus Christ, God's Son,
is both God and human, equally.

He is God from the essence of the Father,
begotten before time;
and he is human from the essence of his mother,

born in time;
completely God, completely human,
with a rational soul and human flesh;
equal to the Father as regards divinity,
less than the Father as regards humanity.

Although he is God and human,
yet Christ is not two, but one.
He is one, however,
not by his divinity being turned into flesh,
but by God's taking humanity to himself.

He is one,
certainly not by the blending of his essence,
but by the unity of his person.
For just as one human is both rational soul and flesh,
so too the one Christ is both God and human.

He suffered for our salvation;
he descended to hell;
he arose from the dead;
he ascended to heaven;
he is seated at the Father's right hand;
from there he will come to judge the living and the dead.
At his coming all people will arise bodily
and give an accounting of their own deeds.
Those who have done good will enter eternal life,
and those who have done evil will enter eternal fire.

This is the catholic faith:
one cannot be saved without believing it firmly and faithfully.[12]

Creed of Chalcedon

We all with one voice confess our Lord Jesus Christ to be one and the same Son, perfect in divinity and humanity, truly God and truly human, consisting of a rational soul and a body, being of one substance with the Father in relation to his divinity, and being of one substance with us in relation to his humanity, and is like us in all things apart from sin (Heb. 4:15). He was begotten of the Father before time in relation to his divinity, and in these recent days was born from the Virgin Mary, the Theotokos, for us and for our salvation. In relation to the humanity he is one and the same Christ, the Son, the Lord, the Only-begotten, who is to be acknowledged in two natures, without confusion, without change, without division, and without separation. The distinction of natures is in no way abolished on account of this union, but rather the characteristic property of each nature is preserved, and concurring into one Person and one subsistence, not as if Christ were parted or divided into two persons, but remains one and the same Son and only-begotten God, Word, Lord, Jesus Christ; even as the Prophets from the beginning spoke concerning him, and our Lord Jesus Christ instructed us, and the Creed of the Fathers was handed down to us.[13]

How Can God Be Three and One?

The doctrine of the Trinity . . . is truth for the heart. The fact that it cannot be satisfactorily explained, instead of being against it, is in its favor. Such a truth had to be revealed; no one could imagine it.

—A. W. Tozer, *The Knowledge of the Holy*

It is the Father who sent the Son to be our sacrifice, the Son who satisfied the just demands and appeased the wrath of the Father, the Holy Spirit who comes into our hearts and gives us the faith to cry: "Abba, Father" as adopted sons and daughters of God.

—Gerald Bray, *The Doctrine of God*

The idea of the Trinity troubles many people. Jehovah's Witnesses reject it:

To worship God on his terms means to reject the Trinity doctrine. It contradicts what the prophets, Jesus, the apostles, and the early Christians believed and taught. It contradicts what God says about himself in his own inspired Word.[1]

The Koran denounces it:

Unbelievers are those that say: 'God is one of three.' There is but one God. If they do not desist from so saying, those of them that disbelieve shall be sternly punished.[2]

The concept of the Trinity even confused Thomas Jefferson:

> When we shall have done away with the incomprehensible jargon of the Trinitarian arithmetic, that three are one, and one is three; . . . and got [sic] back to the pure and simple doctrines [Jesus] inculcated, we shall then be truly and worthily his disciples.[3]

Can God really be three and one at the same time? What does that mean and why should people even bother trying to understand such a strange concept?

The essential Christian doctrine of the Trinity allows the creature to peer ever so slightly into the window of God's infinite nature and personhood. The Trinity stands as one of the most distinctive of all Christian teachings, setting Christianity apart from all other religions, including other monotheistic religions (such as Judaism and Islam). Because the Christian vision of God is unique, mysterious, and inscrutable to the finite mind, it is often misunderstood and misrepresented. Examining what historic Christianity teaches about the Trinity and responding to some critical questions concerning its origin, development, intelligibility, coherence, and importance can help correct these misunderstandings and clear away the confusion.

The Historic Christian Doctrine of the Trinity

The Athanasian Creed, the longest and most philosophical of the ancient ecumenical creeds, sets forth the orthodox doctrine of the Trinity in the following words:

> That we worship one God in trinity and the trinity in unity, neither blending their persons nor dividing their essence. For the person of the Father is a distinct person, the person of the Son is another, and that of the Holy Spirit still another. But the divinity of the Father, Son, and Holy Spirit is one, their glory equal, their majesty coeternal. . . .
>
> Thus the Father is God, the Son is God, the Holy Spirit is God. Yet there are not three gods; there is but one God.
>
> Thus the Father is Lord, the Son is Lord, the Holy Spirit is Lord. Yet there are not three lords; there is but one Lord.
>
> Just as Christian truth compels us to confess each person individually as both God and Lord, so catholic religion forbids us to say that there are three gods or lords.[4]

The word "trinity" refers to "tri-unity" (three in one), thus conveying the biblically revealed truth that there is plurality within the unity of God's nature (one God in three "persons"). The doctrine of the Trinity (or the triunity of God) should properly be understood within the broader context of the Christian theistic view of God.[5] The God unveiled in the Bible (and later described in the historic creeds and confessions of Christendom) is the one sovereign and majestic Lord. Historic Christianity thus affirms belief in one infinitely perfect, eternal, and personal (or superpersonal) God—the transcendent Creator and sovereign Sustainer of the universe. This one God is triune. He exists eternally and simultaneously as three distinct and distinguishable persons (though not separate): Father, Son, and Holy Spirit.

All three persons in the Godhead, or Divine Being, share equally and completely the one divine nature, and are therefore the same God—coequal in attributes, nature, and glory. God has revealed himself as one in essence or substance (being), but three in subsistence (personhood). In terms of what God is (essence), God is one; in terms of who God is (subsistence), God is three. Philosophically speaking, God is therefore "one What" and "three Whos."

To put it in the negative, it is not three different gods (tritheism), for that would divide the essence. Rather it is only one God (monotheism). And it is not one single solitary person (Monarchianism, modalism), for that would blend or confound the persons. Rather it is three distinct and distinguishable persons (triune).

Essential Points about the Trinity

The following ten points convey essential information about the Trinity.[6] These points clarify both what the triunity of God is and what it is not.

1. There exists only one God (one divine essence or being). Trinitarianism is a unique type of monotheism, and the underlying truth of monotheism is rooted in the Old and New Testament Scriptures. Orthodox trinitarianism therefore rejects polytheism in general and tritheism in particular, for they divide the one divine essence.

2. The three persons of the Godhead are each fully divine, all sharing equally and fully the one divine essence (God the Father, God the Son, and God the Holy Spirit). The deity of these three persons is also grounded in the Old and New Testament Scriptures.

3. The three persons of the Trinity should not be understood as three "parts" of God. Each person is fully divine and equally possesses all of God's being.

4. The term "person" in reference to the Trinity is used in a unique sense. It should not be understood to refer to a separate, autonomous entity or being, for this would divide the divine essence.

5. Unlike all finite creatures, God possesses plurality of personhood within his one infinite being. The Trinity is one example of the theological principle known as the Creator/creature distinction.

6. The members of the Trinity are qualitatively equal in attributes, nature, and glory. While Scripture reveals a willing subordination among the divine persons in terms of position or role (for example: the Son submits to the Father, the Holy Spirit proceeds from the Father and Son), there exists absolutely no subordination (inferiority) of essence or nature. The persons are therefore equal in being, but subordinate (or deferential) only in role or position.

7. The members of the Trinity are both eternally and simultaneously distinct as three persons. In other words, the Godhead has forever been, is now, and will forever subsist as three persons: Father, Son, and Holy Spirit. None of the persons came into being or became divine at a given moment in time. Orthodox trinitarianism therefore rejects all forms of Arianism (a teaching that makes the Son a creature and denies the Holy Spirit's personality and deity).

8. The three members of the Godhead are distinct persons and can be distinguished from each other (for example: the Father is not the Son, the Father is not the Holy Spirit, and the Son is not the Holy Spirit). Orthodox trinitarianism therefore rejects all forms of modalism (which blends or confounds the persons by defining them as mere modes of existence or expression).

9. God's "oneness" and "threeness" are in different respects. In other words, the way in which God is one (essence) is different from the way in which God is three (subsistence). Christian theologians and philosophers through the centuries have argued that it is crucial to distinguish between God's essence on one hand, and God's subsistence on the other.

10. The way in which God is one does not violate the way in which God is three, and vice versa. The distinction between God's singular essence (being) and God's plural subsistence (personhood) is essential to eliminating confusion about the Trinity doctrine.

Addressing Critical Challenges

Since the word Trinity doesn't appear anywhere in the Bible, did the early church simply invent the doctrine?

Linguistically, the term *trinity* comes from the Latin *trinitas*. This term was used by the church father Tertullian (ca. AD 160–230) who wrote about "a trinity of one divinity, Father, Son and Holy Spirit."[7] While it is true that the doctrine of the Trinity progressively developed in church history, that doesn't mean the church invented the doctrine. Jehovah's Witnesses, among others, are troubled that the word *Trinity* doesn't appear anywhere in the Bible. But the absence of this word in no way invalidates the doctrine. Many important biblical concepts are conveyed by terms not contained in the Bible—for example: the words *Bible, canon,* and *inerrancy.* Surely nothing in the text itself prohibits the use of extrabiblical terms to express proper meaning. Although the actual word *Trinity* doesn't appear, Scripture clearly reveals the doctrine.

While literally hundreds of passages can be marshaled to support the Trinity doctrine,[8] the biblical basis for this doctrine is briefly summarized in the box, "The biblical basis for the Trinity: five propositions."

The biblical basis for the Trinity: five propositions

1. **There is one, and only one, God.**
   Deut. 4:35, 39; 6:4; 32:39; 2 Sam. 7:22; Ps. 86:10; Isa. 43:10; 44:6–8; 46:9; John 5:44; 17:3; Rom. 3:29–30; 16:27; 1 Cor. 8:4; Gal. 3:20; Eph. 4:6; 1 Thess. 1:9; 1 Tim. 1:17; 2:5; James 2:19; 1 John 5:20–21; Jude 25.
2. **The person of the Father is God.**
   John 6:27; Eph. 4:6; Col. 1:2–3; 2 Pet. 1:17.
3. **The person of the Son is God.**
   John 1:1; 5:17; 8:58; 10:30; 20:28; Phil. 2:6; Col. 2:9; Titus 2:13; Heb. 1:8; 2 Pet.1:1. (Chapter 9 contains further support for Christ's deity.)
4. **The person of the Holy Spirit is God.**
   Gen. 1:2; John 14:26; Acts 5:3–4; 13:2, 4; 28:25; Rom. 8:11; Eph. 4:30.
5. **The Father, Son, and Holy Spirit are distinct and simultaneously distinguishable persons.**
   Matt. 28:19; Luke 3:22; John 15:26; 16:13–15; 2 Cor. 13:14.

Biblical propositions (referenced in the box) logically imply that since there is only one God, and the three distinct persons are all called God, then the three persons must be the one God. The doctrine of the Trinity was not invented by the church at the Council of Nicaea (AD 325) or at any other time. The church fathers saw the doctrine of the Trinity as a necessary inference from Scripture. The doctrine developed in the early church because of the overwhelming scriptural evidence supporting both the deity of Jesus Christ and the deity of the Holy Spirit. Evangelical theologian Alister E. McGrath explains:

> The doctrine of the Trinity can be regarded as the outcome of a process of sustained and critical reflection on the pattern of divine activity revealed in Scripture, and continued in Christian experience. This is not to say that Scripture contains a doctrine of the Trinity; rather, Scripture bears witness to a God who demands to be understood in a Trinitarian manner. . . . Historically, it is possible to argue that the doctrine of the Trinity is closely linked with the development of the doctrine of the divinity of Christ. . . . The starting point for Christian reflections on the Trinity is, as we have seen, the New Testament witness to the presence and activity of God in Christ and through the Spirit.[9]

While no formal or dogmatic statement appears in the Bible concerning the Trinity, the truths that produce the doctrine find their origin uniquely in the pages of Holy Scripture. The apostles and church fathers who followed them were forced to make sense of a single God who was revealed in three persons. Biblical support for the Trinity doctrine can be followed through four strands:

1. Three-in-Oneness in the Old Testament. Truth about God's nature was progressively revealed in Scripture. Therefore, while the Old Testament is limited in what could be considered direct support for the doctrine of the Trinity, the Hebrew Scriptures nevertheless allow for the idea of a plurality of personhood within God's single nature. This allowance of plurality is evidenced in the fact that the Hebrew noun for God (ʾĕlōhîm) is generally found in the plural, and in a handful of Old Testament passages plural pronouns and verbs are used when speaking about God.

Genesis 1 records that just as God was about to create man he said, "Let us make man in *our* image, in *our* likeness" (Gen. 1:26, emphasis added). The very next verse defines "our image" as being "God's image" (Gen. 1:27). Similarly, after Adam and Eve's fall into sin (Genesis 3) God said, "The man has now become like one of *us*, knowing good and evil" (Gen. 3:22, emphasis added). In context, the reference to *us* points back to verse 5 which is identified as "like God." The Old Testament offers two other passages of a similar nature (see Gen. 11:7 and Isa. 6:8). While these passages and others that suggest a divine plurality don't prove the Trinity, they are consistent with the New Testament apostles' modification of the traditional understanding of Jewish monotheism.[10]

2. The Three-in-Oneness Formula in the New Testament. That which is only hinted at in the Old Testament comes into clear view in the New Testament by means of ecclesiastical formulaic references to the Trinity.[11] The following two passages distinguish among the three persons yet link them together in unity and apparent equality:

- "Therefore go and make disciples of all nations, baptizing them in the name of the Father and of the Son and of the Holy Spirit" (Matt. 28:19).
- "May the grace of the Lord Jesus Christ, and the love of God, and the fellowship of the Holy Spirit be with you all" (2 Cor. 13:14).

The language, context, use, and early date of these passages give clear indication that the apostles were well aware that their traditional understanding of Jewish monotheism had to be modified to include the reality of three divine persons. These passages place the Son and the Holy Spirit on an equal level with the Father and are directly connected to the earliest traditions of Christian doctrine and practice (baptism, ecclesiastical benedictions).[12]

3. Listing the Three Persons Together. The listing of the three persons together (Father or God; and Son or Christ or Lord; and Holy Spirit or Spirit)[13] frequently occurs in the New Testament. They are especially linked together in unity with regard to the work of redeeming mankind (Rom. 15:16, 30; 1 Cor. 12:4–6; 2 Cor. 1:21–22, 3.3, Gal. 4:6; Eph. 2:18; 4:4–6; 2 Thess. 2:13–14; Rev. 1:4–6). While this triadic pattern is especially apparent in the Pauline writings, it appears in other parts of the New Testament as well (Acts 2:33, 38; Jude 20–21). The following two passages demonstrate:

- "Peter, an apostle of Jesus Christ, to God's elect . . . chosen according to the foreknowledge of God the Father, through the sanctifying work of the Spirit, for obedience to Jesus Christ and sprinkling by his blood" (1 Pet. 1:1–2).
- "As soon as Jesus was baptized, he went up out of the water. At that moment heaven was opened, and he saw the Spirit of God descending like a dove and lighting on him. And a voice from heaven said, 'This is my Son, whom I love; with him I am well pleased'" (Matt. 3:16–17).

Perhaps the clearest and most profound statements of the unity and coequal nature of the three persons, however, occurs in the Johannine writings (see especially the Gospel of John chaps. 14–16). The threefold listing of names appears frequently (see John 1:33–34; 1 John 4:2, 13–14). (See "The Trinity in the Gospel of John" box for an overview of statements associating the three divine persons of the Trinity.)

The Trinity in the Gospel of John

Father and Word (Son) are together in fellowship from eternity (1:1)
Father and Word (Son) are distinct persons but both divine (1:1)
Father creates the world through the Son (1:3)
Father sends the Son into the world (14:24)
Son becomes incarnate (1:14)
Son is equal to the Father (5:18)
Son is the great I AM (8:58)
Father and Son are one (10:30)
Son shares glory with the Father (17:5)
Son is the way and the truth and the life (14:6)
Knowing the Son is knowing the Father (14:7)
Seeing the Son is seeing the Father (14:9)
Son is in the Father and the Father is in the Son (14:10)
Son's words are the Father's words (14:10)
To hate the Son is to hate the Father (15:23)
He who loves the Son loves the Father (14:21)
Son brings glory to the Father (14:13)

Son prays for the coming of the Spirit (14:16)
Spirit is another Counselor like the Son (14:16; see 1 John 2:1)
Son goes away in order to send the Spirit (16:7)
Son returns to the Father (16:28)
Son will send the Spirit from the Father (15:26)
Father sends the Spirit (14:16)
Father sends the Spirit in the Son's name (14:26)
Spirit of truth guides us into all truth (16:13)
The Spirit's ministry is a continuation of that of the Son (16:13–14)
Spirit brings glory to the Son (16:14)
Spirit bears witness to the Son (15:26)
All that belongs to the Father is the Son's (16:15)

John's Gospel alone provides overwhelming support for the doctrine of the Trinity. Jesus himself, as John records, explains the intimate relationship among the three coequal members of the Trinity in bringing about salvation for sinners:

"When the Counselor comes, whom I will send to you from the Father, the Spirit of truth who goes out from the Father, he will testify about me." (John 15:26)

4. The Three Persons Have the Titles, Attributes, and Perform the Works of Deity. The Bible attests in numerous ways to the full and undiminished deity of the Father, the Son, and the Holy Spirit (see also chap. 9). (See box entitled "Biblical support for deity of the three persons".):

Biblical support for deity of the three persons

All three persons are referred to as God:
Father (1 Pet. 1:2), Son (Heb. 1:8), Holy Spirit (Acts 5:3–4)

All three persons possess divine attributes or qualities:
Self-existence: Father (Acts 17:25), Son (John 5:26), Holy Spirit (Rom. 8:2)
Eternal existence: Father (Ps. 90:2), Son (John 8:58), Holy Spirit (Heb. 9:14)
Immutability: Father (James 1:17), Son (Heb. 13:8), Holy Spirit (2 Cor. 3:18)
Omnipresence: Father (Jer. 23:23–24), Son (Matt.28:20), Holy Spirit (Ps. 139:7)
Omniscience: Father (Isa. 40:28), Son (Col. 2:3), Holy Spirit (1 Cor. 2:10)
Omnipotence: Father (Jer. 32:17), Son (Col. 1:16–17), Holy Spirit (1 Cor. 2:10–11)
Truth: Father (John 7:28), Son (John 14:6), Holy Spirit (1 John 5:6)
Holiness: Father (Lev. 11:44), Son (Acts 3:14), Holy Spirit (John 16:7–8)
Wisdom: Father (Ps. 104:24), Son (Col. 2:3), Holy Spirit (1 Cor. 2:10–11)

All three persons are engaged in the works of God:
Creation of the world: Father (Gen. 2:7), Son (John 1:3), Holy Spirit (Gen. 1:2)
Incarnation of Jesus Christ: Father (Heb. 10:5), Son (Heb. 2:14), Holy Spirit (Luke 1:35)
Resurrection of Jesus: Father (Acts 2:32), Son (John 2:19), Holy Spirit (Rom. 1:4)

Systematic theologian Millard J. Erickson offers the following assessment of the biblical evidence for the Trinity:

Although the doctrine of the Trinity is not expressly asserted, the Scripture, particularly the New Testament, contains so many suggestions of the deity and unity of the three persons that we can understand why the church formulated the doctrine, and conclude that they were right in so doing.[14]

While the Trinity doctrine has clear and persuasive biblical support and stands as the foundation of Christian orthodoxy, four objections are frequently asked. Answering those objections is critically important.

Historically speaking, wasn't there group and individual opposition to the orthodox position concerning the Trinity?

While the Trinity doctrine finds its source in Scripture, its form, structure, and definition developed over the first few centuries of Christianity's history. This formulation took place amidst heretical challenges to the Christian conception of God. The ecumenical creeds of Christendom resulted from the church's sustained reflection on critical doctrinal matters. The creeds were forged through debate and controversy and in response to heresy. The brief explanation of the major Trinitarian heresies that follows includes what they taught about God, how this teaching differed from orthodoxy, and how Christian orthodoxy responded. Modern-day counterparts to these heresies are also briefly mentioned. (Chapter 9 contains a list of christological heresies.)

Arianism: Championed by the influential thinker Arius of Alexandria, Arianism argued that Christ's nature or essence is inferior to the Father's and that Christ is a created being. This position represented a denial of the full and unqualified deity of Christ and of the Holy Spirit. This heresy was first condemned at the Council of Nicaea (AD 325). The christological views of such modern-day groups as Jehovah's Witnesses, Christadelphians, and *Iglesia ni Cristo* are noticeably Arian-like.[15]

Modalism: A type of Monarchianism, this heretical position became popular in the third century. It held that there is only one divine person who merely appears in three different forms or modes (for example: creator, redeemer, sanctifier). Thus, this view denies that the three members of the Trinity are distinct and simultaneously distinguishable persons (confounding the persons). Sabellianism or Patripassianism are historical types of modalism. The modern-day Oneness Pentecostals reflect a type of modalism with their "Jesus Only" view.[16] Unfortunately, even some evangelicals think of the Trinity in modalistic terms.

Monarchianism: Emerging in the second and third centuries AD, this view stressed the absolute unity of God so as to exclude any possibility of God's genuine plurality of personhood (as three distinct persons). In its various heretical forms, Monarchianism holds that God is a single solitary being *and* person.

Polytheism: The popular ancient view that there is more than one, or many, gods is a direct denial of biblical monotheism (dividing the essence). The modern-day sect of Mormonism (the Church of Jesus Christ of Latter-day Saints or LDS) affirms a type of polytheism with its teaching about humans' progression to godhood.[17]

Tritheism: A type of polytheism, this view asserts that God exists as three equal and independent beings; thus as separate gods. Some critics of historic Christianity (such as, Islam) falsely accuse the doctrine of the Trinity as being tritheistic.

Unitarianism: In the tradition of Monarchianism, this view stresses the absolute unity of God's nature and person, thus rejecting the doctrine of the Trinity. In addition, Unitarianism denies the deity of Christ. Such views are expressed today in the Unitarian-Universalist Church.[18]

Isn't the Trinity a mysterious, unintelligible doctrine, and therefore an absurdity?

As creatures, human beings will never know and understand God as God understands himself. And while the Trinity doctrine is to some degree mysterious and ultimately incomprehensible to the finite mind, it can be discussed in a meaningful way and it is not an absurdity. The Trinity is an understandable teaching even though human beings can never fully comprehend just how God is triune. Yet imperfect analogies do provide meaningful insight into his triune nature. For example, a single triangle with three sides or one family with three members is understandable. Reasoned and careful inferences drawn from Scripture about God do make sense, even though they are not ultimately comprehensive. Christian theologian and apologist Robert M. Bowman, Jr. provides a helpful clarification:

> To say that the Trinity cannot be understood likewise is imprecise, or at least open to misinterpretation. Trinitarian theologians do not mean to imply that the Trinity is unintelligible nonsense. Rather, the point they are making is that the Trinity cannot be fully fathomed, or comprehended, by the finite mind of a man. There is a difference between gaining a basically correct understanding of something and having a complete, comprehensive, all-embracing, perfect understanding of it. The way many other theologians would express this difference is to say that the Trinity can be understood, or "apprehended," but not "comprehended."[19]

The difficulty that human beings have in grasping the Trinity doctrine is that God is in certain respects different from anything in the created order. For example, the teaching that one being subsists as three distinct persons is completely counter to all human experience. This is, of course, the difficulty with human analogies of the Trinity—God is in some respects wholly other.

But more truths than just the Trinity are beyond human comprehension. Many things God reveals about himself are unfathomable, including his infinite attributes. Mystery necessarily accompanies human encounters with the biblical, transcendent God. However, the question is whether an individual will accept God as he reveals himself to be, mystery included, or only settle for a being they think they can fully comprehend. Unfortunately, Thomas Jefferson would only accept a God he could comprehend. And yet if the human mind could comprehend God, he wouldn't be much of a God.

As C. S. Lewis points out, some concepts of God are easier than others:

> If Christianity was something we were making up, of course we could make it easier. But it isn't. We can't compete, in simplicity, with people who are inventing religions. How could we? We're dealing with fact. Of course anyone can be simple if he has no facts to bother about![20]

Isn't the Trinity a logical contradiction?

The law of noncontradiction, the foundational principle for all logical thinking, asserts that two contradictory statements cannot both be true at the same time and in the same respect (A cannot equal A and also equal non-A). This law can take a metaphysical cast indicating what is or is not: "Nothing can both be and not be at the same time and in the same respect." This same law can also take an epistemological cast, indicating what is true or false: "A statement cannot be both true and false at the same time and in the same respect."[21] A contradiction in logic reflects a very specific relationship. Two statements are contradictory if they negate or deny each other. Contradictory statements have opposite truth value: exactly one statement is true, the other statement is false.

Skeptics often claim the Trinity is a contradiction in two ways. Some assert that it violates the law of noncontradiction on the ground that the doctrine claims that God is one and not one, and that God is three and not three. This criticism is a straw-man argument, however, for orthodox trinitarianism does not assert that God is one and not one, three and not three. Rather the Trinity doctrine asserts that the way God is one (essence or being), he is not three, and that the way God is three (subsistence or personhood), he is not one. Trinitarians assert that one must distinguish between God's essence on one hand and God's subsistence on the other. God is one in a different respect from the way in which he is three, and three in a different respect from the way in which he is one. Thus the Trinity, as one What (essence) and three Whos (subsistence), is not a formal contradiction.

Other critics claim that the formulation of the Trinity does indeed involve a contradiction. They argue the following: Since the Father is God, the Son is God, and the Holy Spirit is God; and since the Father is not the Son, the

Father is not the Holy Spirit, and the Son is not the Holy Spirit; then the result is that each person is simultaneously God and not God. This is, they reason, a violation of the law of noncontradiction.

This evaluation of the trinitarian formulation is also a straw-man argument, for again it fails to recognize the essence/subsistence distinction. The members of the Trinity all share equally the one divine nature and are thus the one God. However, the relational distinctions in the Godhead (Father, Son, Holy Spirit) do not in any way subtract from each individual person's possession of the divine nature. Thus the three persons are distinct from each other, but they nevertheless remain fully and equally God. How one being can simultaneously be three persons is an unfathomable mystery, but it is not a formal contradiction.

This logical tension may be alleviated if one recognizes what is known as the "predication/identity distinction."[22] To say "Jesus Christ is God" is to predicate to Jesus Christ the divine nature which is an attribute of being, shared equally and fully with the Father and the Son. On the other hand, to say "Jesus Christ is God the Son" is to make an identity claim; namely, that the person of Jesus of Nazareth is the same (identical) person as God the Son, the second person of the Trinity. It is not contradictory to attribute deity to all three members of the Trinity (predication), while simultaneously asserting that they possess distinct personal identities: Father, Son, Holy Spirit (identity). Often misunderstandings can be cleared up if Christians take great care in formulating and articulating the Trinity doctrine.

Critics may question the essence/subsistence distinction, but if they are going to critique the historic doctrine of the Trinity, they must take this critical distinction into account. Throughout the centuries Christians have affirmed that the Trinity may range *above* reason, but never *against* reason. In this way, the Trinity may be called a paradox, but not a contradiction. As Christian theologian Geoffrey Bromiley asserts: "Rationalist objections to the Trinity break down in the fact that they insist on interpreting the Creator in terms of the creature."[23]

Why is the doctrine of the Trinity important?

Too many Christians, living as functional Unitarians, fail to recognize the Trinity's relevance to their Christian faith and life. The Trinity doctrine is crucial because it reveals What and Who God is (one God in three persons), and this insight allows Christians, though in an obviously limited way, to view the inner working of God's nature and personhood. This doctrine allows God's people, as the Athanasian Creed declares, to "worship one God in trinity and the trinity in unity." Christians therefore from ancient times have asserted that to fail to worship the triune God is to fail to worship the true God at all.

Furthermore, the Trinity doctrine brings together in a coherent manner the great truths about God's historical, redemptive actions (completed in and through the Father, Son, and Holy Spirit). For example, the Father sends the Son into the world to offer a propitiatory sacrifice on the cross—that is, a sacrifice that both appeases the Father's just wrath against sin and extends the Father's love and mercy by allowing repentant sinners to escape divine judgment. The Incarnate Son (the second person of the Trinity) is able to provide this atonement because he is both God and man (in this case "two Whats" and "one Who"). The God-man conquers death, sin, and hell through his glorious resurrection from the dead. The Holy Spirit is directly responsible for the repentant sinner's new birth in Christ through regeneration, and the believer's life journey of sanctification. The three divine members of the Trinity make the entire plan of redemption possible. Thus salvation from first to last is directly connected to the doctrine of the Trinity. As theologian Bruce Milne notes: "Just about everything that matters in Christianity hangs on the truth of God's three-in-oneness."[24]

A Cherished Doctrine

Finally, as the greatest of the church fathers, Augustine of Hippo (AD 354–430) explained in his monumental work *De Trinitate* (*On the Trinity*), only a God who has plurality within unity can adequately account for God's being love and for God's knowing. For if God is a solitary being, then before the Creation he had no one to love. Nor could he have distinguished between the knower and the known (a requisite of self-knowledge).[25] In this way the Trinity becomes quite practical. Because human beings are created in the image of the fully relational triune God, concepts such as love, family, and community take on a new dimension of meaning and value. Redemption in Christ is properly understood as adoption into the family of God.

The doctrine of the Trinity reveals God's very nature and personhood and sets Christianity apart from all other religions. Today's believers join with believers of centuries past in worshiping "one God in trinity and the trinity in unity."[26]

Is belief in such a God worth staking a person's life on? Blaise Pascal's Wager, the topic of the next chapter, wrestles with this question and offers significant considerations for anyone willing to pursue the answer.

Discussion Questions

1. What is a clear, concise, and correct definition of the Trinity?
2. Is it problematic that the word *Trinity* does not appear in the Bible?

3. How can the biblical doctrine of the Trinity be stated in five propositions?
4. How does the Trinity differ from modalism and tritheism?
5. How should an awareness of God's triune nature affect a Christian's worship and prayer?

For Further Study

Beisner, E. Calvin. *God in Three Persons*. Wheaton, IL: Tyndale, 1984.

Bowman, Robert M. Jr. *Orthodoxy And Heresy: A Biblical Guide to Doctrinal Discernment*. Grand Rapids: Baker, 1992.

Bray, Gerald. *Creeds, Councils and Christ*. Ross-shire, Great Britain: Mentor, 1997.

McGrath, Alister E. *Understanding the Trinity*. Grand Rapids: Zondervan, 1988.

White, James R. *The Forgotten Trinity*. Minneapolis: Bethany, 1998.

WHY SHOULD I GAMBLE
ON FAITH?

Being unable to cure death, wretchedness and ignorance, men have decided, in order to be happy, not to think about such things.

—Blaise Pascal, *Pensées*

Let us weigh up the gain and the loss involved in calling heads that God
exists. Let us assess the two cases: if you win you win everything, if you
lose you lose nothing. Do not hesitate then; wager that he does exist.

—Blaise Pascal, *Pensées*

Humans differ from animals in the ability to engage in philosophical
reflection, especially reflection about ultimate issues. And yet, many
people avoid thinking about the so-called big questions of life: Does God
exist? Is there an objective meaning to life? What difference does morality
make? Is there life after death?

Several factors may account for indifference to life's big questions. Deep
and complex, these issues make many people feel inadequate to form opinions
about them. Answers have been so hotly disputed over the centuries that
people are tempted to believe no genuinely satisfying answers exist. Some
people fail to recognize any practical significance of these questions to their
daily lives. Whatever the reason for human indifference, these fundamental
philosophical interrogatories won't go away.

The Bible attributes human avoidance of ultimate issues (particularly the human creature's unwillingness to acknowledge his moral accountability to the Creator) to man's fallen sinful state (Rom. 3:23). Cut off from the life of God, sinful people naturally and continually engage in spiritual and moral diversions. In fact, the apostle Paul says that people consciously "suppress the truth by their wickedness" (Rom. 1:18). People fill their lives with activities that allow them to ignore or suppress their innate moral and spiritual responsibilities.

The seventeenth-century Christian thinker Blaise Pascal (1623–1662) came up with a provocative and controversial approach to shake people from their diversions. In his "Wager" argument, Pascal developed a line of practical reasoning with the very purpose of challenging anyone seemingly unconcerned with the perplexing issues of life.

An accomplished scholar in many fields, Pascal is probably best known for his presentation of the Wager. This voluntaristic argument appeals more to the prudential and existential considerations of the human will than to reason per se. However, modern-day skeptics often misunderstand the Wager, viewing it as a stand-alone argument, and thus fail to appreciate its proper epistemological, historical, and existential context. This context is found in the life and thought of Pascal himself. A brief exploration of some of the major events of his life as well as a survey of his conclusions concerning the truth-claims of Christianity provides this important connection.

A Quintessential Renaissance Man

In the short span of Pascal's life (only thirty-nine years), this native of France worked as a mathematician, a physicist, an inventor, a prose writer, a religious philosopher, and, above all, an imaginative and controversial defender of the Christian faith.[1] One of the founding fathers of the "new science," Pascal achieved recognition as one of the most advanced thinkers of his time.[2] As a distinguished Christian apologist, Pascal provided a penetrating and provocative analysis of the broader Christian world-and-life view.[3]

Pascal's fertile mind laid the foundations for infinitesimal calculus, integral calculus, and the calculus of probabilities.[4] German mathematician and philosopher Gottfried Wilhelm Leibniz (1646–1716) credits Pascal's infinitesimal analysis with inspiring his own development of calculus.[5] Pascal also contributed to the study of geometry and number theory. Philosopher Richard H. Popkin writes: "Pascal's analysis of the nature of mathematical systems seems to be closer to twentieth-century mathematical logic than that of any of his contemporaries."[6]

Also considered a first-rate experimental scientist, Pascal diligently practiced the (then emerging) scientific method. He rigorously verified or falsified his observations and conclusions through experimental testing.

Like all great inventors, Pascal's technological intuition and productive imagination propelled him ahead of his time. His creative technological experimentation resulted in such inventions as the syringe, the vacuum cleaner, and the hydraulic press as well as in development of the first public transportation system in Europe. His most famous invention, however, developed from an attempt to help his father avoid the arduous task of calculating taxes. Pascal became convinced that if a clock could calculate the hour, then maybe another device could successfully perform mathematical calculations. His invention of the first digital calculator, or adding machine is considered one of the first "applied" achievements of the early scientific revolution and the precursor to the modern computer.[7]

Philosopher of Science

Pascal showed an astute understanding of and appreciation for the new science born and slowly nurtured in seventeenth-century Europe.[8] An avid supporter of the views of Copernicus and Galileo, he argued that respect for authority should not take precedence over analytic reasoning and scientific experimentation. Pascal explored the nature of the scientific method and scientific progress and specifically addressed the importance of experimental data along with the need to develop sound explanatory hypotheses. He asserted that as scientists continue to explore nature's mysteries, newer and more updated hypotheses would replace older ones.

However, Pascal also recognized the limits of science. He believed that although scientific theories can be confirmed or falsified, they can never be absolutely established. Popkin points out that this position resembles the one advocated by the eminent twentieth-century philosopher of science Karl Popper.[9] Pascal was also aware that scientific progress had not changed human nature, specifically that the process by which human beings form their basic beliefs is rarely a rational or empirical one alone. Contemporary Christian philosopher Peter Kreeft said of Pascal, "He knew the power of science but also its impotence to make us wise or happy or good."[10] Pascal's advanced thinking has caused some to refer to him as the first modern man.

Mystical Religious Experience

Pascal was raised in what might be considered a nominal Roman Catholic family. However, at age thirty-one, while crossing the Seine River during a storm, he had a profound religious experience. This mystical encounter led him to devote the rest of his life to Jesus Christ and to the truths of the Christian faith. While Pascal never spoke publicly of the encounter, he wrote a memoir of it and carried it with him the rest of his life—having the words sown into his clothes. The memoir was discovered only after his death and is referred to as the "Night of Fire." A portion of it reads as follows:

> God of Abraham, God of Isaac, God of Jacob, not of philosophers and scholars. Certainty, certainty, heartfelt, joy, peace. God of Jesus Christ. God of Jesus Christ. My God and your God. Thy God shall be my God. The world forgotten, and everything except God. He can only be found by the ways taught in the Gospels. . . . Jesus Christ. Jesus Christ. . . . Let me not be cut off from him for ever![11]

After this life-changing epiphany, Pascal devoted most of his time to philosophical and religious writing. Some critics of religion have claimed that Pascal turned his back on science and even repudiated his scientific accomplishments. Historian of philosophy Frederick Copleston points out, however, that both these assertions are incorrect: "For in abandoning himself to God he did not renounce all scientific and mathematical interests as 'worldly;' rather did he come to look on his scientific interests in a new light, as part of his service of God."[12]

Defending the Faith

Blaise Pascal was preparing a book on Christian apologetics (*Apologie de la religion chrétienne*) for his skeptical friends when he became seriously ill. The lengthy affliction (possibly carcinomatous meningitis) caused Pascal terrible pain.[13] Unable to work, he gave himself to his devotional life and to helping the poor. He died August 19, 1662, leaving a legacy as one of the great pioneers of modern science and one of the most original Christian thinkers in history.

Pascal's unfinished apologetic work (mostly notes, outlines, and fragments) was subsequently published under the French title *Pensées* (pronounced "Ponsayz," and roughly translated as "Thoughts").[14] While *Pensées* is actually more of an outline than a complete book, its contents are so profound that it remains a perennial bestseller. Three unique Pascalian themes are introduced in the *Pensées*: the enigma of man, the relationship of faith and reason, and his famous Wager.

The Enigma of Man

As an experimental scientist Pascal had a deep appreciation for the value of acceptable explanatory theory. He believed that for a religion or philosophy to be worthy of belief it must account for the meaningful realities of life. One of those central realities is the enigma of man himself, described by Pascal in exclamatory terms: "What sort of freak then is man! How novel, how monstrous, how chaotic, how paradoxical, how prodigious! Judge of all things, feeble earthworm; repository of truth, sink of doubt, and error; glory and refuse of the universe!"[15] According to Pascal, man is a strange mixture of "greatness and wretchedness." Man's greatness is exhibited in his unique ability, as a reflective thinker, to recognize his wretchedness.

The Christian theistic worldview explains man's paradoxical nature by asserting that man's greatness is a direct result of the *imago Dei* (image of God). As a creature made in the image and likeness of God, man reflects the glory of his Maker. Though certainly in a finite way, man nevertheless exhibits certain God-like characteristics.

The wretchedness, on the other hand, can be traced to the first human beings' fall into sin (Genesis 3). Original sin is the biblical doctrine that the entire human race has inherited sinfulness, guilt, and moral corruption from Adam (Ps. 51:5; 58:3; Rom. 5:12, 18–19; 1 Cor. 15:22).

Pascal believed that the ultimate solution to man's contradictory predicament rests in finding redemption through the person of Jesus Christ. In Pascal's words:

> Knowing God without knowing our own wretchedness makes for pride. Knowing our own wretchedness without knowing God makes for despair. Knowing Jesus Christ strikes the balance because he shows us both God and our own wretchedness.[16]

For Pascal, it is in the redemptive encounter with Jesus Christ that man finds both himself and God. Therefore Christianity not only explains the puzzle of man's nature but also provides the solution for man's existential estrangement from God and from himself. Again from the *Pensées*:

> Not only do we only know God through Jesus Christ, but we only know ourselves through Jesus Christ; we only know life and death through Jesus Christ. Apart from Jesus Christ we cannot know the meaning of our life or our death, of God or of ourselves.[17]

Reasons of the Heart

Scholars disagree on how to classify Pascal's views concerning the relationship of faith and reason. Some have called Pascal a fideist (negatively defined as the view that faith has no rational foundation).[18] But Pascal's position is more complicated than simple fideism. He strongly asserted that "religion is not contrary to reason,"[19] and even argued that there are various evidences for the truth of the Christian faith. He lists such evidences as biblical prophecy, miracles (especially Christ's resurrection), the continued existence of the Jews, the Christian church's historical witness in the world, and Christianity's unique explanatory power.

Pascal did assert that reason and scientific investigation have limits and that reason stands in need of the illumination of faith and divine revelation. For him, the traditional proofs for God are religiously inadequate. (Unlike geometry, they are not deductively certain.) He viewed them as too complicated and remote for most people, and though they may provide knowledge about God, they do not provide knowledge of Christ. He proclaimed: "What a long way it is between knowing God and loving him."[20] Thus "proofs" have limited value. They may convince the "mind" but not the "heart."[21]

As Pascal described this distinction, "The heart has its reasons of which reason knows nothing."[22] He also wrote, "It is the heart which perceives God and not the reason."[23] Copleston explains that for Pascal, the heart refers to an "instinctive, immediate, and unreasoned apprehension of truth."[24] Pascal believed that the heart has an intuitive and immediate knowledge of first principles, including God. Rather than being a center of mere emotion, the heart instead conveys a sense of intuition (suggesting immediacy, spontaneity, and directness). Copleston defines Pascal's understanding of the heart as "a kind of intellectual instinct, rooted in the inmost nature of the soul."[25]

It appears that for Pascal, the mind and the heart both play an important role in a person's coming to faith. The heart provides the basic intuition in the process of forming basic beliefs, whereas the mind provides the complementary discursive reasoning. A recent book about the workings of the human mind suggests that Pascal's view of the importance of intuition in human thinking aligns with the latest scientific research.[26]

The Wager

Pascal designed the Wager for his skeptical friends who remained simultaneously unconvinced by the claims of atheism and of Christianity.[27] He believed that the existential realities of life force human beings to make decisions concerning such issues as what awaits a person after death. The uncertainties and risks inherent in the human predicament force individuals to make up their minds about God's existence. How a person decides this ultimate issue has potential consequences in this life and possibly in the next. For Pascal, the question of God's existence and the truthfulness of Christianity cannot be decided by an appeal to reason alone. For him there is "too much to deny and not enough to affirm."[28] Therefore people must make a prudent wager about whether God does or does not exist. Pascal writes in the *Pensées*:

Either God is or he is not. But to which view shall we be inclined? Reason cannot decide this question. Infinite chaos separates us. At the far end of this infinite distance a coin is being spun which will come down heads or tails. How will you wager? Reason cannot make you choose either, reason cannot prove either wrong. . . . You must wager. There is no choice, you are already committed. Which will you choose then? Let us see: since a choice must be made, let us see which offers you the least interest.[29]

Pascal suggests only two possible choices: first, belief in God and the making of a religious commitment (he speaks, of course, about commitment to the Christian God). Two possible outcomes can result from this choice: A person's belief can be correct or incorrect. If a person believes in God and he actually exists, then according to Pascal the believer stands to gain everything. The payoff, so to speak, for a correct wager would involve infinite gain (eternal life with God in heaven). On the other hand, if a person chooses faith and God does not actually exist, then the believer loses nothing. In terms of a cost-benefit analysis, the person who wagers on God has everything to gain and nothing to lose.

The second recourse is to wager against God by disbelieving in him and refusing to make a religious commitment. Two possible outcomes can also result from this choice. A person's disbelief can also be correct or incorrect. If an individual does not believe in God and God does not exist, then the unbeliever gains nothing. On the other hand, if a person does not believe in God but God does actually exist, then the unbeliever stands to lose everything. The loss for wagering incorrectly would involve an infinite loss (hell's eternal exclusion from the life of God). In terms of a cost-benefit analysis, the person who wagers against God has nothing to gain and everything to lose.

In light of these two scenarios, Pascal asserts that the prudent wager is on God. Adopting Christianity over atheism is a judiciously rational decision.[30]

The context in which this wager arose and how Pascal intended its use as an apologetic tool are important. Four points help define his intent.[31] First, the Wager was never intended to function as a rational proof for God's existence, nor as a substitute for Christian evidences. Second, the Wager targets a specific audience, namely those who have suspended judgment on ultimate issues. Third, the Wager emerges in a specific historical and epistemological context. Copleston describes seventeenth-century France as "a society impregnated by deistic humanism and rationalist skepticism and free thought."[32] Fourth, the Wager seems to be intended primarily as a device to help awaken people who are indifferent to ultimate issues (God, death, immortality).

A number of criticisms have been raised against the Wager through the years by skeptics and Christians alike.[33] These reactions, along with some responses (hopefully in the spirit of Pascal) warrant consideration.

1. *The Wager diminishes love for God, and makes faith into a cold, pragmatic gamble.*

Response: The Wager may seem a heartless pragmatic appeal, but it reaches an unbeliever at a realistic starting point. The "tasting and seeing that the LORD is good" (Ps. 34:8) is what transforms a person, by the grace of God. Maybe the Wager should be viewed as a common sense appeal that helps a person mentally prepare for faith (itself a divine gift). Apologetic reasoning is intended to evoke a response and clear away barriers so the heart can then rest confidently and securely in God. Thinking in strongly practical terms about one's relationship with God isn't necessarily unspiritual. The practical desire to avoid God's wrath may be a sign that the person has already experienced God's prevenient grace.

2. *Doesn't the Wager itself run counter to Pascal's own claim that it is God who imparts faith?*

Response: Pascal believed that while a person cannot give himself true faith, a person can begin to prepare himself intellectually. The Wager's greatest force may be its ability to shake a person out of his or her spiritual "indifference." The Wager is simply an apologetic tool, not an end in itself. But if the Wager can be successfully used to awaken a person's consciousness, then it may be a very valuable tool.

3. *Performing a religious task does not make a person a Christian.*

Response: Pascal encouraged those who lacked faith to imitate those who did have faith. While it is true that performing certain religious functions doesn't make a person a believer, many Christians believe that certain actions are a means of grace (reading the Bible, attending church, receiving the sacraments, and so forth). God's grace works through certain actions or activities to change the human heart, and this change is central to a spiritual conversion.

4. *The Wager fails to recognize that the believer loses a great deal by wagering on God if he doesn't actually exist. In fact, the believer loses his autonomy and wastes his life on religious nonsense.*

Response: It may be more accurate to say that the person who wagers on God has everything to gain, and in comparison, little to lose. The Wager line of reasoning does involve a risk-reward analysis. But even if the individual who wagers on God is incorrect about God's existence, he gains a virtuous life and all the comforts and other benefits that accompany a life of faith.

5. *The Wager provides no guarantee, so why wager at all?*

Response: The existential uncertainties of life force people to choose. Life experience provides no absolute guarantees of anything. The person who wagers on God has a realistic guarantee of satisfaction. If wrong about God's existence, he or she will never know because of death (defined in this case as extinction). On the other hand, the person who wagers against God and is right about his nonexistence faces a realistic guarantee of dissatisfaction. If right that God does not exist, he or she will never know because of death (i.e., extinction).[34]

6. *The Wager only works if a person bets on the right (or true) religion. What if you gamble on the wrong God?*

Response: Pascal recognized other religious alternatives, but he believed that Christianity was the most probably true religion in light of prophecy, miracles, and its unique explanatory power. The Wager emerged within a given historical context. An important premise is that no God other than the Christian God is real. That was the original parameter in which the Wager was meant to function. This gamble may not have the same force (or as broad an appeal) in a modern pluralistic age.[35] Today, the Wager may be more appropriately used after a person has conceded the superiority of Christianity's truth-claims as compared to other religions, in the crucible of objective testing.

7. *The Wager works equally for all religions or subjective belief systems that make an infinite claim.*

Response: Few religions make an infinite claim (promise an infinite reward or life), especially pluralistic religions. The Wager is significantly enhanced when joined with an argument for Christianity's uniqueness among the world's religions. Again, the Wager was never intended to serve as a stand-alone argument for Christianity.

8. *The Wager will not convince the hardened or committed atheist.*

Response: No argument will convince anyone (apart from God's grace). There is a difference between evidence and personal persuasion. The Wager was not intended for an atheist audience in the first place. Other Christian apologetic arguments are available for those who deny God's existence (see chap. 1).

9. *The Wager promotes intellectual dishonesty. A person can't pretend to believe when he or she really does not.*

Response: The Wager can promote reflective thought about what lies ahead (death), not dishonesty. Remember, Pascal emphasized the limits of human reason and stressed the importance of, and the need for, revelation and God's gift of faith. Skeptics sometimes overestimate the quantity and quality of what humans know. In addition, if a belief is not contrary to reason and is warranted prudentially then why would a person resist accepting it? To open one's mind to being persuaded is not dishonest.

10. Wouldn't a just God prefer honest skeptics to purely pragmatic believers?

Response: Skeptics fail to see, from a biblical perspective, that "hardness of heart" keeps a person from believing in God. Unbelief is rooted in rebellion and arrogance, which essentially is false worship (1 Sam. 15:22–23). Such evil produces idolatry and immorality. God has given everyone signs of his existence, but some skeptics ignore and/or repress them (Psalm 14; 19; Romans 1). Reflective nonbelievers would do well to consider whether their unbelief springs from rational or nonrational factors.

11. Why gamble a certain finite good (human autonomy) for an uncertain infinite good?

Response: All gamblers risk what is certain for what is uncertain, especially when the benefit significantly outweighs the cost. So much good results from belief in God—even in this life (virtue)—that the autonomy sacrificed seems comparatively insignificant.

12. Doesn't the Wager commit the "ad baculum" fallacy—enticing people to believe by appealing to a threat or harm (i.e., believe so as to avoid hell)?

Response: Some threats are real—the necessary and logical consequences of a person's actions. If God is in actuality the Creator and Sustainer of the universe, then he legitimately sets the rules.

Conclusion

Pascal's writings offer a penetrating analysis of the human condition. They marshal probative evidence for the truth of Christianity. His Wager, though open to criticism, is still worthy of careful consideration on the part of believers and nonbelievers. Part 2, which includes the next five chapters, examines the specifics of faith in Jesus Christ, beginning with the Gospels.

Discussion Questions

1. In what ways, according to Pascal, does Christianity demonstrate superior explanatory power compared with other religions?
2. What does Pascal mean by "reasons of the heart"?
3. What is the context of Pascal's Wager?
4. How should one qualify the Wager as an apologetic tool?
5. What fair criticisms is the Wager susceptible to?

For Further Study

Copleston, Frederick. *A History of Philosophy*. Vol. 4. New York: Image Books–Doubleday, 1994.

Kreeft, Peter. *Christianity For Modern Pagans: Pascal's Pensées; Edited, Outlined and Explained*. San Francisco: Ignatius, 1993.

Morris, Thomas V. *Making Sense of It All: Pascal and the Meaning of Life*. Grand Rapids: Eerdmans, 1992.

Pascal, Blaise. *Pensées*, trans. A. J. Krailsheimer. Rev. ed. New York: Penguin, 1995.

PART TWO

THINKING
THROUGH QUESTIONS
ABOUT FAITH
IN JESUS CHRIST

ARE THE GOSPELS
TRUSTWORTHY ACCOUNTS
OF JESUS' LIFE?

To be skeptical of the resultant text of the New Testament books is to allow all of classical antiquity to slip into obscurity, for no documents of the ancient period are as well attested bibliographically as the New Testament.

—John Warwick Montgomery, *History and Christianity*

The excessive skepticism of many liberal theologians stems not from a careful evaluation of the available data, but from an enormous predisposition against the supernatural.

—Millar Burrows, *What Mean These Stones?*

Is historic Christianity anchored in truth? Was Jesus the divine Messiah, the Lord and Savior of the world? Did he actually fulfill biblical prophecy, perform miracles, suffer and die on the cross, and rise bodily from the dead? Do the facts of history validate his claims?

The truth of the Christian faith depends on the historical nature and accuracy of the unique claims, character, and credentials of Jesus Christ. Since the Gospel writings are the primary source of information about him, historic Christianity can only be true if these writings convey factually reliable information. If, on the other hand, the Gospels contain largely mythical or legendary accounts about Jesus, then the truth-claims cannot be trusted.

History offers valid arguments for why these accounts of Jesus Christ's life should be considered trustworthy. In addition, arguments can be made that show deep flaws in the idea that the Gospels contain mythical accounts. Examining both positions offers substantial reasons for belief in Jesus Christ and his great redemptive work (perfect moral life, atoning death on the cross, and bodily resurrection from the grave).

Historical Reliability of the Gospels

The following arguments[1] analyze the historical and objective evidence for the Gospel accounts. Some of the arguments relate to the New Testament as a whole, while others focus specifically upon the four Gospels.

1. The New Testament documents are the best attested documents of antiquity in terms of total number of manuscripts.

Generally speaking, very few manuscripts of the ancient classical writers (Aristotle, Plato, Caesar, Tacitus, Thucydides, Herodotus, etc.) exist.[2] The best cases average about twenty extant manuscripts for any given historical work. And this number is generally considered an exceptional quantity in terms of manuscript attestation.[3] However, in most instances far fewer manuscripts remain. In fact, for most authors' works the number amounts to a mere handful. Yet by the accepted standards of historiography, even those are not rejected as inauthentic or unreliable on the basis of their sparse number. The reality is that some ancient documents are accepted as authentic texts with extremely thin manuscript attestation.

In stark contrast to these familiar classical works, the New Testament documents are backed by an astounding quantity of manuscript evidence. For example, more than 5,000 individual Greek manuscripts that contain all or part of the New Testament exist.[4] These manuscripts are augmented by more than 8,000 copies of the Vulgate, an important Latin version of the Bible translated by the early-fifth-century Western church father, Jerome. Further attestation comes in the form of several thousand early New Testament manuscripts translated into Eastern languages such as Syriac, Coptic, Armenian, Slavic, and Ethiopic.[5]

Even without these thousands of extant manuscripts, virtually the entire New Testament text could be reproduced from specific scriptural citations within the written (and preserved) sermons, commentaries, and various other works of the early church fathers.[6] These Christian leaders, apologists, and writers served from the second through the fifth centuries. The Patristic writers, as they are also called, included (among others) such prominent Christian figures as Tertullian, Athanasius, Ambrose, Chrysostom, Jerome, and Augustine.

The New Testament stands as the best attested document of the ancient world. This tremendous abundance of manuscript evidence has enhanced the development of a crucial enterprise known as textual criticism. By careful manuscript comparison and analysis throughout history, textual criticism attempts to identify the exact nature of the original text (as written by the New Testament authors).[7]

This powerful manuscript evidence does not intend to prove that the New Testament is factually accurate and trustworthy in its account of Jesus' life, but it does mark the New Testament as a unique historical document worthy of careful consideration.

2. The interval of time between the original authorship and the date of the earliest New Testament manuscript copies is extremely short.

The shorter the time period between the date when a document was originally written (the autograph) and the date of its first extant copy (or manuscript), the more reliable a text is considered. A short time period means there is less time for the document to be corrupted through transmission or interpolation. For most ancient classics, an average gap of over 1,000 years stands between the original work and the date of its earliest existing copy.[8] This gap may extend as wide as 1,400 years in some cases. While even a 700-year gap would be considered good among the great works of antiquity, the textual situation with the New Testament is vastly superior.[9]

Unlike the classical works, a very short period of time exists between the autographs and the earliest New Testament copies. An examination of a few early New Testament manuscripts helps illustrate this point.

The oldest copy of any portion of the New Testament in existence today is the John Rylands' manuscript[10] (so named because it resides in the John Rylands University Library in Manchester, England). This tiny papyrus (primitive paper) fragment contains just a few verses from the Gospel of John (John 18:31–33, 37–38). Discovered in Egypt, this manuscript, also known as P52, has been dated between AD 117–138,[11] and the distinguished philologist Adolf Deissmann has argued that it should be dated even earlier.[12] Depending upon when John's Gospel was written (a rough range between AD 60 and AD 90), the time factor amounts to, at most, only several decades. This remarkably short time span provides potent proof of the text's purity. The discovery of this manuscript also refutes the theory of some higher critics who presumed that John's Gospel had been written after the middle of the second century.[13]

Two early and important collections of papyrus manuscripts of the New Testament are the Bodmer Papyri (P66, P72, and P75) and the Chester Beatty Papyri (P45, P46, and P47). The Bodmer Papyri contain parts of the New Testament (including most of the Gospels of Luke and John) and date to approximately AD 200.[14] The Beatty Papyri contain almost all of the New Testament (including large portions of the four Gospels) and date to about AD 250.[15] These manuscripts therefore are roughly 100 to 200 years removed from their autographs. By textual standards, this time span is very brief for ancient writings and supplies good reason to accept the basic authenticity of the New Testament text.

Five important Greek uncial manuscripts[16] (written in a type of capital letters) also provide critical textual support for the New Testament. Written on parchment (scraped animal skin) rather than on papyrus, these manuscripts took the codex form (arranged more like a modern book) rather than an ancient scroll form. Essential textual information for each codex is listed below.[17]

- **Codex Sinaiticus (א):** contains the entire New Testament and parts of the Old Testament. It resides in The British Museum and dates from about AD 340.
- **Codex Vaticanus (B):** includes almost the entire Bible. It can be found in the Vatican Library and dates from AD 325–350.
- **Codex Alexandrinus (A):** contains most of the Bible and resides in the British Museum. It dates from about AD 450.
- **Codex Bezae (D):** written in Greek and Latin, includes parts of the New Testament (and most of the four Gospels). Kept in the Cambridge University Library, it dates between AD 450–550.
- **Codex Ephraemi (C):** contains part of the Old Testament and most of the New Testament. It resides in the French National Library in Paris and dates from about AD 400.

Many more New Testament texts could be mentioned—texts that run from the early Middle Ages to the Reformation era.[18] However, the ancient texts just discussed illustrate the immense superiority of the New Testament documents to all other classical works of antiquity in terms of the time between autographs and earliest extant copies. An analysis of this data led Sir Frederic Kenyon, an expert on ancient manuscripts, to draw this conclusion:

> The interval then between the dates of original composition and the earliest extant evidence becomes so small as to be in fact negligible, and the last foundation for any doubt that the Scriptures have come down to us substantially as they were written has now been removed. Both the authenticity and gen-

eral integrity of the books of the New Testament may be regarded as finally established.[19]

3. *The historic statements made about Jesus by ancient non-Christian authors comports well with the Gospel record.*

Examination of the following ten historical sources (outside the Bible) reveals information about the life of Jesus that conforms to, and even corroborates, the four New Testament Gospel accounts and also the book of Acts.[20]

- Tacitus (ca. AD 55–120): Roman historian, *Annals*
- Suetonius (ca. AD 120): Roman historian, *Life of Claudius*
- Josephus (AD 37–97): Jewish historian, *Antiquities*
- Pliny the Younger (AD 112): Roman governor, *Epistles X*
- Jewish *Talmud* (commentary on Jewish law, completed AD 500)
- Toledoth Jesu (reflects early Jewish thought, completed fifth century AD)
- Lucian (second century AD): Greek satirist
- Thallus (ca. AD 52): Samaritan-born historian, *Histories*
- Mara Bar-Serapion (ca. AD 73): Letter
- Phlegon (ca. AD 80): historian, chronicles (mentioned by Origen)

These ancient sources draw the following portrait of Jesus and of early Christians:[21] (1) He was a provocative teacher, a wise and virtuous man from the region of Judea. (2) He reportedly performed miracles and made prophetic claims. (3) The Jewish leaders condemned him for acts of sorcery and apostasy. (4) He was crucified by the Roman procurator Pontius Pilate at the time of the Jewish Passover, and during the reign of the Emperor Tiberius. (5) Jesus' followers, called Christians, reported that he had risen from the dead. (6) The Christian faith had spread to Rome where Christians were charged with crimes and met horrific persecution. (7) First-century Christians worshiped Jesus Christ as God and celebrated the Eucharist in their services. (8) While at times the Romans ridiculed the followers of Christ as morally weak, these disciples were often known for their courage and virtue.

Brief and, at times, cryptic statements about Jesus made by ancient non-Christian authors do not prove the claims of the gospel. Yet nothing in them conflicts with what's recorded about Jesus in the Gospels. And these extra-biblical, historical sources are consistent with and confirm the historicity of the gospel message.[22]

4. The authors of the four Gospels were either eyewitnesses of Jesus' life themselves, or were closely associated with eyewitnesses.

In their earliest preaching, the apostles claimed to be direct eyewitnesses of the great events surrounding Jesus' life (Acts 2:32; 3:15; 5:32; 10:39), and this appeal to firsthand information appears throughout the New Testament (Acts 17:30–31; 1 Cor. 15:1–20; Heb. 2:3–4; 2 Pet. 1:16–18; 1 John 1:1–3). The Gospel writers also claimed either to have been with Jesus themselves (John 1:14; 19:35; 21:24–25) or to have relied closely upon the words of those who walked and talked with him (Luke 1:2). The unanimous testimony of early church history is that two of the Gospels were written by Jesus' original disciples (later called apostles), Matthew and John. The other two Gospels, Mark and Luke, rely upon and closely reflect the testimony of the apostles Peter, Paul, and others.[23]

While many contemporary critics reject apostolic authorship (or direct influence) of the four Gospels, there remain good historical and textual reasons for concluding that the apostles either wrote the Gospels themselves or were the guiding source behind them. A brief look at the apostolic witness behind each Gospel lends credence.

The Gospel of Matthew: Though this Gospel nowhere identifies its author in text, from the earliest times in church history the name "Matthew" (an original apostle) was universally associated as its narrator. At least two points favor his authorship:[24] First, manuscript copies of the Gospel circulated from the earliest period (ca. AD 125) with Matthew's name connected to it, and that name (signifying authorship) was never disputed until recent times. Second, a strong ancient tradition stems from the early Christian leader Papias (ca. AD 60–130), that Matthew, one of the original twelve apostles, wrote this particular Gospel. While this tradition is not without dispute, Matthew's authorship was also accepted by such early church fathers as Irenaeus, Origen, and Eusebius.

Gospel of Mark: The early church unanimously agreed that John Mark (Acts 12:12; 13:13; 15:36–41), the cousin of Barnabas and associate of the apostle Paul, was the author of the second (in manuscript order) Gospel.[25] Church fathers Papias, Irenaeus, Clement of Alexandria, Origen, and Jerome (among others) also accepted without dispute that Mark's Gospel reflected the eyewitness testimony of the apostle Peter.[26] This early tradition conveyed that Mark took the basic preached message of Peter (the primitive church's central preacher and an eyewitness) and arranged and shaped that message into the written Gospel of Mark. Textual evidence for Mark's reliance on Peter appears in the Gospel itself. As New Testament scholar F. F. Bruce explains, "Mark's use of pronouns in narratives involving Peter seems time after time to reflect a reminiscence by that apostle in the first person."[27] Apparently

Peter was Mark's source, and Peter's eyewitness testimony undergirds Mark's Gospel.

Gospel of Luke: Belief that Luke was the author of the third Gospel, as well as a close companion of the apostle Paul, appears well supported in church history (by Irenaeus, Clement of Alexandria, Origen, and Tertullian) and best fits the internal textual considerations.[28] The author of Luke's Gospel, also wrote the book of Acts and had to have been a personal companion to Paul. These elements affirm Luke, the physician, as the author of the third Gospel. Though not an original apostle, Luke had access to all the principle apostolic figures including Paul, Peter, and James (the brother of Jesus).[29] Therefore Luke's Gospel relies closely upon the accounts of those eyewitnesses. As the prologue of Luke's Gospel sets forth:

> Many have undertaken to draw up an account of the things that have been fulfilled among us, just as they were handed down to us by those who from the first were eyewitnesses and servants of the word. Therefore, since I myself have carefully investigated everything from the beginning, it seemed good also to me to write an orderly account for you, most excellent Theophilus, so that you may know the certainty of the things you have been taught. (Luke 1:1–4)

Gospel of John: The author of the Gospel of John displays detailed knowledge of first-century Jewish culture, custom, and theology, as well as a keen awareness of the geography of ancient Israel. These details bespeak the recollections of an eyewitness to the events of Jesus' life (John 21:24–25). The author best supported by both church tradition (Polycarp, Irenaeus, Tertullian) and by internal textual evidence is the apostle John,[30] the son of Zebedee (Matt. 4:21; Mark 1:19), affectionately referred to as "the disciple whom Jesus loved" (John 13:23; 19:26). John was not only one of the original twelve apostles, but he was part of the inner circle, being present at Jesus' transfiguration, last supper, and crucifixion. John also saw the resurrected Christ firsthand (John 21:20).

Contemporary critics set forth many objections to the traditional view that eyewitness testimony stands behind the Gospels. However, these objections as a whole prove insubstantial, and the traditional viewpoint remains as the most defensible position on Gospel authorship.[31]

5. *The Gospel writers intended to convey and were capable of conveying historical and factual information about Jesus, and the historical content of their writings has been confirmed to a significant degree.*

Each of the Gospel writers was either a direct eyewitness himself or relayed direct eyewitness testimony concerning Jesus. Either way, each was fully conversant with the facts surrounding Jesus' life, death, and resurrection and thus capable of communicating trustworthy history. Further, since the Gospels reported and described actual events within a generation of their occurrence and since they rely upon early oral and written sources, the credibility of their message must be considered very strong.

While different from modern biographies, the Gospels do fit within the literary genre of biography, especially as understood in the first century.[32] All four Gospels provide detailed information about the life and ministry of Jesus, focusing especially upon the great redemptive events of his life (his death and resurrection). The Gospels are attentive to historical detail (this is especially true of the Gospel of Luke and the book of Acts). John's Gospel provides the most details concerning such things as chronology, geography, and topography.

The basic historical message about Jesus (his extraordinary life, sacrificial death, bodily resurrection) receives corroboration in the limited but probative external sources from ancient non-Christian and later Christian writers. Archaeological discoveries also support the basic reliability of the Gospel accounts. While external sources cannot prove the specific truth-claims of Christianity, they confirm many of the historical facts intertwined in the gospel message.

6. The apostles' credibility as truth-tellers is greatly strengthened when one recognizes they had little to gain and almost everything to lose in proclaiming Jesus as Lord and Savior.

People's actions are frequently motivated by the anticipation of potential gain or loss. The apostles had little to gain and virtually everything to lose by proclaiming Jesus as the risen Savior and Lord. These intimate followers of Jesus were staunch monotheists, part of a centuries-old tradition that practiced strict commitment to the one, true and living God of Israel (Yahweh). Holding aberrant theological views brought costly personal consequences. Creating a hoax about Jesus would only have brought the apostles meaningless hardship, persecution, even martyrdom, not to mention the possible damnation of their souls for blasphemy and apostasy.

If the apostles had, in fact, created a resurrection hoax, what is the likelihood they would have been willing to die as martyrs for what they knew to be false? And, even if the apostles had conspired to create a resurrection deception, that conspiracy would have undoubtedly come apart under extreme pressure. Plenty of adversaries were more than willing to expose any possible deceit. The apostles were hated, scorned, excommunicated, imprisoned, and tortured. Further, if the apostles were deceivers, they violated everything Jesus taught about truth and honesty. Yet nowhere in the Gospels do the apostles appear as charlatans or mythmakers; rather, they are portrayed as simple, honest, truth-telling folk. The apostles' claims about Jesus are strengthened by the fact that they had no discernible motive to lie or deceive.

Solid reasons support the conclusion that the Gospels are historically reliable. However, attempts to classify the Gospels as legendary stories also need to be addressed.

The Gospels: Mythical or Factual?

Popular culture, abetted by some outspoken critics and commentators, either suggests or insists that the Gospels are, to one degree or another, mythical or at best legendary accounts of the life and ministry of Jesus. The following considerations, including time and other practical factors, argue to the contrary.

1. Because of the early emergence of the Gospels and the sources behind them, myths and legends did not have sufficient time to develop and be recorded in their accounts.

Since many of the New Testament books (Gospels and various epistles) were written fairly soon after the reported events, time simply didn't allow legends and myths to enter into them. Good historical and textual reasons exist to conclude that the Gospels were, in fact, written at a very early date.

First, Jesus' death at the hands of Pontius Pilate likely took place sometime between AD 30 and AD 33. Evidence suggests that the synoptic Gospels (Matthew, Mark, and Luke) existed by the early 60s (possibly in the late 50s for Mark)—within one generation of the events surrounding the life, death, and resurrection of Jesus Christ. None of the Gospels mention noteworthy events that transpired between AD 60 and 70.[33] Three such events were: (1) the persecution of Christians instigated by the ruthless Roman emperor, Nero (ca. mid-60s), (2) the martyrdom of three of the early church's central leaders: James (the brother of Jesus), Peter, and Paul (ca. 62–66), and (3) the fall of Jerusalem (including the destruction of the Jewish Temple) under the Roman military leader, Titus (70). Since none of these momentous events, of great interest to Christians, are mentioned in the Gospels as having yet taken place, a growing number of New Testament scholars conclude that the synoptic Gospels must have already been in existence by the early 60s.

Second, since the book of Acts follows the Gospel of Luke as a companion work (written to the same person and in the same writing style), and since Acts makes no mention of the events cited previously, the date of the synoptic Gospels would likely be even earlier, especially if assuming Markan priority (the widely accepted theory that Mark was the earliest Gospel written). If Luke used Mark's Gospel in preparing his own (a reasonable assumption in light of Peter's eyewitness influence upon Mark), then Mark's Gospel may have existed in the late 50s—a very brief time after the events of Jesus' life. Certainly many people were still around at this early stage who had experienced the events surrounding Jesus' life and death. Such firsthand knowledge tends to prohibit the advancement of myth and legend.

Considering that written and oral apostolic sources bridge the gap between the time of Jesus' death and the time the Gospels were written buttresses these two arguments. An official oral tradition of preaching was certainly connected to the apostle Peter. And some of the apostle Paul's epistles (Galatians, 1 and 2 Thessalonians) were written as early as the late 40s and early 50s. Source criticism (the study of sources that stand behind the written text) confirms that there were certainly oral and possibly written sources behind the original Greek Gospels.

New Testament scholar Craig Blomberg states that ample reasons exist to believe that Matthew, Mark, and Luke used such sources, and concludes that those sources provide further credibility to the Gospel writings. "Source criticism cannot demonstrate that the first accounts of the various portions of Jesus' life were entirely trustworthy, but it can suggest that those accounts arose in a time and place in which many who had personally known Jesus still lived."[34]

2. The theory that the Gospels are myth is only plausible if several generations existed over which mythology concerning Jesus could grow.

The idea that myth and legend encrusted the facts surrounding Jesus' life rests on the postulate that several generations passed (between events and records) in which the myths could grow.[35] A. N. Sherwin-White, Oxford scholar of ancient Greek and Roman history, has argued that the span of even two full generations is insufficient for myth and legend to accrue and distort historical fact.[36] Legend expert Julius Muller states that legend cannot replace fact so long as the eyewitnesses remain alive,[37] and given the early dates of the Gospels, eyewitnesses (both believers and nonbelievers) were still around at the time they were written.

3. The apostles of Jesus recognized the difference between myth and factual eyewitness testimony, and they solemnly asserted that they were eyewitnesses of historical events.

Another reason for rejecting the theory that myth and legend crept into the Gospel accounts is that the apostles of Jesus were capable of recognizing the difference between myth and eyewitness testimony, and they declared themselves eyewitnesses of actual historical events (Luke 1:1–4; John 19:35;

1 Cor. 15:3–8; Gal. 1:11–12; 2 Pet. 1:16; 1 John 1 :1–2). Rather than promoting distortion or exaggeration, the apostles actively attempted to squelch rumors and untruths before they could spread (John 21:22–25), further testifying of their intent to report reliable history.

The Gospel writers also gave careful attention to historical aspects. They supplied intimate details of Jesus' time (including names, dates, locations, events, customs, etc.). Historically speaking, the central criterion for including the Gospels in the New Testament canon was that they emerged from within apostolic circles that included eyewitnesses or associates of eyewitnesses.

4. If the Gospel writers had departed from historical fact (either by exaggeration or outright invention), hostile witnesses familiar with the events of Jesus' life could have and would have exposed them.

Good evidence exists to support the conclusion that the Gospels reflect early sources concerning the life and death of Jesus. Therefore, if the Gospel writers had departed from historical facts, hostile witnesses also conversant with the events of Jesus' life would no dcubt have exposed the apostles immediately. As F. F. Bruce writes, it could not have been easy "to invent words and deeds of Jesus in those early years, when so many of his disciples were about, who could remember what had and had not happened."[38] His enemies were even more numerous and socially powerful. The apostles, confident in their testimony, appealed to the firsthand knowledge of unbelievers acquainted with the facts of Jesus life (Acts 2:22; 26:25–27). A person must also bear in mind that the earliest Christian preaching took place in the same area where Christ had lived and died.

5. The Gospel stories do not correspond in style or in content with other known mythical writings.

An analysis of the Gospel accounts reveals that they bear no resemblance either in style or in content to any other well-known examples of mythical writings.[39] For example, biblical miracles are neither bizarre nor frivolous like those depicted in mythological literature (Greek mythology). Jesus' miracles are always done within the context of his ministry, specifically to give glory to God and to meet legitimate human need. The historical and the miraculous stand together side-by-side in the Gospels in a way distinctly different from mythological literature.

6. The arguments for rejecting the Gospels as history are circular.

Typical reasoning for viewing the Gospels as myth is fallacious, usually based on circular argument: The divinity of Christ is rejected because the

Gospel text is rejected. The Gospel text is rejected because it supposedly is based on myth. The Gospels are thought to be myth because of the miraculous events that speak of God becoming man (that is, the divinity of Christ).[40] This reasoning clearly begs the question (the premises illegitimately depend upon the assumed conclusion) and exposes a presumed antisupernatural bias. The problem is one of presuppositions, not of historical fact.

To reject the historicity of the Gospels *a priori* because they contain miracles violates logical and historical standards of reasoning. Since the Gospels are well established historically, the miracle stories they convey deserve serious historical consideration. The only way to know whether there is credibility to a miraculous claim is to investigate it. The cutting edge of science exploration has revealed a universe in which miracles are possible. To reject miracles based on a precommitment to the naturalistic worldview is to engage in circular reasoning.

Conclusion

In summary, an abundance of historical, logical, and textual reasons exist for taking the Gospels at face value. The Gospels convey confirmed historical, factual information about the events surrounding Jesus' life. No good reasons exist for regarding the claims, character, and credentials of Jesus Christ as mere myth. The suggestion that they do arises not from fair-minded historical analysis, but rather from antisupernatural presuppositions and biases. The specific purpose and intent of the Gospels is recorded in John 20:31: "But these are written that you may believe that Jesus is the Christ, the Son of God, and that by believing you may have life in his name."

So, who is this Jesus? His identity forms the topic of the next chapter.

Discussion Questions

1. How does the New Testament compare with other classical works of antiquity in terms of manuscript evidence?
2. How do ancient extrabiblical reports about Jesus compare with the Gospel accounts?
3. What is the relationship of the Gospels to eyewitness testimony concerning Jesus?
4. Why couldn't myth have successfully crept into the Gospel accounts? In what noticeable ways do the Gospels differ from mythical literature?
5. How does the issue of antisupernatural presuppositions affect one's approach to the reliability of the Gospels?

For Further Study

Blomberg, Craig. *The Historical Reliability of the Gospels*. Downers Grove, IL: Inter-
Varsity, 1987.

Bruce, F. F. *The New Testament Documents: Are They Reliable?* Grand Rapids, Eerdmans,
1960. Reprint, 5th rev. ed. Leicester, England: InterVarsity, 1985.

France, R. T. *The Evidence for Jesus*. Downers Grove, IL: InterVarsity, 1986.

Guthrie, Donald. *New Testament Introduction*. Downers Grove, IL: InterVarsity,
1986.

Habermas, Gary R. *The Historical Jesus: Ancient Evidence for the Life of Christ*. Joplin,
MO: College Press, 1996.

Metzger, Bruce Manning. *The Text of the New Testament: Its Transmission, Corruption,
and Restoration*. 2nd ed. New York: Oxford, 1968.

Montgomery, John Warwick. *History and Christianity*. Minneapolis: Bethany, 1965.

Wilkins, Michael J., and J. P. Moreland, gen. eds. *Jesus Under Fire*. Grand Rapids:
Zondervan, 1995.

8

IS JESUS A MAN,
MYTH, MADMAN, MENACE, MYSTIC,
MARTIAN, OR THE MESSIAH?

> But who among his disciples or among their proselytes was capable of inventing the saying ascribed to Jesus, or imagining the life and character revealed in the Gospels?
>
> —John Stuart Mill, *Three Essays on Religion*

> If the life and death of Socrates are those of a philosopher, the life and death of Jesus Christ are those of a God.
>
> —Jean Jacques Rousseau, *Emile*

Who is Jesus Christ? What is his true identity? Jesus himself challenges people to think about this question in the Gospel accounts (Matt. 22:41–46; John 8:24–28; 53–58). He asks his disciples directly:

> "Who do people say the Son of Man is?" They replied, "Some say John the Baptist; others say Elijah; and still others, Jeremiah or one of the prophets." "But what about you?" he asked. "Who do you say I am?" Simon Peter answered, "You are the Christ, the Son of the living God." Jesus replied, "Blessed are you, Simon son of Jonah, for this was not revealed to you by man, but by my Father in heaven." (Matt. 16:13–17)

Historic Christianity is all about Jesus—his identity, message, and mission. For two millennia the Christian church has viewed Jesus as the divine Messiah whose life, death, and resurrection are God's means for forgiving repentant sinners. At the heart of the Christian faith is the assertion that Jesus, precisely because he is God incarnate, can indeed provide redemption on the cross for human beings.

But is it intellectually credible to believe that Jesus Christ was actually God incarnate? Are there other acceptable alternatives to his divine identity? If Christianity's central truth-claim—that Jesus is God—stands the test of reason and history, then faith is powerfully warranted. Understanding how Jesus viewed himself, what Scripture claims about him, and testing those claims by examining six alternative hypotheses strengthens a person's convictions and makes a testimony far more persuasive.

Did Jesus Really Consider Himself to Be God?

There have always been individuals and groups (both past and present) that have denied the New Testament portrayal of Jesus as God incarnate (a single person fully God and fully man). However, a fair assessment of the scriptural data leaves little doubt that the New Testament asserts Jesus' divinity (see chap. 9 for a summary). Viewing Jesus Christ as the God-man is the historic and orthodox consensus of Christendom (Catholic, Orthodox, and Protestant). But, how did Jesus view himself? Some critics assert that he never actually claimed to be God and that the Christian church has erroneously drawn this conclusion.[1]

Jesus never said the exact words "I am God," and yet he was clearly conscious of his deity and deliberately made that awareness known to others. The following four points illustrate:

1. Jesus equated himself with the Father (Yahweh God).

In his public ministry, Jesus identified himself so closely with the Father as to imply that he (Jesus) is God. He made this association in the following ways:[2]

- To *know* Jesus is to know God: "If you knew me, you would know my Father also" (John 14:7).
- To *see* Jesus is to see God: "Anyone who has seen me has seen the Father" (John 14:9).
- To *encounter* Jesus is to encounter God: "Believe me when I say that I am in the Father and the Father is in me" (John 14:11).

- To *trust* in Jesus is to trust in God: "Trust in God, trust also in me" (John 14:1).
- To *welcome* Jesus is to welcome God: "'[W]hoever welcomes me does not welcome me but the one who sent me'" (Mark 9:37).
- To *honor* Jesus is to honor God: "[T]hat all may honor the Son just as they honor the Father" (John 5:23).
- To *hate* Jesus is to hate God: "He who hates me hates my Father as well" (John 15:23).
- To *come* to Jesus is to come to God: "No one comes to the Father except through me" (John 14:6).
- To *love* Jesus is to love God: "He who loves me will be loved by my Father" (John 14:21).
- To *obey* Jesus is to obey God: "If anyone loves me, he will obey my teaching. My Father will love him, and we will come to him and make our home with him" (John 14:23).

2. Jesus made direct claims that many Jewish religious leaders considered blasphemous.

Being strict monotheists, many Jewish contemporaries of Jesus were outraged at his claims to divine authority. Their reaction demonstrates that they understood Jesus to be claiming deity for himself. These admissions make the point:

> Jesus said to them, "My Father is always at his work to this very day, and I, too, am working." For this reason the Jews tried all the harder to kill him; not only was he breaking the Sabbath, but he was even calling God his own Father, making himself equal with God. (John 5:17–18)

Jesus' repeated insistence that he had an intimate and special relationship to God the Father infuriated the crowds. Jesus didn't speak of God as "our Father," but as "*my* Father."

> "I tell you the truth," Jesus answered, "before Abraham was born, I am!" At this, they picked up stones to stone him. (John 8:58–59)

Jesus' use of "I am" (Greek, *egō eimi*) was also tantamount to saying "I am God," for he was applying to himself "one of the most sacred of divine expressions" from the Old Testament.[3] Yahweh had specifically referenced himself as "I am" or "I am he" (Isa. 41:4; 43:10, 13, 25; 46:4; 48:12). Jesus may have also been echoing Exodus 3:14 where Yahweh refers to himself as the great "I AM." Again the reaction on the part of the Jews to stone Jesus (the prescribed penalty for blasphemy, Lev. 24:16) contextually supports the assertion that he claimed deity for himself.

> "I and the Father are one." Again the Jews picked up stones to stone him, but Jesus said to them, "I have shown you many great miracles from the Father. For which of these do you stone me?" "We are not stoning you for any of these," replied the Jews, "but for blasphemy, because you, a mere man, claim to be God." (John 10:30–33)

The Greek word for "one" (*hen*) in this verse is in the neuter form, thus it does not imply that Jesus and the Father are the same person. It could be translated: "I and the Father, *we* are one." Additionally, the oneness between Jesus and the Father is more than a unity of purpose or action. The oneness described here has clear metaphysical overtones (deity).[4] The Jews certainly understood Jesus' statement as a reference to deity, for again they sought to stone him.

> Again the high priest asked him, "Are you the Christ, the Son of the Blessed One?" "I am," said Jesus. "And you will see the Son of Man sitting at the right hand of the Mighty One and coming on the clouds of heaven." The high priest tore his clothes. "Why do we need any more witnesses?" he asked. "You have heard the blasphemy. What do you think?" They all condemned him as worthy of death. (Mark 14:61–64)

The Jewish religious leaders arrested, tried, and sentenced Jesus to die for the crime of blasphemy. His statements before the high priest served as convincing testimony. Notice four things in Jesus' brief exchange with Israel's high priest: (a) he affirmatively identifies himself as Israel's Messiah; (b) he uses the title "Son of Man," which in certain contexts was viewed as a divine title (Dan. 7:13–14); (c) he describes himself as sitting at the "right hand" of God, implying he possesses the authority of God; and (d) he foreshadows his "coming on the clouds," identifying himself as the future judge of humanity.

3. Jesus indirectly claimed to be God by invoking divine prerogatives.

During his ministry, Jesus engaged in functions that are reserved exclusively for God alone.[5] In a context of strict Jewish monotheism, such activities would be blasphemous for anyone other than God.

Jesus claimed the authority to forgive sins, even sins not committed against himself personally:

> When Jesus saw their faith, he said to the paralytic, "Son, your sins are forgiven." Now some teachers of the law were sitting there, thinking to themselves, "Why

does this fellow talk like that? He's blaspheming! Who can forgive sins but God alone?" (Mark 2:5–7)

Jesus received worship from other human beings:

Then the eleven disciples went to Galilee, to the mountain where Jesus had told them to go. When they saw him, they worshiped him. (Matt. 28:16–17)

Jesus claimed power and authority over death—and life:

"For just as the Father raises the dead and gives them life, even so the Son gives life to whom he is pleased to give it." (John 5:21)

Jesus claimed authority to judge humanity:

"Moreover, the Father judges no one, but has entrusted all judgment to the Son. . . . And he has given him authority to judge because he is the Son of Man." (John 5:22, 27)

4. Jesus indirectly claimed to be God by invoking various divine titles.

Jesus used a variety of Old Testament titles in referring to himself that, in certain contexts, carry the implication of deity. This behavior infuriated the Jews. Especially when he described himself as the "Son of God" and "Son of Man." In his trial before the Sanhedrin, it was his use of these titles that (among other things) led the high priest of Israel to condemn him as a blasphemer worthy of death (Matt. 26:62–66). (For more biblical references to examples of Jesus' use of various divine titles, see The Incarnation, chapter 9.)

Much more could be said concerning Jesus' provocative appeals to deity,[6] but the points discussed previously seem sufficient to support the thesis that Jesus of Nazareth claimed to be God. Additional support for the truth of Jesus' claim to deity is found in his matchless moral character, his specific fulfillment of biblical prophecy, and his many miraculous works, which culminated in his own bodily resurrection from the dead.

Is there any other way to explain the life and person of Jesus? Any way to avoid concluding that he was God incarnate? Alternative proposals have been proffered, but a careful evaluation of the New Testament data makes the best interpretation apparent.

What Is the Best Explanation?

Before considering specific alternative views, a review of how to reason to the best explanatory hypothesis can help a person avoid the fallacies that muddle a logical perspective.

Abductive Reasoning

While there are two basic ways of reasoning or arguing in logic (deductive and inductive), logicians sometimes use a lesser known method called abductive reasoning.[7] This third type of reasoning attempts to arrive at the best explanation for an event or a given series of facts. Unlike deduction, abductive reasoning doesn't provide certainty in its conclusion, but instead, like induction, it yields only probable truth. In contrast to induction, however, abductive reasoning doesn't attempt to predict specific future probable occurrences. Rather this method tries to provide the best broad explanatory hypothesis.

Abductive reasoning can be helpful for determining which explanation of a given event is most likely true. For example, an abductive approach may be used in attempting to determine which scenario most likely explains the controversial issue of the assassination of President John F. Kennedy (the lone gunman theory vs. conspiracy theory).[8]

No hard and fast test exists to evaluate one hypothesis over another, but the following seven criteria are generally accepted among logicians.[9] The best explanatory hypothesis (1) is balanced between complexity and simplicity, (2) is coherent, (3) corresponds to the facts, (4) avoids unwarranted presumptions and ad hoc explanations, (5) is testable, (6) yields fruitful predictions, and (7) can successfully adjust to accommodate possible counter evidence. The hypothesis that scores highest on these criteria can be said to have genuine explanatory power and scope. Applying this schema can help evaluate the various explanations for the life of Jesus.

Avoiding the False Alternatives Fallacy

While the logical process of elimination can help sift different theories, a person must be careful to avoid committing the false alternatives fallacy. Logician T. Edward Damer defines this fallacy as "an oversimplification of a problem situation by a failure to entertain or at least recognize all its plausible alternative solutions."[10] A person commits the false alternatives fallacy when he or she simply assumes too few alternatives and then supposes one of these limited choices must be correct.

Some evangelical apologists have been accused of committing this fallacy when they argue the case for Jesus' divinity. For example, an explanatory argument for Jesus' identity is sometimes formulated in terms of a "trilemma."[11] Because Jesus claimed to be God, he must either be: (1) a lunatic, (2) a liar, or (3) the Lord (God). Critics of this argument suggest that it ignores other plausible alternatives (for example, the possibility that Jesus was a mythical figure).

The false alternatives fallacy can be avoided by giving careful consideration to a wider range of options—as long as they constitute *plausible* explanations.

All possible reasonable explanations should be included. However, only a limited number of reasonable explanations exist concerning who Jesus is.

It would also be fallacious to stubbornly reserve judgment concerning a reasonable explanatory hypothesis just because a person hasn't exhausted all possible or conceivable alternatives. Sometimes skeptics commit the *ad futurus* (appeal to the future) fallacy by assuming that the future will undoubtedly reveal a purely natural (or secular) explanation for the life of Jesus. This error exhibits not only a presumptuous and optimistic faith in the future but also ignores that a person must live and reason in the present. To attempt to reason to the best explanatory hypothesis among known alternatives makes sense, and if a new reasonable alternative is discovered, then a critical analysis can take place at that time.

Six Alternative Hypotheses Concerning Jesus' Identity

Jesus' followers placed the messianic claim in his mouth long after the fact. Thus Jesus' claims to divinity are mythical.

This hypothesis, though popular among liberal critical scholars, is highly implausible for the following reasons:

1. Since the Gospels (which present a divine Jesus) were written fairly soon after the events they record (within about a generation), time wasn't sufficient to allow for legends and myths to form and enter biblical accounts (see The Gospels, chap. 7). Further, written and oral apostolic sources bridge the gap between the time of Jesus' death (ca. AD 30) and the time the Gospels were written (ca. AD 70). For example, some of the apostle Paul's epistles (Galatians, 1 and 2 Thessalonians) were probably written as early as the late 40s or early 50s. The mythical hypothesis only becomes plausible if several generations passed between the events and the writing—time for myth to replace the facts. But the narrow time frame between when Jesus lived and when written sources emerged is inadequate to allow this hypothesis. A. N. Sherwin-White, Oxford scholar of ancient Greek and Roman history, has argued that even the span of two full generations is insufficient time for myth and legend to accrue and distort historical fact.[12]

2. The biblical writers recognized the difference between myth and factual, eyewitness testimony, and they solemnly asserted to be eyewitnesses to Jesus' claims and actions (see Luke 1:1–4; John 19:35; Acts 2:22–38; 17:30–31; 1 Cor. 15:3–8; Gal. 1:11–12; 2 Pet. 1:16; 1 John 1:1–2). Additionally, sound arguments can be marshaled to show that the authors of the Gospels were either original apostles of Jesus (and thus eyewitnesses) or were close associates of the apostles.[13]

3. Followers of Jesus had no reason to deify a mere man. First-century monotheistic Jews would have known that to do so would lead to persecution, martyrdom, and even the damnation of their souls.

4. Given the short time frame between events and writing, if the Gospel writers had departed from the historical facts (either by exaggeration or outright invention), hostile witnesses—still alive and conversant with the events of Jesus' life—could and would have exposed them.

5. If the followers of Jesus invented a Messiah, they would likely have created one that corresponded more to the Jewish messianic expectations of the time. The Jesus presented in the Gospels varies in many ways from what first-century Jews anticipated in their Messiah.[14]

6. First- and early-second-century secular and Jewish sources (historians, government officials, and religious writers) report general information about the life and ministry of Jesus that corresponds to and corroborates the Gospels' message. The existence and content of these early extrabiblical and non-Christian sources argue against a myth theory concerning the life of Jesus.[15]

Dismissing Jesus' claims to deity as mere myth ignores the solid historical sources (oral and written) that stand behind those claims. It also ignores the short time interval between the emergence of the Gospel writings and the actual events they purport to describe. Moreover, this view seems rooted in unsupported antisupernatural presuppositions. For these reasons, this view must be considered an implausible, inadequate explanatory hypothesis.

Jesus was simply a "great man," even a "great teacher," but he was not God.

Many people gravitate toward this position because it fits the familiar natural realm and avoids the supernatural. However, because the New Testament portrait of Jesus is based upon sound historical sources, viewing Jesus as a great man becomes intellectually untenable on two counts:

1. A person cannot be "great" and make the kinds of assertions Jesus made about himself. Such claims would have qualified him as a megalomaniac. Why? Because Jesus talked about himself in grandiose ways.[16] A few of his "I am" statements from the Gospel of John illustrate:

- "I am the resurrection and the life. He who believes in me will live, even though he dies; and whoever lives and believes in me will never die. Do you believe this?" (John 11:25–26).
- "I am the way and the truth and the life. No one comes to the Father except through me" (John 14:6).
- "I am the light of the world. Whoever follows me will never walk in darkness, but will have the light of life" (John 8:12).

- "I am the bread of life. He who comes to me will never go hungry, and he who believes in me will never be thirsty" (John 6:35).

A great man (who was only a man) would not say the things Jesus said. Such boasts would have disqualified him from being considered great.

2. A person cannot be "great" and do the kinds of things Jesus did. He offered to forgive the sins of others (including offenses not committed against himself). Jesus allowed other human beings to worship him. He taught that a person's eternal destiny rested upon what that person thought of him personally. A great man (who was only a man) would not do any of these things.

Jesus could not simply be a great man if he claimed to be God and was not. Christian thinker C. S. Lewis makes this insightful comment:

> You can shut him up for a fool, you can spit at him and kill him as a demon; or you can fall at His feet and call him Lord and God. But let us not come with any patronizing nonsense about His being a great human teacher. He has not left that open to us. He did not intend to.[17]

Thus, if Jesus claimed to be God (as the well-attested historical documents convey) but was just a man, then he was perhaps a morally bad man or a mentally sick man. But he certainly was not a great man.

Jesus claimed to be the divine Messiah, but knew he was not. He was, therefore, an intentional deceiver and thus an evil menace.

For Jesus to say and do the things he did, all the while knowing that he was only a mere human being, would make him a very evil man. Intentional spiritual deception is perhaps the worst kind of deceit. Yet in light of everything known about Jesus of Nazareth, to consider him an evil menace is to create a deep and profound dissonance. The Jesus presented in the Gospels reflects an exemplary personal and moral character, one that transcends the frail and imperfect human moral condition.

During his three-year ministry Jesus consistently dealt with challenging moral dilemmas, faced overwhelming personal pressures, and endured incredibly difficult circumstances including physical torture and death itself. Yet he never exhibited even a trace of moral weakness or any of the various vices so common to humankind.

Deceivers, especially diabolical ones, almost always leave clues as to their true motivation—usually among their inner circle of associates and especially when under intense pressure. Yet, Jesus' closest friends and even some of his enemies insisted that he met every circumstance with courage, honesty, and resounding moral virtue (Acts 3:14; 1 Pet. 2:22–23; 1 John 3:4–5). In sharp contrast to known deceivers, Jesus showed no sign of being motivated by wealth, fame, power, or pleasure. Rather, love, truth, and justice prompted his extraordinary life. Viewing Jesus as a charlatan runs completely contrary to both his blameless character and his transcendently insightful ethical reflections and teachings.

Jesus' moral example and teachings laid the foundation for much of the ethical theory embraced and practiced throughout Western civilization. He is widely considered even by non-Christians as the ideal pattern of moral virtue. Is it reasonable to conclude that the person who arguably had the greatest impact on human history in terms of moral virtue was in reality a colossal liar? History, reason, and common sense voice a resounding no![18]

Frankly, for those who have examined the life of Jesus, accepting him as the divine Messiah is much easier than concluding that he was a moral and spiritual fraud. This terribly weak explanatory hypothesis is therefore exceedingly improbable.

Jesus thought he was the divine Messiah but was not. He was a delusional psychotic, a madman.

People who claim to be God generally populate mental health institutions. Delusions of grandeur are symptomatic of severe mental disorders that leave people out of touch with reality. Does Jesus show signs of such derangement? Are there indicators of emotional instability in his life as there are in the case of those suffering mental illness?

Of all men, Jesus seems to have had a secure grip on reality. He consistently exhibited a profound mental and emotional stability. In every crisis that he confronted—whether being mocked and interrogated by his enemies or undergoing the horrific torture of crucifixion—Jesus' mind reflected an amazing clarity, sobriety, and underlying emotional stability. Arguably the world's greatest teacher, he was always clear headed, lucid in thought and eloquent in speech. Jesus rose to every occasion with grace, poise, strength, and balance. It is instructive to read what people who closely observed him at work as a teacher, preacher, and miracle worker said about Jesus.

- "When Jesus had finished saying these things, the crowds were amazed at his teaching, because he taught as one who had authority, and not as their teachers of the law" (Matt. 7:28–29).
- "Coming to his hometown, he began teaching the people in their synagogue, and they were amazed. 'Where did this man get this wisdom and these miraculous powers?' they asked" (Matt. 13:54).
- "'No one ever spoke the way this man does,' the guards declared" (John 7:46).

Even his enemies were amazed at Jesus' teaching and unprecedented authority. Those who knew and observed him did not give the slightest impression that they thought he was psychologically imbalanced.

But maybe Jesus doesn't need to have been a raving madman for this viewpoint to have some explanatory power. Perhaps Jesus was simply wrong about being God, yet still basically sane. Mental illness is not an all-or-nothing proposition. Rather, mental instability is measured in degrees. Other religious figures have made divine claims (Father Divine, Jim Jones, David Koresh) yet didn't appear to be outright insane. So couldn't Jesus have just been simply mistaken about his identity without being a certifiable lunatic? Like many geniuses, maybe he was only eccentric, weird, or just a *little* crazy.

Christian philosopher Ronald Nash brings clarity to this hypothesis: "There are little mistakes and then there are big—*really big*—mistakes."[19] For a first-century Jewish rabbi who had cut his teeth on the strict monotheistic teachings of the Torah to claim to be God would definitely have been a huge mistake. In fact, a mistake of this magnitude would no doubt be perceived within Judaism as a blasphemous claim, and would therefore likely result in a death sentence (Lev. 24:13–16). For Jesus to be mistaken about being the divine Messiah of Israel constitutes a serious departure from reality. For as Christian apologist John Warwick Montgomery asks: "What greater retreat from reality is there than a belief in one's divinity, if one is not in fact God?"[20]

While certain cult leaders have made claims to divinity, there is strong evidence that many, if not all, were intentional frauds. Father Divine, Jim Jones, and David Koresh all gave clear signs of having been motivated by a combination of greed, power, and sexual lust.[21] And none of these cult leaders can be reasonably compared to Jesus in terms of intellectual and moral virtue, let alone divine credentials (miracles, fulfilled prophecy, resurrection).

But what about seemingly noble religious leaders who make extraordinary religious claims? For example, the Dalai Lama, leader of the Tibetan monks, claims to be a *bodhisattva* (the fourteenth successive incarnation of a Buddha-like figure).[22] Yet in spite of this exalted claim, he received the 1989 Nobel Peace Prize. Doesn't he prove that extraordinary religious claims don't have to equate with insanity?

Jesus' situation is, in fact, different from that of the Dalai Lama in three important respects. First, as exalted as the Dalai Lama's claim is, he isn't claiming to be God in human flesh, the transcendent Creator and Redeemer of the world.[23] The Dalai Lama claims only to have an enlightened or awakened consciousness, yet his nature is solely human. Jesus' claim to be the divine Messiah therefore carries greater magnitude. Second, because Jesus' claims to deity were strictly forbidden in the orthodox religious views of the time, he knew he would face fierce opposition, even death. While the Tibetan Buddhists have suffered real persecution in their part of the world, it is not because of the Dalai Lama's personal religious claims. His claims are not out of step with mainstream Buddhist tradition. Jesus' claim therefore carried far greater personal risk. Third, though the Dalai Lama may indeed be a morally decent man (a contrast to various cult leaders), he falls short of Jesus' sterling moral example, and clearly lacks Jesus' divine credentials—notably Jesus' power over wind, waves, disease, and death—including his own historical, bodily resurrection from the dead (see The Resurrection, chap. 10).

And finally, even if mental illness is measured in degrees, Jesus doesn't show the slightest sign of mental instability or eccentricity. In fact, the opposite is true. Psychiatrist J. T. Fisher draws this conclusion:

> If you were to take the sum total of all authoritative articles ever written by the most qualified of psychologists and psychiatrists on the subject of mental hygiene—if you were to combine them and refine them and cleave out the excess verbiage—if you were to take the whole of the meat and none of the parsley, and if you were to have these unadulterated bits of pure scientific knowledge concisely expressed by the most capable of living poets, you would have an awkward and incomplete summation of the Sermon on the Mount. And it would suffer immeasurably through comparison. For nearly two thousand years the Christian world has been holding in its hands the complete answer to its restless and fruitless yearnings.[24]

Could this blueprint for optimum mental health have been laid down by a mentally ill person or even someone only slightly unstable? Reason and informed psychological analysis say no! Jesus transcends all categories concerning human mental health, emotional stability, and moral virtue. A powerful reason for concluding that Jesus was indeed God incarnate is that he was fundamentally different from every other human being that ever lived. Even Socrates, the Buddha, and Confucius pale in comparison to him. In fact, standards of human goodness are measured according to his life and character.

Jesus claimed to be divine, but meant it in an Eastern mystical sense that "all human beings are divine." He was therefore a mystical guru.

With the growth of Eastern religions in the West over the past several decades, along with the rise of the New Age movement,[25] some people (and groups) now suggest that Jesus was really a mystical sage. New Age advocates even suggest that during Jesus' so-called lost years (ages twelve to thirty, prior to his public ministry), he actually traveled to Persia, the Near East, India, and Tibet to learn from various ascended masters.[26] Jesus therefore developed his "Christ consciousness" and his miracle-working ability during his trek through Eastern mysticism. How viable is this view of Jesus as a mystic?

This position is extremely implausible for three reasons:

1. As Christian theologian and New Age specialist Ron Rhodes notes, "The historical, hard evidence for the Jesus-goes-East accounts is virtually non-existent."[27] The various stories that speak of Jesus' alleged journey to the East are contradictory in nature and filled with historical inaccuracies.[28] They also stand in contrast to the well-established historical Gospels that imply Jesus spent his early life in Nazareth, in submission to his parents and Jewish law, and carefully studying the Hebrew Scriptures (Luke 2:51–52). These biblical texts indicate that during Jesus' public ministry, people readily recognized him and his family as local citizens and even acknowledged Jesus as the son of Joseph, the local carpenter (Matt. 13:55–56).

2. The core of Jesus' beliefs as an orthodox Jew, which he strongly affirmed, is directly at odds with many of the essential beliefs of Eastern religions.[29] For example, the Torah explicitly condemns such false religious beliefs as polytheism and pantheism (Exod. 20:3, 23; 34:14–15; Deut. 32:17), teaching rather a strict monotheism (Deut. 4:35, 39; 6:4; 32:39). The Hebrew Scriptures also recognize a sharp distinction between the Creator and the creature (Gen. 1:26–27); thus, in direct opposition to Eastern thought, human beings are not gods. And Old Testament revelation centers on the issue of divine redemption (Ps. 19:14; Isa. 44:6), not mystical enlightenment.

3. New Age advocates consistently misinterpret Scripture by reading Eastern concepts into the text. Such meanings have no objective basis in the Judeo-Christian revelation. Especially evident when New Agers invoke their esoteric system of interpreting the Bible (finding hidden mystical meanings),[30] mysticism overrides rationality and abandons attempts to discover the historical, grammatical, and contextual meaning. Viewing Jesus as a mystical guru or spiritual master has no objective scriptural basis whatsoever.

This explanatory hypothesis is incoherent, fails to fit the facts, and is based almost exclusively on unwarranted suppositions. It cannot therefore be taken seriously as an explanation for the life and identity of Jesus of Nazareth.

Jesus claimed to be God, but in actuality was a "Martian," that is, an extraterrestrial.

Some may be surprised that anyone would actually consider Jesus an extraterrestrial, but various UFO-based religions have been promoting this viewpoint for several decades.[31] Given the growing popularity of UFO-related ideas, the extraterrestrial hypothesis therefore deserves a response. The following four points show this position's weaknesses:

1. The claims of UFO cults concerning Jesus are directly at odds with the basic historical facts of Scripture. According to alleged UFO-based revelations, Jesus is not a man, but rather a visitor from outer space. However, the scriptural account depicts Jesus as a real flesh-and-blood man, though, according to his own claims, not merely a man—rather the God-man. His

humanity is clearly affirmed in the Gospels (see The Incarnation, chap. 9). For example, Jesus was conceived supernaturally, but born naturally. He had human ancestors and experienced normal growth and development as a human being. Jesus lived and died as a real man. He said absolutely nothing about UFOs or other worlds in space.

2. UFO religions are centered on occult beliefs and practices contrary to Jesus' specific views and explicitly condemned in the Jewish Torah. These UFO-related beliefs and practices include mediumistic "channeling" of so-called alien beings, automatic writing, telepathy, teleportation, demateri_ization, levitation, and psychokinesis.[32] All of these practices are explicitly condemned in the Scripture upon which Jesus based his life and ministry (Exod. 22:18; Lev. 19:31; Deut. 18:10–12). Further, the theological messages promulgated by various UFO cults match more closely with New Age mysticism than with the teaching of the Bible.[33]

3. UFO cults read into the biblical text subjective and esoteric interpretations that have no discernible objective basis. In effect, the Bible is interpreted in light of UFO phenomena, rather than according to sound historical and exegetical principles.

4. Many UFO-based groups embrace the extraterrestrial hypothesis concerning flying saucers. This view proposes that UFOs are an objective physical reality, and that literal metallic crafts are piloted by interplanetary space visitors. This viewpoint, however, suffers from insurmountable scientific, philosophical, and evidential problems.[34]

Viewing Jesus as an extraterrestrial is not an intellectually credible theory. It doesn't fit the facts, involves incredible presumptions, and lacks logical coherence.

Was Jesus Actually the Unique, Divine Messiah (God in Human Flesh)?

If the six hypotheses discussed are the only other alternatives concerning the true identity of Jesus of Nazareth, then by the logical process of elimination the historic Christian claim that Jesus was God incarnate stands (see table 8.1). While challenges to the traditional Christian position remain (see The Incarnation, chap. 9), they have been reasonably answered. If a person doesn't arbitrarily presume a naturalistic worldview (which is question begging), then Jesus being God incarnate emerges as the superior explanatory hypothesis. If other seemingly reasonable alternatives arise, then they should be similarly analyzed. Nevertheless, viewing Jesus of Nazareth as the God-man is the one explanatory hypothesis that currently and enduringly corresponds to history, psychology, logic, human intuition, and common sense.

Table 8.1
Identity of Jesus: Who was Jesus?

The Jesus Argument (reasoning to the best explanatory hypothesis)

1. **Myth:** Jesus' life and claims to deity were mythical.
   Rebuttal: This view doesn't fit the solid facts of history surrounding the events of Jesus' life and claims.
2. **Man:** Jesus was simply a good or great man.
   Rebuttal: This view is inconsistent with Jesus' divine claims and actions.
3. **Menace:** Jesus lied about his being God incarnate.
   Rebuttal: This view is inconsistent with Jesus' character and accomplishments (miracles, prophecy).
4. **Madman:** Jesus was psychotic and was therefore mistaken about being God.
   Rebuttal: This view is inconsistent with Jesus' character and life.
5. **Mystic:** Jesus claimed to be God but he meant in an Eastern mystical sense, thus he was a guru.
   Rebuttal: This view is inconsistent with Jesus' beliefs and teachings.
6. **Martian:** Jesus claimed to be God, but he really meant that he was a Martian (an extraterrestrial).
   Rebuttal: This view is based upon unwarranted presumption and is inconsistent with the facts of Jesus' life and teaching.
7. **Messiah:** Jesus was, in fact, the divine Messiah. This view is consistent with the facts, is coherent, is testable, and thus as an explanatory hypothesis it possesses genuine explanatory power and scope.

Jesus' credentials as the divine Messiah are indeed formidable—matchless personal character, incalculable influence upon history, fulfillment of prophecy, power to perform miracles, extraordinary wisdom, bodily resurrection, and so forth. Alternatives that deny his true deity offer no adequate explanation for these credentials. In light of his legacy, it seems reasonable to ask the same penetrating question that he asked of his disciples: "'But what about you?' he asked. 'Who do you say I am?'" (Matt. 16:15).

The intriguing topic of God coming into human history by becoming a man is discussed in the next chapter.

Discussion Questions

1. In what direct and indirect ways did Jesus claim to be God?
2. How can abductive reasoning help in examining the various views of Jesus' identity?
3. Why couldn't Jesus be a good man if he claimed to be God but was not?
4. Can you think of any other reasonable alternatives concerning the possible identity of Jesus?
5. How can a person use Jesus' question "Who do you say I am?" as an effective evangelistic and apologetic tool with nonbelievers?

For Further Study

Corduan, Winfried. *No Doubt about It: The Case for Christianity*. Nashville: Broadman & Holman, 1997.

Evans, C. Stephen. *Why Believe? Reason and Mystery as Pointers to God*. Grand Rapids: Eerdmans, 1996.

Kreeft, Peter. *Between Heaven and Hell*. Downers Grove, IL: InterVarsity, 1982.

Montgomery, John Warwick. *History and Christianity*. Minneapolis: Bethany, 1965.

Nash, Ronald. *Worldviews in Conflict*. Grand Rapids: Zondervan Publishing House, 1992.

Stott, John R. W. *Basic Christianity*. Downers Grove, IL: InterVarsity, 1980.

9

How Can Jesus Christ Be Both God and Man?

For in Christ all the fullness of Deity lives in bodily form.

—Colossians 2:9

The Son of God became a man to enable men to become sons of God.

—C. S. Lewis, *Mere Christianity*

All around the world people celebrate an astounding Christian truth-claim at Christmas—*God became man in Jesus of Nazareth*. Though many holiday participants may not understand its significance, the incarnation is a central doctrine of the Christian faith. God took the initiative and became flesh in order to redeem sinful human beings.

The teaching that the Savior of the world is both divine and human is an extraordinary claim. And yet the truth of the incarnation, while open in certain respects to historical and logical analysis, remains shrouded in mystery. For this reason critics of historic Christianity often misunderstand and misrepresent it. The Watchtower Bible and Tract Society blatantly claims the doctrine contradicts Scripture: "The Bible is clear and consistent about the relationship of God to Jesus. Jehovah God alone is Almighty. He created the prehuman Jesus directly. Thus, Jesus had a beginning and could never be coequal with God in power or eternity."[1]

Pluralist philosopher John Hick questions the incarnation's feasibility: "It has not proved possible, after some fifteen centuries of intermittent effort, to give any clear meaning to the idea that Jesus had two complete natures, one human and the other divine."[2]

Misconceptions and distortions such as these raise a variety of critical questions about the incarnation doctrine's biblical basis, importance, historical development, and coherence. Responding to these issues can help a person grow in understanding of and reverence for the God-man.

Historic Christianity's Doctrine of the Incarnation

The most important creedal statement concerning the incarnation is the Creed of Chalcedon. The Council of Chalcedon (the fourth ecumenical council, AD 451) laid down the basic boundaries for the orthodox view of Christ's person and nature. According to this council, Jesus Christ is one divine person in two natures (divinity and humanity). The Chalcedonian Creed became, and continues to be, the normative standard for the orthodox doctrine of Christ. All of Christendom (Roman Catholic, Eastern Orthodox, and Protestant) affirms the Chalcedonian formula that Jesus Christ is both God and man. This creed enunciates the doctrine of Christ's two natures in the following manner:

> We all with one voice confess our Lord Jesus Christ to be one and the same Son, perfect in divinity and humanity, truly God and truly human, consisting of a rational soul and a body, being of one substance with the Father in relation to his divinity, and being of one substance with us in relation to his humanity, and is like us in all things apart from sin. He was begotten of the Father before time in relation to his divinity, and in these recent days was born from the Virgin Mary, the *theotokos* [God-bearer], for us and for our salvation. In relation to the humanity he is one and the same Christ, the Son, the Lord, the Only-begotten, who is to be acknowledged in two natures, without confusion, without change, without division, and without separation. The distinction of natures is in no way abolished on account of this union, but rather the characteristic property of each nature is preserved, and concurring into one Person and one subsistence, not as if Christ were parted or divided into two persons, but remains one and the same Son and Only-begotten God, Word, Lord, Jesus Christ; even as the Prophets from the beginning spoke concerning him, and our Lord Jesus Christ instructed us, and the Creed of the Fathers was handed down to us.[3]

The Chalcedonian formulation does not explain exactly how the two natures are united in one person, but it sets the crucial theological parameters for orthodox biblical Christology (doctrine of the person and nature of Christ). In other words, this statement generally tells what the doctrine of the incarnation means and doesn't mean, but remains silent about how Christ is actually God and man.

The Christian Theistic View of God

The doctrine of the incarnation can be properly understood only within the broader theological framework of the Christian theistic view. The God disclosed in Scripture and later enunciated in the historic creeds and confessions of Christendom is the one sovereign and majestic Lord. Historic Christianity thus affirms belief in one infinitely perfect, eternal, and yet tri-personal God, the transcendent Creator and sovereign Sustainer of the universe. This one God is triune, existing eternally and simultaneously as three distinct and distinguishable persons, though not separate, autonomous individuals: Father, Son, and Holy Spirit (see chap. 5). All three persons in the Godhead, or Divine Being, share equally and completely the one divine nature, and are therefore the same God, coequal in attributes, nature, and glory. The doctrine of the incarnation then properly emerges from this explicit trinitarian teaching.

Latin in origin, the term *incarnation* literally means "becoming flesh" (Lat. *in carne*, Gk. *en sarki*). While the term is not contained in Scripture per se, the Greek equivalent is (1 John 4:1: "Jesus Christ has come in the flesh" [*en sarki*]). The doctrine of the incarnation is at the core of the biblical message, for it reveals the true person and nature of the Lord and Savior Jesus Christ.

This doctrine teaches that the eternal *Logos* (Word), the second person of the Trinity, without diminishing his deity took to himself a fully human nature. To be more specific, this doctrine explains that a full and undiminished divine nature and a full and perfect human nature were inseparably united in the one historical and divine person, Jesus of Nazareth. According to Holy Scripture, Jesus Christ is God the Son in human flesh (*theanthrōpos*, the God-man).

The Hypostatic Union

As the incarnate Son of God, Jesus Christ is one person with two natures. In accord with the Chalcedonian definition, these two natures (divinity and humanity) "remain distinct, whole, and unchanged, without mixture or confusion so that the one person, Jesus Christ, is truly God and truly man."[4] Christ is one in substance (*homoousios*) with the Father in regard to his divine nature and one in substance with humanity in regard to his human nature. The two natures are perfectly united forever in the one person (*hypostasis*) of Jesus Christ. The resulting hypostatic union refers therefore to the union of the two distinct natures in the one person of Jesus Christ (neither dividing the person nor confounding the natures). Philosophically speaking, as the

God-man, Jesus Christ is "two Whats" (that is, a divine "what" [or nature] and a human "what" [or nature]) and "one Who" (that is, a single "person" or "self").

Kenosis

The concept of kenosis[5] (from Gk. *ekenosen*: Phil. 2:7 "made himself nothing," or "emptied himself") is an attempt to explain just how the two natures of Christ related to each other in God becoming man. While there have been many so-called kenotic theories in the modern era, two models are briefly considered here.

The first contemporary model states that in order for Jesus to have been truly human he must have divested himself of such divine attributes as omnipotence, omniscience, and omnipresence. This kenotic theory interprets "emptied himself" in Philippians 2:7 as meaning that Christ relinquished divine attributes. Thus the incarnate Christ is someone less than God, and therefore not truly equal to God.

This position must be regarded as heresy, however, for if God the Son is deprived of any divine attribute then he is obviously not deity. Christian theologian Bruce Milne identifies the equation for this heretical kenotic theory as "Incarnation = God minus."[6] This position runs contrary to Scripture, not to mention contrary to the creeds, and is therefore rejected by theologically orthodox Christians.

The second model suggests that instead of Christ divesting himself of divine attributes, Jesus retained all divine attributes through his divine nature. However, in union with his human nature he could freely choose not to exercise certain attributes (or exercise them only intermittently) in his earthly sojourn as a man. According to this position, Jesus' deity remains undiminished. This view understands Philippians 2:7 as not a literal emptying of attributes, but as a sign of Christ's humility in which he voluntarily gave up the status and glory that were his in heaven. This act involved a surrendering of divine position rather than of divine power. Milne identifies the equation for this approach as "Incarnation = God Plus,"[7] for Christ retains his deity and yet takes to himself a truly human nature. This second model has biblical support and holds consistent with creedal orthodoxy.

Ten Essentials about the Incarnation

The following ten points summarize vital information about the incarnation and can help a person think through the most important elements of the doctrine:[8]

1. Jesus Christ is one person possessing two distinct natures: a fully divine nature and a fully human nature (a unity of person and a duality of natures). The historic person of Jesus of Nazareth is therefore the God-man.

2. While Christ has two natures, he nevertheless remains a single unified person (not two different persons). His human nature subsists only for the purpose of this union; it has no independent personal subsistence of its own. Christ is the same person both before and after the incarnation. The difference is that before the incarnation he had but one nature, namely divine. After the incarnation, this very same God the Son added to himself another nature—a human one—that subsists together with the divine nature he already had and continues to have. While Jesus Christ has a divine and a human consciousness (and two wills, divine and human, due to the two natures), he nevertheless remains one person. Christian orthodoxy rejects the Nestorian heresy that taught that there were two separate persons in Christ.

3. Through his divine nature, Jesus Christ is God the Son, the incarnated second person of the Trinity, who shares the one divine essence fully and equally with the Father and the Holy Spirit. Christian orthodoxy rejects the Arian heresy that viewed Jesus merely as a God-like creature.

4. Through his human nature, Jesus Christ is fully human, possessing all the essential attributes of a true human being. Christian orthodoxy rejects Docetism, which denies the true humanity of Christ.

5. The properties or attributes of both natures may be properly predicated of the one person. In other words, the one person of Jesus Christ retains all of the attributes of both natures (for example, through his divine nature he is omniscient while simultaneously through his human nature he may lack knowledge). Through Christ's miraculous conception by the Holy Spirit, he did not inherit a sinful human nature.

6. The union of the two natures is not an indwelling, nor a mere contact or occupancy of space, but a personal union. This is similar to the union of body and soul in human beings.

7. The two natures coinhere or interpenetrate in perfect union so the human is never without the divine or the divine without the human, but the natures do not mix or mingle.

8. The two natures, divine and human, are distinct, but inseparably united in the one person. The two natures retain their own attributes or qualities and are thus not mixed together. Christian orthodoxy rejects the Eutychian heresy that blended the two natures of Christ together to form one hybrid nature (Monophysitism: one nature).

9. The human nature is not deified, and the divine nature is not humanized, or subject to human limitations.

10. The word nature refers to essence or substance, and these two natures are inseparable, unmixed, and unchanged.

Critical Questions

From these ten essential points as a foundation, several important questions about the doctrine of the incarnation arise.

Since there is no passage in the New Testament where Jesus Christ actually says "I am God," how did Christianity formulate the doctrine of the incarnation?

The doctrine resulted from the Christian church's sustained and critical reflection upon the overwhelming scriptural evidence that Jesus is indeed both God and man. Jesus' apostles were Jewish monotheists; they nevertheless became convinced that while Jesus was indeed a man, he was far more than just a man. In fact, these same apostles placed Jesus on the level of Yahweh in their scriptural writings. They came to the astounding conviction that to encounter Jesus of Nazareth was to encounter none other than God in human flesh. While there is no specific passage that records Jesus saying "I am God," at least seven (and possibly as many as ten) specific New Testament references refer to Jesus as God (Gk. *theos*).[9] The Bible thoroughly supports both the deity and humanity of Jesus Christ.

Literally hundreds of passages support the doctrine of the incarnation.[10] A brief survey of that material undergirding this distinctive and essential Christian doctrine is offered in the box "Biblical support for Christ's deity." A second box offers "Biblical support for Christ's humanity." In addition to these texts, four specific passages explicitly teach the doctrine of the incarnation (but see also Rom. 1:2–5; 9:5; 1 Tim. 3:16; Heb. 2:14; 5:7; 1 John 1:1–3):

Biblical support for Christ's deity

The Bible attests in numerous ways to the full and undiminished deity of Jesus Christ. The following material represents only a portion:[11]

Divine titles proclaimed by or attributed to Jesus Christ[12]
God (John 1:1, 18; 20:28; Rom. 9:5; Titus 2:13; Heb. 1:8; 2 Pet. 1:1)
Lord (Mark 12:35–37; John 20:28; Rom. 10:9–13; 1 Cor. 8:5–6; 12:3; Phil. 2:11)
Messiah (Matt. 16:16; Mark 14:61; John 20:31)
Son of God (Matt. 11:27; Mark 15:39; John 1:18; Rom. 1:4; Gal. 4:4; Heb. 1:2)
Son of Man (Matt. 16:28; 24:30; Mark 8:38; 14:62–64; Acts 7:56; cf. Dan. 7:13–14)

Prerogatives or actions of God in the Old Testament proclaimed by or attributed to Jesus Christ
Worship of God (Isa. 45:23 / Phil. 2:10–11)
Salvation of God (Joel 2:32 / Rom. 10:13)
Judgment of God (Isa. 6:10 / John 12:41)
Nature of God (Exod. 3:14 / John 8:58)
Triumph of God (Ps. 68:18 / Eph. 4:8)

Divine names, actions, or roles proclaimed by or attributed to Jesus Christ
Creator (John 1:3; Col. 1:16; Heb. 1:2, 10–12)

Sustainer (1 Cor. 8:6; Col. 1:17; Heb. 1:3)
Universal Ruler (Matt. 28:18; Rom. 14:9; Rev. 1:5)
Forgiver of sins (Mark 2:5–7; Luke 24:47; Acts 5:31; Col. 3:13)
Raiser of the dead (Luke 7:11–17; John 5:21; 6:40)
Object of prayer (John 14:14; Acts 1:24; 7:59–60; 1 Cor. 1:2; 2 Cor. 12:8–9)
Object of worship (Matt. 28:16–17; John 5:23; 20:28; Phil. 2:10–11; Heb. 1:6)
Object of saving faith (John 14:1; Acts 10:43; 16:31; Rom. 10:8–13)
Image and representation of God (Col. 1:15; Heb. 1:3)

Divine attributes or qualities proclaimed by or attributed to Jesus Christ
Eternal existence (John 1:1; 8:58; 17:5; 1 Cor. 10:4; Col. 1:17; Heb. 13:8)
Self-existence (John 1:3; 5:26; Col. 1:16; Heb. 1:2)
Immutability (Heb. 1:10–12; 13:8)
Omnipresence (Matt. 18:20; 28:20; Eph. 1:23; 4:10; Col. 3:11)
Omniscience (Mark 2:8; Luke 9:47; John 2:25; 4:18; 16:30; Col. 2:3)
Omnipotence (John 1:3; 2:19; Col. 1:16–17; Heb. 1:2)
Sovereignty (Phil. 2:9–11; 1 Pet. 3:22; Rev. 19:16)
Authority (Matt. 28:18; Eph. 1:22)
Life in himself (John 1:4; 5:26; Acts 3:15)

Biblical support for Christ's humanity

The Bible attests in numerous ways to the full and essential humanity of Jesus Christ. The following material represents biblical support for Christ's humanity:[13]

Jesus Christ calls himself (or others speak of him as) a man
During his earthly ministry (John 8:40; Acts 2:22; 1 Cor. 15:21; Phil. 2:7–8)
After his resurrection (Acts 17:31; 1 Cor. 15:47; 1 Tim. 2:5; Heb. 2:14)

Jesus Christ was conceived supernaturally, but born naturally (Matt. 1:25; Luke 2:7; Gal. 4:4)

Jesus Christ had an ancestral lineage (Matthew 1; Luke 3)

Jesus Christ experienced normal growth and development (Luke 2:40–52; Heb. 5:8)

Jesus Christ was subject to real physical limitations
Weariness (John 4:6)
Hunger (Matt. 21:18)
Need for sleep (Matt. 8:24)
Thirst (John 19:28)
Sweat (Luke 22:44)
Temptation (Matt. 4:1–11)
Lack of knowledge (Mark 5:30–32; 13:32)

Jesus Christ experienced physical pain and death (Mark 14:33–36; Luke 17:25; 22:63; 23:33; John 19:30)

Jesus Christ manifested the full range of human emotions
Joy (Luke 10:21; John 17:13)
Sorrow (Matt. 26:37)
Friendship Love (John 11:5)
Compassion (Mark 1:40–41)
Weeping (John 11:35)
Astonishment (Luke 7:9)
Anger (Mark 3:5; 10:14)
Loneliness (Mark 14:32–42; 15:34)

Jesus Christ possesses all the essential qualities of a human being
Body (Matt. 26:12)
Bones (Luke 24:39)
Flesh (Luke 24:39)
Blood (Matt. 26:28)
Soul (Matt. 26:38)
Will (John 5:30)
Spirit (John 11:33)

In addition to the texts cited in the boxes above, four biblical passages specifically teach the doctrine of the incarnation.

1. **"The Word became flesh and made his dwelling among us"** (John 1:14). John's Gospel explicitly reveals that the Word (the preincarnate Christ), who was with God and was God (John 1:1), has now become in-fleshed (*sarx egeneto*). The Greek passage can be literally translated, "The Word became in-fleshed as a man and pitched His tent temporarily among us."[14]

2. **"Your attitude should be the same as that of Christ Jesus: Who, being in very nature God, did not consider equality with God something to be grasped, but made himself nothing, taking the very nature of a servant, being made in human likeness"** (Phil. 2:5–6). In this passage, the apostle Paul speaks of Jesus Christ as possessing the very nature or form of God (*en morphē theou*) in his preincarnate state. The One who possessed (not needing to "grasp") the prerogatives and status of deity humbled himself and, as an act of service, took to himself a fully human nature.

3. **"For in Christ all the fullness of the Deity lives in bodily form"** (Col. 2:9). The apostle Paul states unequivocally here that the full essence of deity resides in union with the human nature of Jesus Christ. In context, Paul was responding directly to the Gnostic heresy, which categorically denied that Christ had come in the flesh. The doctrine of the incarnation was clearly a central feature of the apostle Paul's teaching.

4. **"This is how you can recognize the Spirit of God: Every spirit that acknowledges that Jesus Christ has come in the flesh is from God"** (1 John 4:2). Here the apostle John also responds to Gnostic teaching by affirming that true Christian teaching must include the doctrine of the incarnation. In fact, he asserts that the incarnation is a test of Christian orthodoxy (correct belief).

If Jesus Christ is God and therefore equal to the Father in nature, then how can the handful of passages in the New Testament that seem to subordinate Christ to the Father be explained?

Certain groups both past and present reject the deity of Christ (and therefore the doctrine of the Trinity) because they believe Christ is subordinate (inferior) to the Father in nature or essence. Those who hold this view (subordinationism) usually appeal to a few verses that, at first examination, appear to suggest Christ is less than God the Father. However, when understood in their proper theological context these verses provide no support for such a position. Before examining some of these passages, two points of theological qualification must be underscored.

First, during his earthly sojourn Jesus Christ humbled himself, taking the role of a servant. As a man, Jesus chose not to retain the status and glory of deity. Therefore, in his role as servant, he submitted to the Father and could say that the Father was greater than he. However, the Father was greater only in position, role, or "rank" (function), but not greater in nature (essence).

Second, as a man (through his human nature) Jesus Christ always honored his Father as his God. The Athanasian Creed states that Christ is "equal to the Father as touching his Godhood and inferior to the Father as touching his manhood."

Four so-called subordinationist verses, and responses to them, follow:[15]

1. "The Father is greater than I" (John 14:28). When Jesus uttered these words to the disciples during his upper room discourse (John 14), he wasn't implying an inferior nature or essence. On numerous occasions recorded in the Gospel of John, Jesus had clearly placed himself on Yahweh's level (John 5:17; 8:58; 10:30). Rather, he spoke in this instance of the Father being greater because in becoming incarnate, Jesus had humbled himself in service to the Father for the sake of fulfilling the divine plan of redemption. By relinquishing the prerogatives of deity and veiling his divine glory, Jesus accepted a role or position as a man, below the Father in rank, but never in essence.

2. "My God and your God" (John 20:17). After Jesus rose from the dead and appeared to Mary, he subsequently declared: "I am returning to my Father and your Father, to my God and your God" (John 20:17). How could Jesus call the Father "my God" if he was himself God? The answer is quite simple. Jesus Christ also possessed a human nature, and as a man was capable of referring to the Father as his God. The Chalcedonian and Athanasian Creeds state that with respect to Christ's humanity, he was less than the Father in nature. This passage need not pose any challenge to historic Christianity's designation of Jesus Christ as God the Son.

3. "The firstborn of creation" (Col. 1:15). The apostle Paul, speaking of Jesus Christ proclaimed: "He is the image of the invisible God, the firstborn over all creation." Some interpret this verse as an assertion that Jesus Christ had a beginning in time and was thus a *creature* made by God. However, careful examination of this verse shows such an interpretation to be erroneous. The word "firstborn" (Gk. *prōtotokos*) in this context doesn't mean "first child born." Rather, firstborn is a reference to first in rank, the heir, or preeminent one. Like the firstborn heir in a Jewish family, the Son (Christ) is the heir of all creation.

4. "The head of Christ is God" (1 Cor. 11:3). The apostle Paul wrote in 1 Corinthians 11:3, "Now I want you to realize that the head of every man is Christ, and the head of the woman is man, and the head of Christ is God." This verse does not teach that Christ is subordinate in essence to the Father. The passage teaches about appropriate functional authority, not an inferiority of being. Paul says the head (authority) of woman is man even though men and women are exactly equal in terms of being, for both are made in the image of God (Gen. 1:26–28) and thus equally possess inherent dignity and moral worth. However, this verse indicates that functional and/or voluntary submission is consistent with an equality of being. Christ is subordinate to the Father, but the submission is voluntary and a feature of Christ's role as servant while on Earth.

Why is the doctrine of the incarnation important?

It has been said that "Christianity is Christ." This statement means that Christ is the center and heart of the historic Christian faith. The gospel message is all about the person, nature, and work of Jesus Christ. In contrast, if Buddha or Confucius, for example, were taken away from their respective religions, the religions would retain the essence of their moral instruction. However, take the person of Christ away from Christianity and nothing distinctive remains.

In light of this christocentric focus, the doctrine of the incarnation has enormous significance for Christians. Directly because of his identity (as the God-man) Jesus was able to perform his work of redemption (see chap. 11). God the Son, second person of the Trinity, assumed a human nature and entered the time-space world. Living and acting in a way open to historical investigation, he provided the atoning sacrifice for sinful mankind. As the God-man, Jesus alone was able to represent both God and mankind and provide redemption through his perfect life, sacrificial death, and glorious bodily resurrection from the dead.

Since Christ is the center of Christian doctrine and truth, his identity is of vital importance. It follows therefore, that the doctrine of the incarnation, which reveals his identity, is the foundation on which all Christian doctrine is built. Close analysis of some of Christianity's central tenets shows this core relationship:[16]

- **God's existence and characteristics:** A person may know many important things about God via general revelation (through the created order, the providential ordering of history, and the human conscience). However, without the incarnation, talking about God on such a basis alone is highly speculative and knowing God personally is virtually impossible. God is disclosed personally, intimately, uniquely, and decisively in the incarnation of Jesus Christ. The attributes of God are manifest personally in his life.

- **The Trinity:** The two other persons of the Godhead, the Father and the Holy Spirit, are uniquely understood and appreciated in light of the revealed person and nature of Christ. The incarnation illumines the great truth about the triune nature of God.

- **Atonement:** Only Jesus Christ, both God and man, is able to offer himself as an efficacious sacrifice reconciling a holy God with sinful mankind. Christ can do what he did redemptively (as Savior) because of what he is ontologically (God-man).

- **Resurrection:** A mere creature has no power over death. A bodily resurrection that conquers death is only possible for the God-man (John 2:19; Acts 2:24; Rom. 1:3–4).

- **Justification:** Human beings are justified before God through faith (personal trust) in the person of Jesus Christ. The basis of humanity's acquittal before the Father is directly tied to the actions of the divine-human Savior on the cross.

The doctrine of the incarnation touches and influences every area of Christian theology. To change or distort the identity of Jesus Christ is to distort and destroy the essence of the Christian faith (2 Cor. 11:3–4; Gal. 1:6–9). Jesus specifically instructs his disciples and others to consider and reflect upon his true identity (Matt. 16:13–16; 22:41–46, cf. Psalm 110). Jesus warned some of the Jewish leaders of his time that their eternal destinies rested on whether they would acknowledge and accept him for who he really was (John 8:23–24, 28, 52–53, 57–58). Jesus and the apostles also warned the church about the ever present danger of counterfeit Christs (Matt. 24:4–5, 11, 23–24; 2 Cor. 11:3–4, 13–14; Gal. 1:6–9; 1 Tim. 4:1–2; 2 Tim. 4:3; 2 Pet. 2:1–2; 1 John 2:22–23; 4:1–3; Jude 3).

Weren't there individuals and groups that initially challenged and/or rejected the orthodox view of the person and nature of Christ?

The major doctrinal controversies of the first several centuries of Christian church history focused on christological issues (questions concerning the person and nature of Christ). A brief explanation of these heresies, including what they taught about Christ, how they differed from orthodoxy, and how Christian orthodoxy responded (see chap. 5 for Trinitarian heresies) follows:

Ancient Christological Heresies

- **Docetism:** An early kind of Gnosticism, this view affirmed a type of dualism (the belief that matter is evil and spirit is good).[17] Docetists insisted that Jesus only *seemed* human (Gk. *dokeō*—"to seem"), asserting that Jesus had a "phantom-like body" and denying that he was truly human. The apostles encountered this heresy in the first century and their response appears in 1 John 4:1–3.

- **Ebionism:** According to this view, Jesus was a mere man, a prophet, but the natural son of Joseph and Mary (no virgin birth). Thus Ebionism (a view traced to the second century) flatly denied the true deity of Christ. This position was rejected in subsequent Christian creeds.

- **Arianism:** Arius of Alexandria (AD 256–336) argued that Jesus was of *like* substance (*homoiousios*) with the Father but not of the *same* substance (*homoousios*). Jesus was viewed as the first and greatest creation of God, thus not as a true deity. This influential heresy, which the ancient church father Athanasius (ca. 296–373) successfully battled, was first formally condemned at the Council of Nicaea (AD 325).

- **Apollinarianism:** Following Apollinarius (born ca. 310), the Bishop of Laodicea, some theologians taught that in the incarnation the divine Logos took the place of the human soul or psyche of Christ. Jesus was human only with respect to his physical body, but not in any other way. Apollinarianism thus affirmed Christ's deity but denied his true, full humanity. This heresy was condemned at the Council of Constantinople (AD 381).

- **Nestorianism:** This view, associated with Nestorius (died AD 451), affirmed both Christ's deity and humanity, but saw the union between the natures as only a moral and/or sympathetic union, not a real, personal union. This position represents an overemphasis upon the distinctiveness of the two natures. As a result, Jesus became two persons with two natures, rather than the orthodox position of one person with two natures. This heresy was condemned at the Council of Ephesus (AD 431).

- **Eutychianism:** Fostered by Eutyches (ca. AD 378–454), this view held that Christ had one mixed or compound nature. The two natures merged to form a single nature that was neither divine nor human (a third substance). This position represents an overemphasis upon the unity of the natures. This heresy was condemned at the Council of Chalcedon (AD 451) and again at the third Council of Constantinople (AD 680).

- **Monophysitism:** This view held that Christ had only one nature, arguing that his human nature was absorbed into his divine nature. This heresy was condemned at the third Council of Constantinople (AD 680).
- **Monothelitism:** This view held that Christ had only one will. The orthodox position is that if Christ had two natures he must have had two wills, though his human will conformed in every way to his divine will. Monothelitism was also condemned at the third Council of Constantinople.

Isn't the very concept of the incarnation (one person as God and man) logically incoherent?

The doctrine of the incarnation, in which the nature of God unites with the nature of man in one person, Jesus Christ, remains an unfathomable mystery. It may indeed be the most profound Christian mystery of all. But while the incarnation is incomprehensible to the finite mind, it cannot be rejected as incoherent or absurd. Divinely revealed truth may indeed move above reason, but never against reason, for God is the source and ground of rationality itself.

Some people argue that the incarnation is absurd because it asserts that the infinite (divine nature) is contained in the finite (human nature). But the incarnation does not make this assertion.[18] The criticism is clearly a straw man (distortion or misrepresentation). The divine nature of Christ was not confined or limited to the human nature (or Christ's physical body). While the divine nature is in union with the human nature in the one person, the divine nature certainly extends beyond the bounds of the human nature.[19] Protestant reformer John Calvin explains:

> For even if the Word in his immeasurable essence united with the nature of man into one person, we do not imagine that he was confined therein. Here is something marvelous: the Son of God descended from heaven in such a way that without leaving heaven, he willed to be born in the virgin's womb, to go about the earth, and to hang upon the cross; yet he continuously filled the world even as he had done from the beginning.[20]

The incarnation should be understood as "God plus" (God the Son plus a human nature), not as "God minus" (loss of deity or divine attributes) or "God limited" (the infinite limited in the finite). The incarnation should be thought of as the divine Logos, a preexistent (eternal) person, assuming a human nature unto himself, without laying his deity aside.

The incarnation nevertheless remains a mystery. Just how the person of Christ had a divine consciousness and a human consciousness and yet remained a single person cannot be fully comprehended by human beings.

However, the doctrine has been formulated in church history in such a way that it avoids logical contradiction. The idea of two natures united in one person may be difficult to conceive and is truly paradoxical, but it is not a contradiction.

The True Meaning of Christmas

During the Christmas season, Christians celebrate the great event—and truth—of the incarnation. In the Christ child of Bethlehem, God entered human history and revealed himself up close and personal. The astounding truth is that in Jesus Christ, humanity encountered God in a real, personal, historical, and tangible way. The ultimate significance of Christmas is that the infinite, eternal God the Son left his glorious throne in heaven. He accepted life—and death—as a human to personally offer his love and forgiveness to sinners. The next chapter offers evidence of Christ's deity as found in his death and resurrection.

Discussion Questions

1. How can the doctrine of the incarnation be stated?
2. What does the term *hypostatic union* mean?
3. How can one answer the charge that Christ is less than God because he was subordinate to the Father?
4. Why is the doctrine of the incarnation important to the rest of Christian theology?
5. Why is the incarnation a paradox rather than a logical contradiction?

For Further Study

Erickson, Millard J. *The Word Became Flesh*. Grand Rapids: Baker, 1991.

Grudem, Wayne. *Systematic Theology*. Grand Rapids: Zondervan, 1994. See pages 529–67.

Morris, Thomas V. *The Logic of God Incarnate*. Ithaca, NY: Cornell, 1986.

Reymond, Robert L. *Jesus, Divine Messiah: The New Testament Witness*. Phillipsburg, NJ: Presbyterian and Reformed, 1990.

Rhodes, Ron. *Christ before the Manger: The Life and Times of the Preincarnate Christ*. Grand Rapids: Baker, 1992.

Warfield, Benjamin B. *The Person and Work of Christ*. Philadelphia: Presbyterian and Reformed, 1950.

10

DID JESUS CHRIST
ACTUALLY RISE FROM THE DEAD?

Christianity does not hold the resurrection to be one among many tenets of belief. Without faith in the resurrection there would be no Christianity at all.

—Michael Green, *Man Alive*

The meaning of the resurrection is a theological matter, but the fact of the resurrection is a historical matter.

—Wilbur Smith, *Therefore Stand: Christian Apologetics*

From a historic Christian perspective, both the uniqueness and truth of Christianity rest on Jesus Christ's bodily resurrection from the dead. That Jesus Christ rose to life three days after being executed is both central to the Christian gospel (doctrine) and is Christianity's ultimate supporting fact (apologetics).

Almost two thousand years ago the apostle Paul recognized that Christianity stands or falls on Christ's resurrection. In his words: "If Christ has not been raised, our preaching is useless and so is your faith . . . If Christ has not been raised, your faith is futile, you are still in your sins" (1 Cor. 15:14–17).

Since the truth-claims of Christianity hinge so closely on the resurrection, the New Testament accounts of it warrant careful analysis and reflection. New Testament writers not only report the resurrection as a factual event, but also place the phenomenon within a theological context and explain its overall significance in God's historical redemptive plan. Summarizing the theological importance of the resurrection, exploring its meaning, and critiquing some alternative naturalistic explanations is necessary to properly evaluate the validity of Christian faith.

The Resurrection's Theological Significance

If Christ rose from the dead then all of Christianity's foundational truth-claims prove true. Jesus' identity, mission, and message rest on the reality of the resurrection. The entire New Testament was written in light of it and each book bears witness to its factuality. Indeed, the essential function of the apostles was to bear witness to this event (Acts 1:22; 1 Cor. 9:1).

According to Scripture, the resurrection was not merely a coming back from the dead—a resuscitation or near-death experience. Nor was it something akin to reincarnation. Rather, Jesus was resurrected to a new type of human life—eternal life with a transformed, glorified physical body no longer subject to weakness, pain, sickness, or death. In his resurrection, Jesus Christ fully and completely conquered death forever.

Ten Essential Truths about the Resurrection

The following ten points convey essential theological information about the resurrection of Christ[1] and reveal its christological implications.

1. The resurrection is the ultimate confirmation of Jesus' identity as the divine Messiah, Savior, and Lord (Rom. 1:3–4; 14:9). It proves that Jesus is who he said he is. By raising Jesus from the dead, God the Father vindicated Jesus Christ's redemptive mission and message (Matt. 16:21; 28:6). The resurrection confirms the truth of everything Jesus said.

2. Because Jesus Christ rose from the dead as a man—with a physical body as part of his human nature—he permanently identified with humanity and is the God-man forever. The resurrection was not a flight from the human condition but rather its glorious restoration and fulfillment.

3. When God raised Jesus Christ from the dead (Acts 2:24; 3:15) all three members of the Trinity were involved: Father (Rom. 6:4; 1 Cor. 6:14; Gal. 1:1; Eph. 1:20), Son (John 10:17–18; 11:25; Heb. 7:16), and Holy Spirit (Rom. 8:11). The resurrection confirms God's full involvement—as Father, Son, and Spirit—in salvation.

4. The resurrection designates Jesus Christ as the forever-living head of the Christian church (Eph. 1:19–22). The historic Christian church therefore worships and takes direction from a living Savior.

5. Christ's resurrection power is active in, and ensures, the believer's eternal salvation (Rom. 4:25; 10:9–10; Eph. 2:5–6; Phil. 3:10). The gospel message of salvation in Christ rests on the truth of the resurrection.

6. Christ's resurrection power is available to empower all believers as they seek to live in obedience and gratitude to God (Rom. 6:12–13). The debilitating power of sin over mankind has been broken by the resurrection.

7. Christ's resurrection is the pledge and paradigm for the future bodily resurrection of all believers (1 Cor. 6:14; 15:20; 2 Cor. 9:14; Phil. 3:21; Col. 1:18; 1 Thess. 4:14). Just as he rose, believers will also rise.

8. Christ's resurrection is the answer to mankind's greatest existential predicament, being stalked by death. Here in death's shadow, the resurrection provides hope, purpose, meaning, and confidence in the presence of death (John 11:25–26; Rom. 14:7–8).

9. The resurrection of Jesus Christ is the major theme of the apostles' original preaching and teaching (Acts 1:22; 2:31; 4:2, 33; 17:18), and the chief doctrinal tenet of the New Testament as a whole. "He is risen" is the confessional cry of the early church.

10. The truth or falsity of the Christian gospel rests squarely upon the bodily resurrection of Jesus Christ (1 Cor. 15:14–18). Christianity's truth-claims can be tested through examining the facts of Jesus' historical resurrection from the dead.

A Sketch of the New Testament Resurrection

The four Gospels and various New Testament Epistles reveal the following narrative of Jesus Christ's death and resurrection[2] (see Matt. 26:47–28:20; Mark 14:43–16:8; Luke 22:47–24:53; John 18:1–21:25; Acts 9:1–19; 1 Cor. 15:1–58).

Jewish religious leaders (chief priests and elders) arrested Jesus of Nazareth and tried him for blasphemy. Subsequently found guilty before the Sanhedrin, Jesus was taken by the Jews to the Roman governor of Judea, Pontius Pilate, insisting on his execution. Pilate reluctantly condemned Jesus to death as an insurrectionist. He was beaten and crucified at the hands of Roman soldiers and finally died.

Jesus' lifeless body was taken down from the cross, covered with a burial cloth, and placed in the newly cut tomb of Joseph of Arimathea (a wealthy and prominent member of the Sanhedrin). A large boulder was placed at the entrance of the tomb, and Roman guards were stationed there to ensure that Jesus' body was not disturbed.

Three days later on Sunday morning ("the first day of the week") at dawn, a violent earthquake shook the tomb. An angel of the Lord appeared and rolled away the stone. Terrified at the sight of the angel, the guards were paralyzed.

Later (after the guards ran away), some women followers of Jesus arrived at the tomb and discovered it empty. The women encountered the angel who informed them that Jesus was no longer there, that he had risen from the dead. Upon hearing about the women's encounter, some of Jesus' apostles raced to the tomb and also found it empty of Jesus' body.

Over a forty-day period of time after these events, starting on that original Easter Sunday, Jesus appeared, physically alive, to a variety of people in a variety of places. According to the New Testament Gospels and Epistles, the resurrected Jesus appeared to individuals, small groups, large assemblies, friends and enemies, believers and unbelievers, women and men, in public and in private. The New Testament specifically mentions twelve different resurrection appearances: to Mary Magdalene (John 20:10–18), to Mary and the other women (Matt. 28:1–10), to Peter (Luke 24:34; 1 Cor. 15:5), to two disciples on the way to Emmaus (Luke 24:13–35), to ten apostles (Luke 24:36–49), to eleven apostles (John 20:24–31), to seven apostles (John 21), to all of the apostles (Matt. 28:16–20), to five hundred disciples (1 Cor. 15:6), to James (1 Cor. 15:7), again to all the apostles (Acts 1:4–8), and finally, later, to Paul (Acts 9:1–9; 1 Cor. 15:8).

Characteristics of Jesus' resurrection body can also be cataloged. His hands, feet, and side still bore the marks of his crucifixion (John 20:20). His body of flesh and bone could be seen and touched (Matt. 28:9; Luke 24:37–40; John 20:20). He even invited Thomas to touch and examine his wounded hands and side (John 20:27). Jesus also ate and drank with his disciples after the resurrection (Luke 24:41–43; Acts 10:41). His resurrection body was certainly material and physical in nature, yet it had been transformed into a glorious, immortal, and imperishable body capable of things that ordinary bodies are not: Jesus could appear in and disappear from a closed room and he could violate gravity (moving upward through the clouds). Therefore, both a continuity and a discontinuity existed between Jesus' preresurrection body and postresurrection body.

Six Strands of Evidence

As support for the historical and factual nature of the resurrection of Jesus, Christian apologists through the centuries have appealed to several potent strands of evidence.[3]

The Empty Tomb

One of the best supported facts surrounding Jesus' resurrection is the empty tomb. Most New Testament scholars, even some liberal scholars, agree that solid historical fact stands behind the Gospels' claim that Jesus' tomb was empty on that original Easter morning. The story's natural details conform well to what is known historically. Far from being a myth or legend, the report of the empty tomb has a very early date, fits with archaeological data (burial customs, construction of tombs, timing of ceremonial events), and was never challenged, let alone refuted, by the contemporary enemies and critics of Christianity.

In addition, the Jews or Romans could have immediately squashed Christianity by producing Christ's body. The disciples could not have proclaimed a bodily resurrection if the body could be brought forth. In ancient Judaism, the concept of resurrection was considered only in physical, not spiritual terms. Since Judaism only knew of a "bodily" resurrection, there had to be a "real tomb" that was really empty. This empty tomb needed an adequate explanation. Christians have argued for two thousand years that the only consistent explanation for the empty tomb is that Jesus arose bodily from the dead (see examination of naturalistic theories below).

The Postcrucifixion Appearances

According to the New Testament, numerous people (as many as 500) had intimate, empirical encounters with Jesus Christ after his death on the cross. These appearances were reported by a variety of people, at various times, places, and circumstances. The witnesses of the resurrection claimed to have seen, heard, and touched the glorified Christ. The same person whom they had seen executed three days before was now alive and in their midst. He even manifested the physical marks of crucifixion. These in-time-and-space physical appearances, reported soon after the actual encounter, cannot reasonably be dismissed as mythical or psychological in nature (see examination of naturalistic theories below). The multiple postcrucifixion appearances of Jesus, combined with the empty tomb evidence, weigh heavily in demonstrating the objective truth of the resurrection and thus of the overall Christian gospel message.

The Transformation of the Apostles

The book of Acts describes a dramatic and enduring transformation of eleven men. Terrified, defeated cowards after Jesus' crucifixion (as revealed in the Gospels), the apostles turned into courageous preachers and, in some cases, martyrs. These men became bold enough to stand against hostile Jews and Romans even in the face of torture and death. Such radical and extensive change deserves an adequate explanation, for human character and conduct do not transform easily or often. The fact that the apostles fled and even denied knowing Jesus following his initial arrest makes their courage in the face of persecution even more astounding. The apostles attributed the strength of their newfound character to their direct personal encounter with the resurrected Christ. In Christ's resurrection, the apostles found their unshakable reason to live and die.

The Conversion of Saul of Tarsus

Saul of Tarsus was a distinguished first-century Hebrew scholar of the Torah (Law), a member of the Jewish party of the Pharisees, and a Roman citizen (Acts 21:37–22:3). Zealous in his devotion to God and in his desire to protect ancient Judaism from what he perceived as false and dangerous teaching, he became the principal antagonist of the primitive Christian church. Saul expressed his intense hatred toward Christians by having them arrested. He even instigated and approved the physical persecution and execution of believers, including Stephen (Acts 7:54–8:3; Gal. 1:13–14). Traveling on the road to Damascus (ca. AD 33) to carry out plans for persecuting the church, Saul experienced a life-changing encounter. He claimed to have seen and spoken with the resurrected Jesus of Nazareth (Acts 9:1–30; 22:5–13). Following a dramatic conversion to the faith he once loathed, Saul used the gentile name "Paul," and became the greatest protagonist of the emergent Christian church.

The apostle Paul is probably the second most important figure in the history of Christianity (after Jesus Christ). Paul became Christianity's greatest missionary, theologian, and apologist, and the inspired author of thirteen books of the New Testament. What brought about Paul's conversion—perhaps the greatest religious conversion in history? According to Paul himself, the incredible transformation was due to his blinding face-to-face meeting with the resurrected Jesus Christ. This startling conversion, and the apostle Paul's subsequent astonishing life and accomplishments, seem truly inexplicable apart from the fact of the resurrection.

Emergence of the Christian Church

What specific event in history could have started a movement that within 400 years came to dominate the entire Roman Empire and, over the course of two millennia, all of Western civilization? In a very short time Christianity developed a distinct cultural and theological identity apart from traditional Judaism. According to the New Testament, this unique faith (Christianity) came into being directly because of the resurrection of Jesus Christ. The extraordinary, historical emergence of the Christian church demands an explanation. According to the New Testament, the apostles changed the course of the world by preaching the truth of the resurrection, and thus, the historic church emerged.

A Switch to Sunday as a Day of Worship

The Jews worshipped on the Sabbath—the seventh day of the week (sundown Friday to sundown Saturday). However, the early Christian church gradually changed the day of their worship from the seventh to the first day of the week (Sunday: "the Lord's Day," Acts 20:7; 1 Cor. 16:2; Rev. 1:10).[4] This change was instituted to commemorate Jesus' resurrection from the dead. His being raised to immortal life transformed (through reflection) Christian worship, uniquely influencing the formulation of the sacraments of the early church (baptism and communion), and thus distinguished the Christian faith in its theology and practice from that of traditional Judaism. Apart from the resurrection, there was no reason for the early Christians (as a sect of Judaism) to view Sunday (the first day of the week) as having any enduring theological or ceremonial significance, no impetus for departure from the worship practices of Judaism.

Alternative Naturalistic Explanations

Skeptics, particularly those with a strong antisupernatural bias, often attempt to explain the events surrounding Christ's resurrection as purely natural phenomena. Six naturalistic hypotheses have gained some popularity over the years, but each can be critiqued by objective standards. Logical consistency, explanatory power and scope, fidelity to known facts, avoidance of unwarranted assumptions, and testability (making claims that can be tested and proven true or false) characterize good explanatory hypotheses.

Hypothesis 1: The resurrection of Jesus could have simply been a legend or myth.

Since the question of mythical accounts is fully addressed in chapter 7, only some of that material is summarized here. Many New Testament books (the Gospels and the various Epistles) were written fairly soon after the events they report and describe. There simply wasn't sufficient time for legends and myths to enter the biblical accounts.

While Jesus' death took place in either AD 30 or AD 33, there are good reasons to believe that the synoptic Gospels (Matthew, Mark, and Luke) were in existence by the early 60s (possibly in the late 50s for Mark), within a generation of the events surrounding the life, death, and resurrection of Jesus Christ. Neither the Gospels nor the book of Acts mentions three historic events which transpired between AD 60 and 70: the persecution of Christians by the Roman Emperor Nero (ca. mid-60s), the martyrdom of the apostles Peter and Paul (ca. 64–66), and the fall of Jerusalem under the Roman military leader Titus (70).[5] Since none of these events, undoubtedly of great interest to Christians, are mentioned in the Gospels, some New Testament scholars argue convincingly that the synoptic Gospels were already in existence by the early 60s.

In addition, the book of Acts follows the Gospel of Luke as a companion work. Since Acts makes no mention of these enormously significant events the synoptic Gospels may date even earlier than the early 60s, especially assuming Markan priority is correct (the dominant theory in modern scholarship that Mark was the earliest Gospel written).

Not only were the Gospels written too early to be mythical, but also they were connected to the reported events by a sturdy bridge of both oral and written sources. Some of the apostle Paul's epistles (Galatians, 1 and 2 Thessalonians) were probably written as early as the late 40s or early 50s. Source criticism (the study of the sources behind the written text) indicates that oral and possibly written information predates the Greek Gospels, which would bridge the gap even more closely between the events of Jesus' life and the written records. New Testament scholarship reveals ample reasons for belief that Matthew, Mark, and Luke used such sources.[6]

The demythologizing theory (the idea that myth has encrusted the facts of Jesus' life) only seems possible by postulating several generations over which that mythology could have grown.[7] A. N. Sherwin-White, Oxford scholar of ancient Greek and Roman history, has argued that the span of two full generations is insufficient for myth and legend to accrue and distort historical fact.[8] As noted previously, given the short interval of time between Jesus' life and the emergence of the Gospel records, there simply wasn't sufficient time for them to become distorted. Legend expert Julius Muller states that legend cannot replace fact so long as the eyewitnesses remain alive.[9]

A further reason for rejecting the myth and legend theory is that the apostles of Jesus recognized the difference between mythical and factual eyewitness testimony, and they unswervingly asserted (at great personal risk) that they were eyewitnesses of actual historical events (Luke 1:1–4; John 19:35; 1 Cor. 15:3–8; Gal. 1:11–12; 2 Pet. 1:16; 1 John 1:1–2). Rather than embellishing their stories, the apostles actively attempted to squelch rumors and untruths before they could spread (John 21:22–25). They were honest enough to report their own incredulity when initially confronted with evidence for Christ's resurrection.

The Gospel writers exemplify careful attention to historical details. They recorded intimate details about the historical time period of Jesus (including names, dates, events, customs, etc.). Historically speaking, the central criterion for including the Gospels in the New Testament canon was that they emerged from within apostolic circles (eyewitnesses or associates of eyewitnesses).

The Gospel accounts also stand apart in style and in content from known mythical writings.[10] Biblical miracles are neither bizarre nor frivolous as those found in mythological literature (for example, in Greek mythology). Jesus' miracles are always performed within the context of his ministry, specifically to the glory of God, and usually in response to legitimate human need. The historical and the miraculous stand together side by side in the Gospels in a way unlike other mythological literature.

Some people attempt to tie the resurrection of Jesus to the worship of allegedly resurrected fertility gods in ancient pagan religions (Osiris, Adonis, Attis, Mithra, and so forth).[11] However, these comparisons prove superficial, inexact, and often based on late sources. Thus, they have no historical connection with, or influence upon, Christianity. None of these pagan religious stories has the historical foundation that supports the resurrection of Jesus Christ.

Since good evidence supports the conclusion that the Gospels reflect early sources concerning the life and death of Jesus, if their writers had departed from the historical facts of the resurrection, hostile witnesses familiar with the events of the time could have and would have exposed them.

Viewing the resurrection of Jesus Christ as a legend or myth ignores the solid historical support behind the event, seems deeply rooted in unsupported antisupernatural presuppositions, and fails to recognize the short interval of time between the emergence of the Gospel writings themselves and the actual events they purport to report and describe. Accordingly, this must be considered a highly inadequate explanatory hypothesis.

Hypothesis 2: The disciples could have stolen the body and created a hoax.

According to the Gospel records, after the resurrection some Jewish religious leaders bribed the guards to say they had fallen asleep at the tomb and that Jesus' apostles had come during the night and stolen the body (Matt. 28:11–15). Regardless of how this story began, it became in effect the earliest alternative, naturalistic theory to explain Jesus' resurrection. On that basis it deserves analysis.

Were the apostles capable of stealing the body? The need to bypass the guards and move the large stone which sealed the tomb makes this theft highly unlikely, especially since the apostles acted cowardly after Jesus' initial arrest. Moreover, if the guards were asleep, then how did they know who stole the body?

And what possible motivation would the apostles have had for stealing the body? They had nothing to gain and everything to lose by doing so. Creating a hoax about Jesus' resurrection could only bring them meaningless hardship, persecution, martyrdom, and even possible damnation for blasphemy. If the apostles had, in fact, stolen the body and then created a hoax concerning the resurrection appearances, would they then be willing to die as martyrs for what they knew was false? Such a conspiracy would likely have come apart under pressure. Plenty of adversaries were more than eager to expose any potential fraud. The apostles were hated, scorned, excommunicated, imprisoned, and tortured. Furthermore, if Christ's closest followers were deceivers then they went against everything Jesus taught about truth and honesty. The image portrayed of them in the Gospels is one of honest, truth-telling folk.

If the apostles or later members of the church had invented the story of Christ's resurrection, that story would never have included his appearance to women. First-century Israel did not consider women to be credible witnesses. And the apostles would not present themselves in such an unfavorable light. These peculiar details seem inconsistent with invention, yet consistent with the facts.

Apologists Peter Kreeft and Ronald K. Tacelli note: "If they [the apostles] made up the story, they were the most creative, clever, intelligent fantasists in history, far surpassing Shakespeare, Dante, or Tolkien. Fishermen's 'fish stories' are never that elaborate, that convincing, that life changing, and that enduring."[12]

This hypothesis overall seems extremely implausible, fails to fit the facts, and lacks true explanatory power and scope. It cannot explain the dramatic change in the apostles. Nor does it explain the resurrection appearances to individuals other than the apostles.

Hypothesis 3: The women went to the wrong tomb.

It seems possible that in their grief and confusion following Jesus' crucifixion, the women who loved him might have mistakenly gone to the wrong tomb. On the other hand, according to the Gospel account, the women knew the tomb's precise location. But even if they went to the wrong place, Joseph of Arimathea certainly knew the correct site of his own tomb. And, it seems reasonable that the apostles would have insisted upon correcting any doubt or confusion about location.

Since both the Jewish and Roman officials were motivated to discredit Christianity, if Jesus' body were actually lying in another tomb, they had both the ways and the means to find and exhume it. Without the resurrection, Christianity would have been finished before it really began. Yet the body was never produced.

The wrong tomb hypothesis offers no explanation for the resurrection appearances, the transformation of the apostles, or the formation of the Christian church in a religiously and politically hostile environment. This hypothesis plays fast and loose with the facts, is simplistic, and lacks explanatory power and scope.

Hypothesis 4: Maybe Jesus wasn't really dead. Perhaps he only looked dead, but subsequently revived in the tomb and appeared to his disciples as the "risen Lord."

The Roman executioners were very good at their task. They operated under the constant threat of the death penalty themselves if they allowed a prisoner to escape. According to the Gospel accounts, the Roman soldiers confirmed that Jesus was in fact dead on the cross by thrusting a spear into his side. The blood and water flowed from his pierced heart (John 19:34–35). In light of this confirmation of death, they found no need to break his legs in order to hasten death through suffocation (John 19:36–37).

Could Jesus have survived after suffering severe torture, crucifixion, and exposure in a cold tomb with no medical attention? Could the guards—or the massive stone—have been overcome by a near corpse? Could Jesus have then convinced his disciples that he had gloriously and triumphantly risen from the dead when his medical condition was, at best, "critical"? And if this incredible story was somehow true, where did Jesus go?

This so-called swoon theory raises many questions without answers. It makes Jesus of Nazareth out to be a fraud, an intentional deceiver. But nothing about the historic Jesus would lead to the belief that he was a charlatan. This hypothesis doesn't fit the facts, is extremely implausible, and lacks any real explanatory power.

Hypothesis 5: The followers of Jesus could have simply hallucinated rather than actually seeing him after his death.

Hallucinations are understood to be private, subjective, and individual mental experiences (or projections) that do not correspond to objective reality. Hallucinations are also typically brief experiences (lasting seconds or minutes), often induced by drugs or the extreme deprivation of food, drink, and sleep.[13] They typically happen to people who are extremely nervous and/or high strung. The resurrection appearances were experienced by various people, at various times, in various places, under various circumstances over a period of forty days. The hallucination hypothesis simply cannot reasonably account for the consistency of data from such a diversity of sources. Grieving Mary in the garden may have been momentarily susceptible to hallucination, but what about those ambivalent to the cause of Jesus, such as his brother James, or the openly hostile Saul of Tarsus? It seems impossible that the more than 500 people who reportedly witnessed the resurrected Christ (1 Cor. 15:6) all had the same hallucination.

The disciples describe intimate encounters with the risen Jesus in which they repeatedly saw, heard, touched, conversed, and even ate with him. These personal encounters fit with and correspond to their relationship with Christ prior to the resurrection. These kinds of experiences differ from what is known of hallucinatory states.

The apostles, being orthodox Jews, were not prepared to believe in a risen Messiah. Their concept of resurrection was limited to the general resurrection of mankind in the future divine judgment. Since hallucinations are mere projections of what is already in the mind, and since the apostles had no resurrection expectations, they would not have hallucinated a resurrection. This hypothesis fails to account for the empty tomb, and like most of the other hypotheses fails to account for other facts as well. It therefore lacks any real explanatory power.

Hypothesis 6: Jesus could have had an identical twin brother who was separated at birth but later returned to impersonate the resurrected Christ.

Imagine the incredible state of affairs this hypothesis would demand.[14] A Jesus look-a-like would have to discover somehow his amazing resemblance to Jesus of Nazareth. He would no doubt have to study the public ministry of Jesus and then lurk in the shadows awaiting Jesus' death, only then to present himself as the resurrected Christ. But first he would need to bypass the guards and move the large stone sealing the tomb to steal Jesus' body. Would conspirators help him? Would the marks of crucifixion on his hands, feet, and side be self-inflicted? And how would he manage to appear and disappear within closed rooms? After forty days of appearances, this man would then have to disappear completely and permanently. How? Why? And what would motivate a man to do such things?

This recent and "inventive" naturalistic hypothesis has no basis in the Gospel accounts. In fact, it contradicts the personal details revealed about Jesus' birth (a single child born to Mary and Joseph in Bethlehem, Luke 2:1–20). Like some of the other hypotheses examined, it is nothing more than an *ad hoc* hypothesis emerging from antisupernatural presuppositions. When someone assumes miracles can't and don't happen, the only recourse is to offer a natural explanation, no matter how bizarre and implausible.

After almost two millennia, the only genuinely reasonable explanation for the events surrounding Jesus' death is that the apostles told the truth, and Jesus rose bodily from the dead. The resurrection corresponds to the specific claims of Christ. Not only did Jesus predict his own resurrection numerous times (Matt. 16:21; Mark 9:10; Luke 9:22–27; John 2:19–22), but it also makes sense in light of Jesus' matchless personal character, fulfillment of Old Testament messianic prophecy, and his supernatural power. Jesus' followers claimed to be historical eyewitnesses of the resurrection (Acts 2:32; 3:15; 5:32; 10:39), and their changed lives further testify to the truth of that claim.

The proper way to examine such a miraculous claim is to scrutinize the evidence and follow wherever it may lead. To reject the resurrection *a priori* is logically illegitimate based upon a preconceived commitment to naturalism (question begging). As amazing as it may be, the resurrection rings true on many different levels.

Genuine explanatory power makes the resurrection of Christ, as proclaimed by the apostles, superior to all naturalistic alternatives. Christian apologist William Lane Craig explains: "One of the greatest weaknesses of alternative explanations to the resurrection is their incompleteness: they fail to provide a comprehensive explanation of all the data. By contrast the resurrection furnished one, simple, comprehensive explanation of all the facts without distorting them. Therefore, it is the better explanation."[15]

The question of the resurrection holds enormous practical significance. A person's contemplation of inevitable and imminent death can quickly lead to existential angst, fear, and despair. Only the promise of the resurrected Lord, whose resurrection is a fact of history, can deliver a person from this dreadful human predicament.

> "I am the resurrection and the life. He who believes in me will live, even though he dies; and whoever lives and believes in me will never die. Do you believe this?" (John 11:25–26)

This rescue from death takes place not only through the truth and power of the resurrection, but also due to the efficacy of Christ's atonement—the topic of the next chapter.

Discussion Questions

1. Why is the resurrection important to the veracity of Christ's claims?
2. How is the resurrection of critical importance to the individual believer?
3. Can you list and explain the strands of evidence in favor of Christ's resurrection?
4. What is the basic problem with the alternative explanations of Jesus' resurrection?
5. How does the resurrection meet man's greatest existential need?

For Further Study

Craig, William Lane. *Knowing the Truth about the Resurrection.* Ann Arbor, MI: Servant, 1988.

Habermas, Gary R. *The Resurrection of Jesus.* Grand Rapids: Baker, 1980.

Habermas, Gary R., and Antony G. N. Flew. *Did Jesus Rise from The Dead? The Resurrection Debate*. Ed. Terry L. Miethe. San Francisco: Harper & Row, 1987.

Ladd, George E. *I Believe in the Resurrection of Jesus*. Grand Rapids: Eerdmans, 1975.

Tenney, Merrill C. *The Reality of the Resurrection*. New York: Harper & Row, 1963.

11

WHY DID JESUS CHRIST
HAVE TO DIE?

The Atonement is rooted in the love and justice of God: love offered sinners a way of escape, and justice demanded that the requirements of the law should be met.

—Louis Berkhof, *Summary of Christian Doctrine*

The Atonement is at the very heart of the Christian faith. Christ died in our place, becoming the object of the wrath of God and the curse of the law, and purchased salvation for all believers.

—John Jefferson Davis, *Handbook of Basic Bible Texts*

Christianity is a religion, not of self-help, but of divine rescue. The central message of the New Testament is that God the Son came to Earth in the person of Jesus Christ to rescue sinful human beings from God the Father's just wrath. Thus the gospel reveals that man is saved by God, from God. It also reveals that salvation is provided specifically through the death of Jesus Christ upon the cross. The cross of Christ is thus the crux of Christianity (*crux* in English means "the crucial point," but in Latin it means "cross").

To understand "the atonement," a person must first understand both humanity's sinful condition and God's just wrath against sin. For without sin there is no divine wrath, and without divine wrath there is no need for salvation. This important context makes the significance of Jesus' death on the cross all the more comprehensible.

Sin Exposed

According to Scripture, a person's need for salvation stems from the fact that he or she is a sinner. But this immediately raises several important questions about sin, such as what it is and where it came from. The Bible answers critical questions concerning sin's nature, origin, type, effects, and extent.[1]

What is sin?

At its core, sin is an assertion of spiritual autonomy (a declared independence, even of God)—an offense committed primarily against God (Ps. 51:2–4), though it is also perpetrated against human beings. The Bible uses a number of Hebrew and Greek terms to describe the various aspects and shades of sin.[2] However, the most prominent terms—Hebrew *ḥaṭaʾ* and the Greek *hamartia*—generally describe sin as missing the mark set by God, going astray from God, and actively rebelling against God. This willful departure from God on the part of man often takes the specific form of violating God's expressed commands (Rom. 2:12–14; 4:15; 5:13; James 2:9–10; 1 John 3:4). Because the moral law revealed in Scripture is the extension of God's holy and righteous character, to transgress his law is an affront to God himself. In light of this, sin might rightly be defined as anything (including actions, attitudes, and nature) contrary to the moral character and commands of God.[3] Other ways of referring to sin include unrighteousness, godlessness, and lawlessness.

- "Wash away all my iniquity and cleanse me from my sin. For I know my transgressions, and my sin is always before me. Against you, you only, have I sinned and done what is evil in your sight, so that you are proved right when you speak and justified when you judge" (Ps. 51:2–4).
- "The sinful mind is hostile to God. It does not submit to God's law, nor can it do so" (Rom. 8:7).
- "Everyone who sins breaks the law; in fact, sin is lawlessness" (1 John 3:4).

Where did sin come from?

Sin originates in the will of the creature (see chap. 19 on the problem of evil). Satan—after having led an earlier angelic revolt against God (Isa. 14:12–20)—appeared as a serpent in the Garden of Eden and tempted

Adam and Eve to eat of the tree of the knowledge of good and evil (Gen. 3:1–5). They rebelled against God by doubting his word and transgressing his expressed command not to eat of that particular tree (Gen. 2:17). The first humans therefore misused their freedom by willfully disobeying their Creator. Adam and Eve sinned by doing what they wanted (autonomy) instead of what God wanted.

- "And the LORD God commanded the man, 'You are free to eat from any tree in the garden; but you must not eat from the tree of the knowledge of good and evil, for when you eat of it you will surely die'" (Gen. 2:16–17).
- "When the woman saw that the fruit of the tree was good for food and pleasing to the eye, and also desirable for gaining wisdom, she took some and ate it. She also gave some to her husband, who was with her, and he ate it" (Gen. 3:6).

What are the two types of sin mentioned in Scripture?

Original sin: While some important differences concerning the doctrine of original sin exist among the various theological traditions within Christendom,[4] the following discussion provides a widely accepted biblical perspective.

Adam, in his relationship to God, was not just a private individual. He was not only the *first* man, he was also *representative* man.[5] He embodied all of humanity in the covenant between him and God, often referred to as the covenant of works.[6] God chose as part of this covenant to treat Adam's action (either in obedience or disobedience) as representative of all humanity's actions. In other words, when Adam was placed in the garden, he acted on behalf of all mankind. Therefore, when Adam disobeyed God, it wasn't just Adam who broke favor with God, but all his descendants as well. Sin and guilt transferred from the fall of Adam to all Adam's progeny (Rom. 5:12, 18–19). Thus, through Adam, all people sinned and are morally accountable to God. Accordingly, original sin, as theologian John Jefferson Davis defines it, refers to "the sinfulness, guilt, and susceptibility to death inherited by all human beings (Christ excepted) from Adam"[7] (Ps. 51:5; 58:3; 1 Cor. 15:22; Eph. 2:3).

The doctrine of original sin also implies that all of Adam's progeny are conceived in sin and inherit a sin nature—a severely debilitating force permeating the core of a person's being (Ps. 51:5; 58:3; Prov. 20:9). Consequently, humans are not sinners simply because they happen to sin; rather, they sin because they are sinners by nature. The underlying nature of sin produces specific sins. Man's problem with sin, therefore, should be thought of more as a condition, than as just a set of specific actions.

- "Surely I have been a sinner from birth, sinful from the time my mother conceived me" (Ps. 51:5).
- "Even from birth the wicked go astray; from the womb they are wayward and speak lies" (Ps. 58:3).
- "Therefore, just as sin entered the world through one man, and death through sin, and in this way death came to all men, because all sinned" (Rom. 5:12).

Personal sin: The vast variety of sinful acts and of failures to act righteously—these constitute personal sin. Such sins are distinct from but nevertheless flow from the inherited sin nature, which stems from Adam's original sin (1 Kings 8:46; Prov. 20:9; Rom. 3:23; 1 John 1:8). All people frequently commit such sins in thought, word, and deed (in omission as well as commission).

- "Who can say, 'I have kept my heart pure; I am clean and without sin'?" (Prov. 20:9).
- "If we claim to be without sin, we deceive ourselves and the truth is not in us" (1 John 1:8).

What are the effects of sin on human beings?

First and foremost, according to the Bible, sin negatively affects a person's relationship with God. It produces discord and disconnection. However, sin also impacts relationships with one's self, with other people, and to some extent even with nature. As mentioned earlier, sin is not merely a bad habit. Rather, it is, as theologian John Stott describes, a "deep-seated inward corruption."[8] The sinful nature produces spiritual blindness, enslavement to moral corruption, hardness of heart, lawlessness, and subsequently physical and spiritual death (Rom. 1:18–22; 5:10; 6:17; 8:7; 2 Cor. 4:4; Eph. 2:1–3; 4:11–19). Sin has indeed alienated man from God resulting in a hostile relationship with the Creator. Because of sin, man stands as the deserving object of God's judgment, his holy wrath.

- "We know that the law is spiritual; but I am unspiritual, sold as a slave to sin. I do not understand what I do. For what I want to do I do not do, but what I hate I do" (Rom. 7:14–15).
- "So I tell you this, and insist on it in the Lord, that you must no longer live as the Gentiles do, in the futility of their thinking. They are darkened in their understanding and separated from the life of God because of the ignorance that is in them due to the hardening of their hearts" (Eph. 4:17–18).

What is the extent of sin?

Sin is universal, affecting each and every human being (Ps. 143:2; Eccles. 7:20; Jer. 17:9; Gal. 3:22; James 3:2; 4:4). This sin nature, inherited from Adam, resides at the very core (inner being) of mankind (Jer. 17:9; Matt. 15:19), and affects the entire person—including the human mind, will, affections, and body (Eph. 2:3; 4:17–19). Human beings are thus totally depraved.[9] The doctrine of total depravity doesn't mean that people are completely or utterly evil, but it means that people are pervasively sinful (sin has affected their total being). This condition of total depravity makes it impossible for human beings to merit the favor of God (Jer. 17:9; John 5:42; 6:44; Rom. 7:18; 1 Cor. 2:14; Titus 1:15). While fallen human beings are capable of doing certain morally good acts (under the influence of God's goodness), their sin nature renders them incapable of living in a way completely pleasing to God.

- "There is not a righteous man on earth who does what is right and never sins" (Eccles. 7:20).
- "For all have sinned and fall short of the glory of God" (Rom. 3:23).
- "For out of the heart come evil thoughts, murder, adultery, sexual immorality, theft, false testimony, slander" (Matt. 15:19).

Given man's sinful condition and God's holy and righteous character (Deut. 32:4; Ps. 98:9; Isa. 6:3), man unavoidably faces the just wrath of God (Rom. 1:18; Eph. 2:3). A just God must condemn the responsible sinner. Yet in the midst of man's desperate state (divine judgment), God intervened and provided a way of escape.

Divine Rescue

God in his infinite love and compassion provided a way for sinful human beings to avoid eternal condemnation—and it comes exclusively in Jesus Christ (John 14:6; Acts 4:12). Salvation can be attained by repenting of (turning away from) sin and believing (having confident trust) that Jesus Christ is the divine Messiah, that he died on the cross as a sacrifice to atone for sin, and that he rose bodily from the dead (1 Cor. 15:3–4). Salvation is a direct and exclusive gift of God's grace (unmerited kindness), apprehended through faith alone, and totally on the account of Jesus Christ (Eph. 2:8–9).

A brief discussion of the Christian doctrine of the atonement[10] (the redemptive work of Christ upon the cross) follows.

Why the Atonement Was Necessary

God's perfectly holy, righteous, and just character demanded that he punish sin, hence sinners, appropriately. He couldn't simply pardon sin with a word because his infinite justice had to be genuinely satisfied. Instead, God expressed his lovingkindness and chose to punish a fully adequate substitute, thus allowing sinners to receive mercy. The substitute who suffered divine wrath in the place of sinners was God's own incarnate Son, Jesus Christ. The redemption of man clearly came at God's expense. His decision to punish his own Son, humanity's obedient "Adam," instead of disobedient creatures manifested God's amazing love.

On the cross Jesus Christ, the willing substitute, became the object of God's just wrath against sin. This incredible atoning sacrifice fully satisfied God's justice. In granting fallen human beings the opportunity to receive appropriate forgiveness, his love was fully manifested.

Biblical Word Pictures

Like many Christian doctrines, the atonement contains considerable divine mystery. The truth about Christ's sacrifice on the cross is inexhaustible through human reflection. The following six biblical metaphors depict the meaning of Christ's atonement:[11]

1. Vicarious (substitutionary) penalty. Jesus Christ died in the place of sinners (suffering alienation from God in their stead). Yet in this process he exchanged his righteousness (derived from perfect law-keeping) for their unrighteousness. As heirs of salvation, Christians enjoy both the forgiveness of their sin and the imputed righteousness of Christ, credited to them through faith. The German reformer Martin Luther called the substitutionary death of Christ the "great exchange."

- "God made him who had no sin to be sin for us, so that in him we might become the righteousness of God" (2 Cor. 5:21).
- "For Christ died for sins once for all, the righteous for the unrighteous, to bring you to God" (1 Pet. 3:18).

2. Propitiation. The basic redemptive theme in the Old Testament centered on the idea of *propitiation*—the averting of God's holy wrath against God's people when they sinned. This idea is expressed primarily in two ways: First, in the plight of Israelites who flagrantly violated God's law, angered him, and deserved to die. In some cases, especially in the wilderness, God did bring death on some of the people (e.g., Num. 11:1, 10; 25:3–4), though he spared the nation as a whole in response to Moses' mediation (Exod. 32:10–14,

30–35). These incidents underscore the point that ultimately human sin must be punished.

Second, God provided for "atonement" (covering) of his people's sins through the blood sacrifice of ritually clean animals (Lev. 4–6; 16:1–34; 23:26–32). These Old Testament sacrifices did not actually avert God's wrath, but prefigured the final and ultimate sacrifice offered by the Messiah, who was Jesus (Heb. 9:11–14, 28; 10:1–14). By shedding his own blood on the cross at Calvary, Jesus Christ bore the wrath of God intended for the sinner.

- "My dear children, I write this to you so that you will not sin. But if anybody does sin, we have one who speaks to the Father in our defense—Jesus Christ, the Righteous One. He is the atoning sacrifice for our sins, and not only for ours but also for the sins of the whole world" (1 John 2:1–2).
- "God presented him as a sacrifice of atonement, through faith in his blood" (Rom. 3:25).

3. Reconciliation. Sin created a barrier between God and man, completely alienating man from God. Enmity and hostility, deservedly so on God's part, characterize that relationship. Scripture refers to sinners as enemies of God and objects of his holy wrath. However, the death of Christ assuaged God's wrath and broke down the wall between man and God. God's love for human beings was manifested even when they were still hopelessly sinful.

- "Since we have now been justified by his blood, how much more shall we be saved from God's wrath through him! For if, when we were God's enemies, we were reconciled to him through the death of his Son; how much more, having been reconciled, shall we be saved through his life!" (Rom. 5:9–10).
- "God was reconciling the world to himself in Christ, not counting men's sins against them" (2 Cor. 5:19).

4. Redemption. According to Scripture, the potent force of sin holds man in its grip. Human beings are, so to speak, held hostage by sin and cannot break free themselves. Much as in a kidnapping case, Jesus Christ's death on the cross paid a ransom price to secure the release of human beings from sin and death and the devil. Christ's atoning sacrifice set free those taken captive by sin.

- "For even the Son of Man did not come to be served, but to serve, and to give his life as a ransom for many" (Mark 10:45).

- "[H]e has died as a ransom to set them free from the sins committed under the first covenant" (Heb. 9:15).

5. Justification. As confirmed violators of God's perfect law, human beings stand guilty before their holy Creator and sentenced to eternal separation from him. The divine Judge, however, made a ruling in light of Jesus Christ's atoning sacrifice. Justification refers to the judicial (legal) act of God whereby he acquits the believer of wrongdoing and accepts the believer as righteous in his sight based upon the perfect imputed (and alien) righteousness of Jesus Christ (Luke 18:14; Acts 13:39; Rom. 3:20, 23–24, 28; 5:1–2; Gal. 2:16; 3:24; Titus 3:5, 7). This divine declaration of justification comes exclusively by God's grace, through the means of human faith alone, and solely because of the merit of Christ.

Justification means that for those who trust in Jesus' full payment of sin's penalty, God will not hold their sins against them ever. Sinners, through faith in Christ, receive right standing with God as a gift. He now views his children "just as if they'd never sinned." Justification by grace, through faith, on account of Jesus Christ's atoning work on the cross is a central point of the historic Christian gospel.[12]

While justification involves a change in a person's legal status before God (his being declared righteous), sanctification, by distinction, is the lifelong process of inward moral renewal (being made righteous) initiated by the Holy Spirit. (The process of Christian sanctification is discussed further in chapter 15.)

- "So the law was put in charge to lead us to Christ that we might be justified by faith" (Gal. 3:24).
- "Therefore, since we have been justified through faith, we have peace with God through our Lord Jesus Christ, through whom we have gained access by faith into this grace in which we now stand" (Rom. 5:1–2).
- "Through him everyone who believes is justified from everything you could not be justified from by the law of Moses" (Acts 13:39).

6. Adoption. Because sin disinherits a person from sonship to God that person becomes, in a sense, an orphan. Scripture indicates, however, that a person's trust in Jesus Christ brings about adoption into the family of God (John 1:12; Rom. 8:15–16; Gal. 4:6; 1 John 3:1). The redeemed are granted the full status of being God's children and hence enjoy all the privileges granted to sons and daughters of the Most High King. Adoption provides a familial perspective on God's gracious gift of salvation.

- "Yet to all who received him, to those who believed in his name, he gave the right to become children of God—children born not of natural descent, nor of human decision or a husband's will, but born of God" (John 1:12–13).

Jesus Christ, the Solution to Man's Greatest Problem

The death of Jesus Christ by crucifixion at the hands of Pontius Pilate is a well-attested historical fact (see chap. 7). The person who died on Calvary's cross, however, was no ordinary person, and his death was no ordinary execution. The divine Messiah died on that Roman cross and his death provided a once-for-all sacrifice for sins. The solution to man's greatest problem, the sin that separates a person from God, is found in the perfect life, sacrificial death, and glorious resurrection of the God-man, Jesus Christ. Christians can be comforted that no matter how great their sin, God's gracious gift of salvation in Christ's atoning death is completely sufficient and permanent. God's perfect love and justice meet together for all to see in the atonement. As the apostle John declared:

> This is love: not that we loved God, but that he loved us and sent his Son as an atoning sacrifice for our sins. (1 John 4:10)

Christian truth-claims, however, are not without competitors. Couldn't all religions lead to the same God? A discussion of religious pluralism, the topic of the next chapter, leads off Part 3—objections to the Christian faith.

Discussion Questions

1. What exactly is sin? How is *sin* distinct from *sins*?
2. What is original sin and how does it affect human beings?
3. What does the death of Christ actually save believers from?
4. How does Christ's death resolve God's wrath against sin?
5. How does Jesus' identity affect the efficacy of his atoning work?

For Further Study

Hoekema, Anthony. *Saved By Grace*. Grand Rapids: Eerdmans, 1989.

Milne, Bruce. *Know The Truth*. Downers Grove, IL: InterVarsity, 1982.

Morris, Leon. *The Atonement: Its Meaning and Significance*. Downers Grove, IL: InterVarsity, 1983.

————. *The Apostolic Preaching of the Cross*. Grand Rapids: Eerdmans, 1955. Reprint, 1992.

Murray, John. *Redemption: Accomplished and Applied*. Grand Rapids: Eerdmans, 1955. Reprint, 1975.

Piper, John. *Counted Righteous in Christ*. Wheaton, IL: Crossway, 2002.

PART THREE

THINKING THROUGH OBJECTIONS TO THE CHRISTIAN FAITH

DON'T ALL RELIGIONS
LEAD TO GOD?

In the sphere of matters subject to individual thought and decision, pluralism is desirable and tolerable only in those areas that are matters of
taste rather than matters of truth.

—Mortimer J. Adler, *Truth in Religion*

Pluralism is one of the three or four most serious threats to the integrity
of the Christian faith at the end of the twentieth century.

—Ronald H. Nash, *Is Jesus the Only Savior?*

Following the catastrophic events of September 11, 2001, President
George W. Bush called for a national day of prayer. He urged people of
all faiths to pray for America. Interfaith religious services included clerics
from Judaism, Christianity, Islam, Buddhism, and Hinduism. Prayers collectively addressed God as "the God of Abraham, the God of Muhammad,
and the Father of Jesus Christ." A service held in New York City was led by
popular television personality Oprah Winfrey, who boldly declared that all
people pray to the same God.

Is Oprah right? Do we all pray to the same God? Does this mean all religions are equally valid spiritual paths?

Religious pluralism is the view that all religious roads—certainly all major
or ethical ones—lead to God or to ultimate reality and salvation. Given the

161

current cultural milieu, characterized by globalism, multiculturalism, relativism, and a postmodern perspective on truth, religious pluralism poses a serious and growing challenge to the Christian faith. By identifying two specific types of religious pluralism and critiquing each from both a logical and theological standpoint, a sound response to this formidable issue develops.

Social versus Metaphysical Pluralism

Significant ethnic, racial, cultural, and religious diversity can be found within most major cities in America and many others around the globe. Next-door neighbors might come from Southeast Asia, Australia, India, Africa, Europe, or the Middle East. Democratic nations in particular place great value on the principle of tolerance, especially the tolerance of religious expression. In the United States, for example, the Bill of Rights guarantees citizens the right to free exercise of religion.

Unfortunately, some people take the notion of equal toleration of religious expression to mean that all religions are equally true, thus equally valid paths to God. In effect, democracy has been applied to ultimate truth.[1] This seemingly "politically correct" approach to religion, though popular, represents deeply convoluted thinking. The acceptance of *social* pluralism (tolerance of diverse religious expression) does not logically imply the truth of *metaphysical* pluralism (that all religious truth-claims are equally valid and simultaneously true).

Response to Metaphysical Pluralism

The popular notion that all religions are true ignores three crucial issues. In order to think through and respond to the idea of religious pluralism, these three must be recognized and understood.

1. The world's religions are fundamentally different. While many religions share some common beliefs and especially moral values, fundamental and irreconcilable differences clearly divide them on many core issues. These distinctives include the nature of God, the source and focus of revelation, the human predicament, the nature of salvation, and the destiny of mankind.[2] A plethora of views exists concerning the nature of God (or ultimate reality) alone. Some religions affirm monotheism (one God); others, polytheism (many gods); still others affirm pantheism (all is God); and at least one even affirms atheism (no God).[3] In Judaism[4] and Islam, God is personal (and singular); in Christianity God is more than personal and singular (superpersonal and triune; see chap. 5); in strands of Hinduism and Buddhism, God is less than personal and singular (apersonal and diffuse).[5]

Some of the world's religious traditions view God as wholly transcendent (beyond the world), others as wholly immanent (within the world), and still others as both transcendent and immanent. Some religions view God as infinite in nature and distinct from the world, whereas in other religions God is finite and identical with the world. Clearly, no universal agreement exists among the world's religions as to who or what God really is. As missionary scholar Harold A. Netland states, "Careful examination of the basic tenets of the various religious traditions demonstrates that, far from teaching the same thing, the major religions have radically different perspectives on the religious ultimate."[6]

Beliefs about mankind's ultimate problem (sin, ignorance, lack of enlightenment) and the necessary human response (faith, obedience, meditation), not to mention how that dilemma must be resolved in terms of encountering the divine (salvation, liberation, enlightenment) represent stark contrasts among religions. The most dramatic differences exist between the dominant religion of the West (Christianity) and the dominant religion of the East (Hinduism).[7]

Christianity affirms that humanity's ultimate problem is separation from God due to the willful disobedience of Adam and Eve (humanity's original parents), with guilt and moral corruption being passed through them to the rest of the human race (original sin). Forgiveness of sin and reconciliation to God comes only through the loving redemptive sacrifice of God personally carried out by the God-man Jesus Christ. That gift of forgiveness, however, must be received through repentance and faith. Salvation for the believer culminates then in an eternal, personal relationship with God extending into the afterlife.

Hinduism, on the other hand, declares that man's ultimate problem is not so much sin, but rather ignorance, a lack of enlightenment. Human beings must undergo a cycle of rebirths in order to eliminate karma (the effect of unjust conduct in previous lives). This succession of lives ultimately leads to *moksha*, the absorption of one's individual consciousness into "God," or ultimate reality (impersonal Brahman). From this perspective, all is God and God is all.

The comparison of these two religions illustrates the stark worldview difference between theism and pantheism. And, one thing is painfully obvious: these distinct visions of ultimate reality and truth cannot both be right, for they are logically irreconcilable.

2. Attempts to reduce all religions to a common meaning are futile. The religions of the world are so diverse in belief and in worldview orientation that they defy attempts to reduce them to a single common theme or essence. Indeed, in light of this vast and complex array of religious perspectives, religious reductionism would appear to be a dubious, if not altogether impossible, venture. Oxford theologian Alister E. McGrath notes, "There is a growing consensus that it is seriously misleading to regard the various religious traditions of the world as variations on a single theme."[8] Netland draws a similar conclusion about attempts to show that all religions share the same objective of saving mankind: "It is highly misleading to speak as if all religions share a common soteriological goal and simply differ on the means to reach it."[9]

Attempts to reduce all religions to their lowest common denominator usually succeed only in distorting them. Homogenizing religions is a costly price to pay to eliminate religious diversity, for in the end the religions must sacrifice the very features that make them unique and appealing in the first place.

Moreover, the various religions do not readily conform to any particular reductionistic category. While some rightly identify similar ethical values as a common motif, closer inspection reveals that even the similar moral principles are motivated by, and grounded in, fundamentally different views of the nature of reality. Religion cannot be reduced simply to ethics, for they are rooted in claims about the ultimate nature of reality (metaphysics), to which ethical systems appeal for justification. The renowned authority on world religions, University of California–Berkeley professor Huston Smith, concludes that all religions are not basically the same: "For as soon as [the notion of sameness] moves beyond vague generalities—'every religion has some version of the Golden Rule'—it founders on the fact that the religions differ in what they consider essential and nonnegotiable."[10]

Similar ethical values shared by religions such as Christianity, Buddhism, Hinduism, and Confucianism cannot be separated from the distinctive doctrines that define these particular religions. This distinctiveness is especially true for historic Christianity, which is not primarily a system of ethics. Christian ethics flow from a redemptive relationship with God through the person of Jesus Christ. Therefore the ethical teachings of Jesus in the New Testament cannot be separated from the unique Christian doctrines that emerge directly from the great redemptive events of Jesus' life (incarnation, atonement, and resurrection). In other words, the truth of Christian ethics is inextricably tied to the truth of Christian theology.

3. Different religious beliefs remain logically irreconcilable. The formal laws of logic demonstrate the impossibility of all religious truth-claims' being true at the same time and in the same way. For example, Jesus Christ cannot be God incarnate (Christianity) and not God incarnate (Judaism, Islam) at the same time and in the same respect (the law of noncontradiction: A cannot equal A and non-A).

Contradictory religious claims have opposite truth value, meaning that they negate or deny each other. Therefore exactly one is true and the other false. And, accordingly, Jesus Christ must either be God incarnate or not be God incarnate; there is no middle position possible (the law of excluded middle: either A or non-A).

Since Jews, Christians, and Muslims all conceive the identity of Jesus of Nazareth differently (human teacher, thus blasphemer; God incarnate, human prophet), logically speaking, their conceptions cannot all be true. While it is logically possible in a contrary relationship that all three positions are false (for example, if he never existed at all), they definitely cannot all be true. Thus, the claims of popular religious pluralism fail to comport with the self-evident laws of thought. This observation led Christian philosopher Ronald H. Nash to conclude that "any one who would become a pluralist must first abandon the very principles of logic that make all significant thought, action, and communication possible."[11]

In direct contrast to the "tolerant" sentiment often expressed by popular pluralists, the laws of logic insist that one must be rigidly "intolerant" when it comes to the morass of contradictory religious truth-claims (see chap. 17 for more on tolerance). Whenever the claims of one religion directly contradict (negate or deny) the claims of another religion, then both claims cannot be true.

Some people argue that logic does not apply to religion. They insist that ultimate truth comes only through some type of nonrational intuition. Their argument betrays them, however, because in arguing against logic they must first presuppose the laws of logic to attempt a refutation. To do so is self-contradictory. For even those who claim, "Logic does not apply to God," must use logic in the formulation of that very statement. It is not reasonable to use logic to disparage or reject logic.

Is it possible that the laws of logic apply to all other areas of life *except* religion? The answer cannot be yes. To divorce oneself from the self-evident laws of thought when it comes to ultimate reality is to resign oneself to irrationality. Netland replies that this price is too great, for it requires the "forfeiture of the possibility of meaningful affirmation or statement about anything at all—including statement about the religious ultimate. One who rejects the principle of noncontradiction is reduced to utter silence, for he or she has abandoned a necessary condition for any coherent or meaningful position whatsoever."[12]

An Attempt to Rationalize Pluralism

Some philosophers and religious scholars believe a way does exist of making religious pluralism intellectually tenable. They suggest that perhaps the contradictions among the world's religions are only apparent rather than real. Maybe all religions experience the same divine reality, but in different ways. After all, an encounter with a mysterious and unfathomable God is at the core of most religions. Surely God transcends the finite human mind.

Prominent pluralist thinker John Hick[13] employs a common Eastern way of illustrating this possibility, called the elephant analogy. In this word picture, several blind men encounter an elephant for the first time. Each feels a different part of the animal and then attempts to determine truth about the essence of its being. One man pats a leg and *envisions* the elephant as a "living pillar." Another man grasps the trunk and *discovers* a snake. The man who rubs the tusk describes the elephant as a "sharp plough share." Though each individual expresses one important aspect of the whole reality, none comprehends the complete entity.[14]

According to this analogy, the differences among the world's religions may be attributed to mankind's inability to grasp the infinite reality of God. Hick applies the famous Kantian objective/subjective distinction of the *world as it is* (the objective, noumenal world), from the *world as it appears* to human consciousness (the subjective, phenomenal world) to the problem of religious diversity. He argues that one must distinguish between ultimate reality as it is (the divine noumena), from ultimate reality as experienced by finite human beings (the divine phenomena).[15]

Hick's pluralistic theory places the ultimate divine reality beyond the particular deities of the various religions. This divine ultimate is not experienced directly, but instead is filtered through the different historical and cultural lenses of mankind. Thus people encounter the same divine reality (through Muhammed, Krishna, or Jesus) differently because of their differing historical, cultural, or philosophical perceptions and biases. He further argues:

> These different *personae* are thus partly projections of the divine Reality into human consciousness, and partly projections of the human consciousness itself as it has been formed by particular historical cultures.[16]

Each religion is valid, according to Hick, because each faith provides a genuine, though obviously limited, encounter with ultimate reality. The world's religions represent "different 'faces' or 'masks' or *personae* of God, the Ultimate Reality."[17] And, since Hick thinks that religion is ultimately about existential transformation (ethics) and not about specific doctrinal beliefs, then all religious paths are acceptable because all the major religions are capable of transforming a person from being "self-centered" to being "divine-centered." Hick views religious pluralism as a much more attractive hypothesis than either total "skepticism" toward religion or traditional religious "dogmatism" (such as historic, orthodox Christianity).

A Critique of Hick's Approach

While Hick's pluralistic vision appeals to many for its apparent tolerance and its attempted unification of religion, his conception is nevertheless fraught with serious problems. They begin to emerge from careful scrutiny of the elephant analogy.

Although no one questions the reality of biases and of limited knowledge on the part of mankind when encountering God, these concessions do nothing to shore up the elephant analogy's central weaknesses as related to pluralism. The elephant analogy implies a radical skepticism concerning knowledge of God; namely, that no one, or in this case no religion, can really know God satisfactorily.[18] But if God is by and large unknowable, then how is a person able to know that God is unknowable?[19] In fact, for that matter, would anyone even know that God exists? How does a human philosopher know so much about the inner workings of the incomprehensible ultimate reality? Especially since this ultimate reality—in Hick's view—does not reveal itself in nature or in propositions.

Ironically, while the elephant analogy attempts to validate the truth of all religions, if taken to its logical conclusion the story really shows that all religions fail to identify God adequately. So rather than affirming religious truth, the analogy implies that all religions, at least in large measure, are based on false or misleading claims.[20]

Religions may indeed provide core ethical values, but as noted previously, these moral values are motivated by, and grounded in, essentially different views of the nature of reality. In religion, ethics cannot be divorced from metaphysical truth-claims. What is good must be understood in light of what is *real* and *true*. Actions do not exist in a vacuum apart from truth.

The elephant analogy is especially flawed when viewed from the standpoint of historic, orthodox Christianity. According to Christianity, God has personally revealed himself by entering the world of time and space in the historical person of Jesus Christ (John 1:1, 14, 18; Col. 2:9; Phil. 2:6–8). This same Jesus makes exclusive claims to divine authority and possesses the prerogatives of deity (e.g., John 8:58; 10:30) which are incompatible with the homogenizing and accommodating views of religious pluralists (see chap. 9 on the incarnation).

To accommodate pluralism's unknowable God, Christianity would be forced to give up its revelatory foundation, the Bible, and all of its distinctive doctrines including the incarnation, the Trinity, and the atonement. As Alister McGrath noted, "The identity of Christianity is inextricably linked with the uniqueness of Christ, which is in turn grounded in the resurrection and Incarnation."[21] If the analogy were to reflect historic Christianity, the elephant would heal the men's blindness and personally introduce himself, for Christianity claims that God is personally, intimately, uniquely, and decisively disclosed in Jesus Christ.

The only way the elephant analogy can work to validate religious pluralism is if the claims of historic Christianity are false. According to Jesus' words in the New Testament, "Anyone who has seen me has seen the Father" (John

14:9). "If you really knew me, you would know my Father as well" (John 14:7). Again, central to the message of historic Christianity is the astounding claim that God came to Earth in human flesh and has been personally known among human beings.

The apostle Paul's words directly summarize this central Christian truth: "For in Christ all the fullness of the Deity lives in bodily form" (Col. 2:9). Moreover, a fair reading of the New Testament reveals that faith in Jesus Christ is considered the unique and only way of encountering God. "Jesus answered, 'I am the way and the truth and the life. No one comes to the Father except through me'" (John 14:6). The apostle Peter declared concerning Jesus, "Salvation is found in no one else, for there is no other name under heaven given to men by which we must be saved" (Acts 4:12).

Hick's expressed reasons for embracing religious pluralism over historic, orthodox Christianity (the faith of his youth) spring from his rejection of the Bible as a propositional revelation from God and in his conclusion that the Christian doctrine of the incarnation is both unhistorical and logically incoherent.[22] He argues vociferously that the incarnation is a myth.[23] Hick also views historic Christianity's position of religious exclusivism as intellectually narrow and morally unacceptable. But Hick's bold rejection of the truth-claims of historic Christianity creates a logic problem for his broad pluralistic view.

Christian philosopher C. Stephen Evans points out that "it is an essential part of Christian faith that Jesus is God in a unique and exclusive way. It follows from this that all religions cannot be equally true. If all religions are equally true, then Christianity is false, and therefore not all religions are true."[24] In the end, the correct position must be one of these two: (1) Christianity and all other exclusive religions are wrong, and all other religions, which are inclusive, are right; or (2) all religions are metaphysically wrong. In other words, pluralism redefines religion along the lines of ethical transformation and simply dismisses any concrete truth-claims that might end up creating contradictions among the religions. In a very real sense a pluralist cannot take the truth-claims of any religion seriously.

While Hick apparently considers the exclusive claims of historic Christianity provincial and arrogant, in reality his own pluralistic claims are dismissive of virtually all of the religions' distinctive features. This brings the tolerance of this pluralistic position into question. Rather than representing a neutral or objective analysis of religion, this idea of an unknowable ultimate reality is closely connected to an Eastern monistic understanding of the divine. But why prefer monism over theism? Pluralists such as Hick seem to presume that they, unlike the religions of the world, really know the elephant. The claims of historic Christianity seem much more credible than any politically correct reinvention of religion.

Mythical Claims or Factual Truth?

Another approach to pluralism, advocated by Joseph Campbell (among others) argues that all religions can be simultaneously true because all religions merely make mythical and/or poetical claims, not historical, factual truth-claims. This assertion means that the religions of the world, like mythology overall, are metaphorically true but literally false.[25]

In his best-selling book *The Power of Myth*, Campbell commits many of the same logical errors Hick makes. Campbell boldly reinvents and/or redefines all religions (even historical religions) as myth. In one fell swoop he dismisses religious (including propositional) truth-claims altogether. He, too, ends up accomplishing the opposite of what he intended. Rather than offering a way for all religions to be true, he shows that in the most important way—concerning universal, objective, absolute truth—all religions are instead utterly false. While personally arguing that God or ultimate reality is wholly transcendent and unknowable, "beyond names and forms,"[26] Campbell nevertheless affirms an impersonal and amoral deity not unlike the monistic and pantheistic concepts of Eastern religion. One cannot resist wondering how Campbell presumes to know so much about the supposedly unknowable realm. In the end, Campbell's sweeping conclusions about all religions and about ultimate reality itself seem more presumptuous and arrogant than the exclusivistic religious fundamentalists and literalists he chastises.

Whether a person is inclined to accept them or not, the truth-claims of Christianity are historical and factual in nature. The Gospels assert that a person named Jesus of Nazareth was born under the reign of Roman emperor Caesar Augustus and that Jesus suffered and died at the hands of an equally real Roman governor, Pontius Pilate (archaeological finds have unequivocally confirmed Pilate's historical existence). The Gospels and the book of Acts present themselves as historical narratives, not as poetic or mythical literature (Luke 1:1–4).

The historic Christian faith consistently resists and defies all attempts to homogenize and mythologize its central characters and truth-claims. The apostles had an empirical encounter with the resurrected Jesus and reported it as a historical-factual event (1 Cor. 15:3–8). The disciples consistently referred to themselves as "witnesses" or "eyewitnesses" of the great events of Jesus' life (Acts 2:32; 3:15; 5:32; 10:39). As the apostle Peter proclaimed, "We did not follow cleverly invented stories when we told you about the power and coming of our Lord Jesus Christ, but we were eyewitnesses of his majesty" (2 Pet. 1:16).

The apostle Paul's sobering words to the Corinthian church declare that factual truth really does matter: "If Christ has not been raised, our preaching is useless and so is your faith . . . if Christ has not been raised, your faith is futile, you are still in your sins" (1 Cor. 15:14, 17).

According to the laws of logic and the historical realities of Scripture, religious pluralism (no matter how popular and appealing) cannot be true. The next chapter proposes an appropriate way to view the world's religions through the lens of Christianity.

Discussion Questions

1. What is the difference between social pluralism and metaphysical pluralism?
2. What are the chief problems with religious pluralism?
3. How does Hick's philosophical pluralism seek to rescue religious pluralism?
4. From a historic Christian perspective, what's wrong with the elephant analogy?
5. What is wrong with Campbell's claim that all religions are metaphorically true yet literally false?

For Further Study

Adler, Mortimer J. *Truth in Religion*. New York: Macmillan, 1990.

Green, Michael. *"But Don't All Religions Lead To God?"* Grand Rapids: Baker, 2002.

Nash, Ronald H. *Is Jesus the Only Savior?* Grand Rapids: Zondervan, 1994.

Okholm, Dennis L., and Timothy R. Phillips, eds. *More Than One Way? Four Views on Salvation in a Pluralistic World*. Grand Rapids: Zondervan, 1995.

13

HOW SHOULD CHRISTIANS RESPOND
TO THE WORLD'S RELIGIONS?

Is God's grace limited to the relatively few who, often through accidents of time and geography, happen to have responded to the gospel?

—Clark H. Pinnock, *More than One Way?*

Salvation is found in no one else, for there is no other name under heaven given to men by which we must be saved.

—Acts 4:12

Billions of people around the world adhere to distinctly different belief systems. Ten major non-Christian world religions are identifiable today: Buddhism, Confucianism, Hinduism, Islam, Jainism, Judaism, Shintoism, Sikhism, Taoism, and Zoroastrianism.[1] The so-called minor religions are too numerous to count (these include Native American, South American, African, Asian, and various other basic or folk religions).[2]

Jesus said, "I am the way and the truth and the life. No one comes to the Father except through me" (John 14:6). In light of his words, how should Christians respond to all these other religions and the people who embrace them?[3] And where does this confusing, conflicting morass of religious claims stand alongside Christianity's own truth-claims?

Given the present cultural climate of pluralism, multiculturalism, relativism, and postmodernism, a careful answer to these perennially perplexing questions can equip a Christian with an appropriate response to troubling religious differences. Without oversimplifying the central apologetic issues, sound biblical principles can build a foundation for an appropriate Christian perspective on—and relationship to—the world's religions. A brief critique of pluralism and inclusivism from the perspective of historic Christian exclusivism, along with answers to common objections to exclusivism, helps build on that foundation.

A Biblical Perspective on the World's Religions

To assess and classify the world's religions from a distinctly Christian perspective is a complex task. Not all Christians agree as to the proper system or approach. However, God's special revelation in Scripture gives guidelines for wading through such complicated issues. Ten identifiable theological principles in the Bible can help form a cogent Christian analysis of the various religions of mankind. These biblical truths are enumerated and referenced from Scripture, and their apologetic and evangelistic importance briefly explained. The formulation and articulation of these theological principles reflects the Augustinian–Reformed theological tradition or consensus.

1. God has revealed himself.

The world's Creator and Redeemer has taken the initiative dynamically and decisively to reveal himself to mankind (Ps. 19:1–4, 7–11; Acts 14:17; Rom. 1:18–20; 2 Tim. 3:16–17; Heb. 1:1–3). Thus, revelation was divinely initiated, not a human effort.

The doctrine of revelation is a central feature of historic Christianity. This unveiling of something either previously unknown or not yet fully known (God's self-disclosure) is unique to Christian doctrine. The Christian faith proclaims that God has revealed himself clearly and meaningfully to mankind. Christianity is thus a religion of revelation and that revelation is essential for knowing God.

According to historic Christianity, God has revealed himself in two distinct ways (described more fully in chap. 3): (1) through his world in what is called general revelation (which communicates knowledge of God via the created order) and (2) through his Word in what is called special revelation (which communicates knowledge of God via redemptive history).

The truth and reality of God's revealing himself to mankind is critical in forming a Christian viewpoint on the world's religions. From a biblical perspective, God did not hide away in the heavens leaving man to wander and grope aimlessly in the dark concerning his existence, nature, characteristics, and will. In this respect a stark contrast can be seen between religion and revelation.[4]

Religion, as traditionally understood, typically reflects man's speculative and uncertain search for an undisclosed or not fully disclosed deity (the divine mystery). The initiative to discover truth about God in such religions resides in the limited and imperfect creature. Biblical revelation, on the other hand, reflects God's reaching toward man, whereupon he clearly and specifically discloses himself in acts of creation and of redemption. According to Scripture, the initiative to discover truth about God springs not from man but from God himself, who, though being infinitely perfect, nevertheless reveals himself in ways that the creature can meaningfully apprehend.

Another important difference between generic religion and biblical revelation resides in the definition of *truth*. In many of the world's religious traditions, especially Eastern ones, so-called truths about God are mystical and esoteric in nature and therefore cannot qualify as propositional (factual, logical) truth-claims. For this reason, logical contradictions and factual inconsistencies among the religions are viewed as being of little ultimate consequence (or even as being indicative of spiritual profundity).

By contrast, while the God of the Bible is mysterious and ultimately unfathomable to the finite human mind, he nevertheless has communicated sufficiently and understandably in propositional form (statements that contain true-or-false assertions). Even before coming in person, he also specifically made man in his own expressed image with a mind capable of grasping propositional truth. Therefore, in Christianity, truths about God must correspond to rational and logical categories, and God, because of his rational nature, cannot contradict himself. Contradictory religious truth-claims (which abound in the world's religions) are thus inconsistent with the biblical concept of divine "truthful" revelation.

2. General revelation is available to all.

Basic knowledge about the one true God's existence and nature is clearly revealed to all people (see Ps. 19:1–4; Rom. 1:18–20; Acts 17:25–27; Rom. 2:14–15). According to Christian theology, God's general revelation takes two forms (see chap. 3 on revelation):[5] first, the external general revelation, which consists of the created order, or nature, and God's providential ordering of history; second, internal general revelation includes an innate sense or awareness of God's existence and of his moral law, that is, a conscience. Thus, every person and culture has access to it.

Internal general revelation is directly connected to the Christian understanding of the *imago Dei* (image of God: Gen. 1:26–27). As the crown of God's creation, mankind with his rational capacities, moral volition, relational aspects, and distinct spiritual qualities uniquely reflects God's image. As a creature made in the image and likeness of God, man mirrors in a finite way the glory of his Maker, though since man's fall into sin this reflection has certainly been obscured.

Because of general revelation, both internal and external, certain features of non-Christian religions can be true. Since God created the universe and subsequently created each specific human being in his image—authentic traces of him can be found in all cultures, among all peoples, and, with some important qualifications, even among all religions.[6] Creation powerfully, perpetually, inaudibly, and universally reflects the Creator.

Scripture also reveals that as God's special creation, individuals surely know in the core of their being that there is a God to whom they are morally accountable. This inherent and intuitive sense of the divine explains mankind's deep-seated religious and moral impulse. Humans have even been called *homo religiosus* because of their intrinsic religious tendencies. Anthropological and sociological findings confirm that religion has been a universal phenomenon throughout human history.[7] Even avowed atheists tend to pursue and promote existential answers to life's ultimate questions, often in a virtually "religious" manner (the philosophies of atheistic existentialism and Marxism provide examples). General revelation explains this powerful phenomenon of human religiosity (or what is often today called "spirituality") and illuminates why many of the world's religions find common ground in certain issues, particularly in core ethical issues.

3. Sin produces distortion.

Man's fallen (sinful) condition has impaired his noetic (cognitive and/or belief-forming) faculties resulting in moral and spiritual obtuseness. Thus man's natural predisposition is to suppress and distort the knowledge of God available in general revelation (see Rom. 1:18–25; Eph. 4:17–19).

While adherents to the world's religions have a real (though rudimentary) knowledge of the biblical God via general revelation, their present sinful condition (on account of the Fall, Genesis 3) causes them to suppress this truth. Fallen human beings thus suffer from a type of malady one might call "spiritual schizophrenia,"[8] both desiring and resisting God simultaneously. While man was made for fellowship with his Creator, his sinful nature keeps him from acknowledging, or worshipping, the true God and accepting moral accountability before him. Augustine insightfully expressed mankind's need for relationship with God in what may be his most famous prayer: "The thought of you stirs him so deeply that he cannot be content unless he praises you, because you made us for yourself and our hearts find no peace until they rest in you."[9]

Since this powerful divine awareness within man cannot be completely shut down, it inevitably comes forth. But apart from divine grace, this impulse takes a wrong turn, often down the path of an idolatrous distortion. The result of this spiritual perversion is seen in the various belief systems of the world: animism, syncretism, polytheism, pantheism, finite godism, occultism, and humanism. In his famous encounter on Mars Hill (Athens), the apostle Paul dealt with a similar pluralistic religious scenario in the first century (Acts 17:16–34).

So, while a human being knows there is a God via general revelation, apart from the special grace of God working in his life he will surely choose not to believe in the true God (Rom. 3:10–12).[10] Ironically, in rejecting God, man's religious impulse may in fact impel him to exalt almost any and every idol or "deity" in God's place. For these reasons, most Protestant evangelicals hold that general revelation in and of itself cannot save—though it can and does remove all excuses for rejecting God. Since people in non-Christian religions have access to true revelation, that very revelation ultimately holds them accountable before their Creator.

4. Satan causes more distortion.

While some religious notions may be the product of mere human speculation, at least some forms of religion are energized by Satan and his minions (Matt. 24:24; 1 Cor. 10:14–22; 2 Cor. 4:4; 2 Thess. 2:9–10; 1 Tim. 4:1; Rev. 2:9; 12:9).

Scripture indicates that Satan and/or his demonic followers (fellow angels who sided with him in rebellion) stand behind pagan idolatry and actively blind the minds of unbelievers. Their intent is always to deceive mankind with a powerful spiritual counterfeit. Heresies and false doctrine are sometimes associated with demonic influence (1 Tim. 4:1–2). Certain hidden practices are explicitly condemned in Scripture as abominations to God (Deuteronomy 18), because these practices are connected to demonic activity. In other words not all non-Christian religions are the product of misguided human striving, but rather some have a truly malevolent spiritual source.

As a result of human sin and satanic activity, no human being stands on purely neutral spiritual ground. While the satanic dimension of various pagan religions can be overstated, spiritual warfare must be recognized as a reality behind the scenes of the world's religions, especially those deeply rooted in occult practices.[11]

5. Christ and his exclusive claims in special revelation are unique.

The New Testament reveals Jesus Christ as God in human flesh (John 1:1; 8:58–59; 10:29–31; 14:8–9; 20:28; Phil. 2:5–7; Col. 2:9; Titus 2:13; Heb. 1:8; 2 Pet. 1:1), and thus as the only possible Savior of mankind (Matt. 11:27; John 1:18; 3:36; 14:6; Acts 4:12; 1 John 5:11–12).

God's more specific and particular self-disclosure—special revelation—comes in and through his unique redemptive actions, events, and words (see chap. 3). This form of revelation comes at special times, in special places, and in two stages. First, God manifested himself through his covenant people such as the Hebrew patriarchs, prophets, and kings (Old Testament). Second, God's revelation culminated decisively in the incarnation of Jesus Christ, the God-man. God's climactic entrance into human history is chronicled in the life, death, and resurrection of Jesus Christ (New Testament).

According to the New Testament (including his own recorded words), Jesus Christ is not one way among many ways to God (see table 13.1). Nor is he merely a prophet or messenger who points others to God. Rather, Jesus is God the Son, the Second Person of the Trinity, in human flesh, who has come personally to Earth to reconcile the world to himself through his sacrifice on the cross (2 Cor. 5:19). Jesus Christ is not only uniquely declared Lord and Savior of the world (Rom. 10:9–13; Phil. 2:5–11), but also like Yahweh in the Old Testament, he is declared Lord and Savior to the exclusion of all other so-called lords and saviors (1 Cor. 8:5–6; 1 Tim. 4:10).

Table 13.1
Comparing the leaders of the world's religions

Religion	Leader	Status	Mission
1. Buddhism	Buddha (Gautama)	Enlightened one	Lead others to Nirvana
2. Confucianism	Confucius	Ethical teacher	Build moral society
3. Hinduism	Krishna	Divine Avatar	Inspire as a hero
4. Taoism	Lao-Tzu	Sage	Teach the Tao (way)
5. Jainism	Mahavira	Heroic figure	Teach asceticism
6. Judaism	Moses	Prophet	Communicate the will and law of Yahweh
7. Islam	Muhammad	Final prophet	Communicate the will of Allah
8. Zoroastrianism	Zoroaster	Prophet	Communicate the will of Ahura-Mazda
9. Christianity	Jesus	God Incarnate (Lord, Messiah, Savior)	Redeem mankind

Jesus' exclusionary remarks concerning other possible ways of salvation are unequivocal: "I am the way and the truth and the life. *No one* comes to the Father *except* through me" (John 14:6, emphasis added). The apostle Peter affirms this same christological exclusivity: "Salvation is found in *no one else*, for there is *no other name* under heaven given to men by which we must be saved" (Acts 4:12, emphasis added).[12]

The unique identity and exclusive claims of Jesus Christ are different from the identity and claims of all other great religious leaders. Only Jesus makes claims to divine authority and backs them with the prerogatives and proofs of deity. The christocentric doctrines of the incarnation, atonement, and resurrection form the heart of Christianity, and these same truths set Christianity apart from all other religions.[13] There can be no other savior, for God is personally, intimately, uniquely, decisively, and eternally disclosed in the person of Jesus Christ. All people everywhere, regardless of culture, race, or religious heritage, must look to him alone for salvation. As his apostles proclaimed: "He who has the Son has life; he who does not have the Son of God does not have life" (1 John 5:12).

6. Faith in Christ is a necessary response to the gospel.

People experience salvation by conscious faith in response to the explicit preaching of the gospel (Luke 24:46–47; John 3:15–16; 20:31; Acts 4:12; 11:14; 16:31; Rom. 10:9–10, 13–18; 1 Cor. 15:1–4; Gal. 3:2, 5, 16; Eph. 1:13; 1 Tim. 2:5–6; 2 Tim. 3:15; Heb. 4:2; 1 Pet. 1:23–25; 1 John 2:23; 5:12).

God brings about salvation through the gospel, the good news of Christ's sacrificial atonement for sin. People respond in conscious faith to the proclaimed message about Jesus Christ's life, death, and resurrection. Scripture directly connects the hearing of the gospel proclamation with conscious faith on the believers' part, which then results in salvation. Nowhere does the New Testament say or even suggest that a person can be saved apart from explicit faith in Christ. In fact, the apostle Paul seems to argue the necessity for someone to *hear* the gospel message in order to be saved:

- "How, then, can they call on the one they have not believed in? And how can they believe in the one of whom they have not heard? And how can they hear without someone preaching to them? And how can they preach unless they are sent? As it is written, 'How beautiful are the feet of those who bring good news!' . . . Consequently, faith comes from hearing the message, and the message is heard through the word of Christ" (Rom. 10:14–15, 17).

7. God's sovereign grace brings people to faith in Jesus Christ.

God the Father calls and supernaturally draws people to Jesus Christ (John 6:37, 44, 65; 12:32; 15:16; Acts 13:48; Rom. 8:29; Eph. 1:4) and the Holy Spirit imparts to them the gift of faith through the preaching of the gospel

(Rom. 10:17; 12:3; 1 Cor. 12:3; 2 Cor. 4:13; Eph. 6:23; Phil. 1:29; 1 Thess. 2:13; Heb. 12:2).

Because of the Fall, human beings suffer from total depravity, meaning sin has enslaved the total person—soul, mind, will, and body (Ps. 51:5; Matt. 15:19; Rom. 7:14–15; Eph. 4:17–19). The inevitable result of this depravity is total inability (sinners are in and of themselves incapable of responding in faith to God, Rom. 8:7–8; 1 Cor. 2:14). Thus it is divine grace, specifically the work of the Holy Spirit through the content of special revelation (the preaching of the gospel of redemption in Christ, John 20:31; Rom. 10:17), that results in man's response of faith (Eph. 2:8–9; Titus 3:5). God's grace heals the fallen human will, illumines the mind, softens the heart, and through special revelation corrects people's inevitable distortions of general revelation (Eph. 2:4–6; 4:17–24; Phil. 2:12–13). The human response of faith is therefore rooted in the initiative and regenerative power of God.

God is described as the author and finisher of salvation, and Scripture promises that all whom God calls will be saved (Acts 13:48). His sovereign grace and will are in effect, regardless of how it may seem, even in the fate of the unevangelized.

8. Correct belief (truth) is important.

Salvation depends on the objective correctness, the truth, of what a person believes (John 3:36; 8:24; 2 Cor. 11:4; Gal. 1:8–9; 1 Tim. 1:3–4, 18–19; 6:3; Titus 1:9; 2 Pet. 2:1; 1 John 2:22–23; 4:1–3; 2 John 7–11; Jude 3–4).

According to Scripture, salvation demands more than personal sincerity. It also requires the objective correctness of the belief(s) in which a person places his faith. Doctrinal correctness matters, for false doctrine shipwrecks faith and imperils the soul. Faith in a false God or a false Christ or a false gospel simply cannot result in salvation. It is necessary to salvation to have faith in the genuine Lord and Savior; to place trust in Christ's true person, nature, and work.

Believers may not fully comprehend or may have genuine misunderstandings or even limited exposure to and about Christian truth, but there are doctrinal parameters outside of which a person cannot cross without suffering apostasy and divine judgment. Embracing a false Christ and/or a false gospel leads to dire consequences. Paul's warning to the Galatian church concerning a different gospel dramatically underscores the importance of sound (biblical) doctrine:

- "But even if we or an angel from heaven should preach a gospel other than the one we preached to you, let him be eternally condemned! As we have already said, so now I say again: If anybody is preaching to you a gospel other than what you accepted, let him be eternally condemned!" (Gal. 1:8–9)

The world's religions draw people toward false gods, false Christs, and false gospels. The ultimate spiritual watershed is a person's response to Jesus Christ. As the apostle John declares, "Whoever believes in the Son has eternal life, but whoever rejects the Son will not see life, for God's wrath remains on him" (John 3:36).

9. Christianity necessitates an apologetic response.

In order to guide people past faith barriers and expose fallacious religions for the danger they represent, Christians bear a responsibility to study the teachings and perspectives of the world's religions and offer a sound, respectful critique (Acts 17:22–31; 2 Cor. 10:4–5; Titus 1:9; 1 Pet. 3:15; Jude 3).

Christian apologists must take the religions of the world seriously. To do so requires diligent study of religious history and origins, sources of authority, categories, teachings, arguments, and worldview orientation. The effective apologist will come to know other religions and their adherents with an insider's mastery. Only then can he or she graciously expose a given religion's flaws in light of essential Christian truth.[14] Not an easy task for the apologist, a well-done exposé can have a powerful effect. This endeavor seems to be what Scripture calls for in terms of the apologetics enterprise. "We demolish arguments and every pretension that sets itself up against the knowledge of God, and we take captive every thought to make it obedient to Christ" (2 Cor. 10:5). The serious challenge posed by the world's non-Christian religions deserves Christianity's best apologetic effort in response.

10. People deserve proper respect.

Because all people bear God's own image, the Christian must show people of other religions proper personal respect (Gen. 1:26–27; 9:6; James 3:9).

As creatures of God, all people bear the *imago Dei* and therefore have inherent dignity and moral worth. Every person consequently deserves respectful treatment regardless of race, sex, social class, or religious belief. Christians are called by God to guard the individual right of others to believe what they choose, whether their particular beliefs are wrong, absurd, or contrary to Christian truth. This regard basically amounts to respecting human personhood, volition, and individual moral responsibility. Christians should even tolerate the practices (religious and otherwise) of others, so long as those practices are legal, moral, and prudential. However, respecting another person's beliefs must not be misconstrued as approving those beliefs. Christians are responsible to use their powers of persuasion to convince others of truth, especially the ultimate truth of Jesus Christ. While being *socially tolerant*, Christians must at the same time be *intellectually intolerant* of conflicting truth-claims (see chap. 17 on the issue of tolerance).

How people are treated leaves a powerful and lasting impression—for or against the gospel witness. The Bible calls believers to speak the truth in love (Eph. 4:15)—motivated by love and expressing love in words, actions, and attitude.

Contemporary Rivals to Christian Exclusivism

The scriptural data discussed previously supports what historically has been called Christian exclusivism. Some evangelicals today prefer to call it "particularism."[15] Whatever a person chooses to call it, three theological points affirm this view: (1) The Christian faith is the one exclusively true faith; (2) Jesus Christ is the only Savior of mankind; and (3) Having conscious faith in Jesus Christ is necessary to be saved. This historical position of the Christian church can be distinguished from two competing current-day positions concerning Christianity's relationship to other religions—pluralism and inclusivism.

The Problems with Religious Pluralism

Because a thorough critique of pluralism is provided in chapter 12, this section contains only a brief summary of criticism.

First, a reminder of some definitions: Popular pluralism (so called because of its popularity in present-day culture) asserts that all religions are equally valid and simultaneously true. Philosophical pluralism (presented and affirmed by philosophers of religion) asserts that all major or ethical religions are equally valid paths to God or ultimate reality. Philosopher of religion John Hick is the most prominent representative of philosophical pluralism.[16] In affirming that all major religions are true, philosophical pluralism denies all three points that define Christian exclusivism.

Fundamental and irreconcilable differences, however, separate the world's religions on many crucial issues. Because of these differences, the religions defy attempts to reduce them to a single common theme or essence. In light of this religious diversity, popular pluralism must be false in its assertion that all religions are simultaneously true, for in the morass of religious truth-claims, abundant and blatant contradictions can be seen. For example, it is not logically possible for Jesus Christ both to be God incarnate (Christianity) and not to be God incarnate (Judaism, Islam). He either is God incarnate or is not; no other logical options are available. Logically scrutinizing the claims of popular religious pluralism shows that they reduce to absurdity.

Philosophical pluralism's attempt to avoid these logical difficulties nevertheless results in still more problems: Pluralism implies a radical skepticism about God, results in showing all ultimate religious truth-claims to be false, arbitrarily redefines the nature of religion, refuses to take historic Christian truth-claims seriously, and contradicts its pluralistic assertion by ultimately embracing one particular religious perspective (usually a type of Eastern monism).

Pluralism is clearly at odds with historic Christianity's distinctive doctrines of revelation, the Trinity, the incarnation, the atonement, and the resurrection. These doctrines simply do not comport with pluralism's homogenizing and accommodating agenda.

Religious Inclusivism

While religious inclusivism is affirmed in many other (non-Christian) religious traditions, the focus here is upon Christian inclusivism. Though differences clearly exist among its advocates, inclusivism affirms two essential points: (1) Salvation is found in its fullness in Christianity, through the Savior Jesus Christ, *but* (2) people can encounter the grace of God in all cultures and religions and be saved by Christ anonymously, that is, without knowing specifically about Christ (and therefore without exercising conscious Christian faith).[17]

In affirming that explicit faith in Jesus Christ is not necessary for salvation, inclusivism rejects the idea (defined in exclusivism) that a person must have conscious faith in Jesus Christ in order to be saved (and some forms of inclusivism deny much more).[18] The most prominent advocate of Christian inclusivism was the German Catholic theologian Karl Rahner. His views influenced the Second Vatican Council to adopt an inclusivist position:[19] "Those who through no fault of their own are still ignorant of the Gospel of Christ and of his Church yet sincerely seek God and, with the help of divine grace, strive to do his will as known to them through the voice of their conscience, those men can attain to eternal salvation."[20] Theologian Clark H. Pinnock has expressed a somewhat more "evangelically oriented" but closely similar type of inclusivism.[21]

The Problems with Christian Inclusivism

To assert that God's saving grace in Christ is operative in non-Christian religions goes counter to what Scripture reveals about the idolatrous nature and, at times, demonically influenced nature of humanly derived religion (see points 3 and 4, pp. 174–75 under "A Biblical Perspective").

Even if non-Christian religion is viewed corporately as a mixed bag (good and bad, noble and ignoble), criteria are needed to sort out the theologically good from the theologically bad (a role only Scripture can play, 2 Tim. 3:15–16).[22] Mixing genuine divine grace with pagan beliefs and rituals raises serious questions as to whether inclusivism may not be a trapdoor to religious pluralism. This possibility represents a very serious problem, especially in Rahner's quite liberal approach to inclusivism.

It could be reasoned that asserting the truth of inclusivism renders Christian missions and evangelism unnecessary, certainly not mandatory. In fact, if inclusivism is true, no essential reason to be Christian remains. Rahner makes reference to "anonymous Christians," but the term contradicts historic Christian doctrine. One must also wonder, could there be "anonymous Buddists" or "anonymous Hindus"?

According to Scripture, salvation depends upon correct beliefs. It is the object of belief that saves, not mere personal sincerity. False beliefs can lead to damnation (see point 8, pp. 178–79 under "A Biblical Perspective").

A strong biblical case can be made that conscious and explicit faith in Christ is necessary for salvation (see point 6, p. 177 under "A Biblical Perspective"). If this case is correct, inclusivism is necessarily false.

The anthropology of inclusivists seems to have an overly optimistic view of man and a weak view of sin (inconsistent with the biblical doctrine of total depravity and total inability—see point 3, pp. 174–75 under "A Biblical Perspective").

Finally, inclusivism lacks strong exegetical support from Scripture, and its major inferences seem forced upon the text. This life-and-death issue reasonably could be expected to have solid backing in Scripture.

Challenges to Exclusivism

Some people appear to entertain inclusivism primarily because of the perceived weaknesses in the position of exclusivism. A list of typical objections to exclusivism along with an exclusivist response follows. However, that there are differences among those who embrace exclusivism must be kept in mind. The form of exclusivism defended in this chapter reflects a commitment to the Augustinian–Reformed theological tradition or consensus. Arminian-oriented exclusivists may answer some of these challenges quite differently.

Exclusivism implies that God plays favorites. He restricts his grace in that some people are exposed to the gospel and others are not. Isn't this unfair?

Response: Biblically speaking, all people have already rejected God's authority through their association with Adam (via original sin, Rom. 5:12,

18–19). So what people actually require is a second chance at God's grace, and he gives it, at his discretion. Ultimately everyone who comes under God's judgment will get exactly what he or she deserves (justice). In fact, God could have damned all people, and he would still be just. He doesn't owe anyone a second chance, let alone a first chance. God's distribution of grace may not seem equitable, but that doesn't make him unjust. It is God's discretion and prerogative as a sovereign King to extend his mercy and grace to whomever he will. This perspective may not be popular today, but Scripture supports the idea that God's gracious salvation is particular in focus rather than universal (see point 7, pp. 177–78 under "A Biblical Perspective").

Exclusivism asserts that conscious faith in Christ is necessary for salvation. But Jews in the Old Testament were saved apart from conscious faith in Jesus Christ, so why can't that be true of people today?

Response: Believers in the Old Testament were saved under the covenant of grace. They trusted in the mercy of Yahweh and had at least a rudimentary understanding that God's Messiah would provide an atoning propitiatory or substitutionary sacrifice (Psalm 22; Isaiah 53).[23] Jews were saved through prospective faith (looking forward to the coming of Christ), whereas Christians today are saved through retrospective faith (looking back upon Christ). Questions relating to the progressive nature of revelation and to salvation history (Old Testament to New Testament, Judaism to Christianity) do not apply to the world's religions as a whole because they are not based on that revelation.

Since there were some so-called holy pagans in the Bible (Melchizedek, Job, Jethro, Naaman) who lived prior to the Jewish worship of Yahweh and certainly prior to Christ, couldn't there be some today?

Response: These individuals were given special revelation (not merely general revelation) by God and knew many things about Yahweh and his promise of redemption.[24] They were a unique part of salvation history (possessing prospective faith) and the Scriptures offer no basis for thinking that what was true of them must be true of the unevangelized person today. Special revelation is given to a special few.

If salvation is exclusive to Christianity, there's no way to account for the saintly people in other religions (Buddha, Gandhi, the Dalai Lama, and so forth).

Response: Three points apply: First, an appeal to morality does not answer the truth question.[25] Simply because people seem morally admirable doesn't mean that their beliefs are true. Second, Christianity is not principally a system of ethics, but rather a religion of divine redemption. The question is not how ethical one is in comparison with other human beings, but whether one can match God's moral perfection. No mere human is without sin. Scripture teaches that all have sinned and need God's gracious forgiveness in Christ. According to Scripture, Christians can come into the presence of the Father because they are clothed in the imputed righteousness of Christ (2 Cor. 5:21). Third, no so-called saint of the world's religions compares morally with Jesus Christ in perfection or in power.

A God of love would not allow all the people in history apart from the narrow religions of Judaism and Christianity to be lost. Nor would he condemn people today who have never heard about Christ (the unevangelized). That would not be love.

Response: The following seven theological points come to bear on Christian conclusions about the fate of the unevangelized.

1. In terms of numbers, the vast majority of people who have ever lived on Earth are alive today. It is possible to reach more people with the gospel now than ever before.

2. It is unbiblical to think of the unevangelized as spiritually open and/or neutral to the things of God. The natural man's sinful predisposition is to be closed and even hostile to the truth of God (see point 3, pp. 174–75 under "A Biblical Perspective"). Since most people who *are* exposed to the gospel reject it, there is no reason to think that it would be different among those who haven't heard.

3. The unevangelized have already sinned in Adam, thus rejecting God's grace and suffering spiritual alienation. It is biblically incorrect to say that the unevangelized perish through no fault of their own.

4. God's general revelation, far from being a means of rescue, actually condemns the unevangelized whose natural predisposition is to suppress the truth in unrighteousness (see point 3, pp. 174–75 under "A Biblical Perspective").

5. Reports of the unevangelized having knowledge of Christ (redemptive analogies, and so forth) prior to encountering Christian missionaries are highly anecdotal. They are an inadequate basis for establishing doctrine, especially in the absence of strong scriptural support.

6. Scripture explicitly teaches that conscious faith in Christ is necessary for salvation (see point 6, p. 177 under "A Biblical Perspective").

7. Exclusivists lack complete agreement regarding the fate of the unevangelized. Three positions remain open to consideration.

Restrictive exclusivism: Affirming that conscious faith in Christ is not merely normative, but necessary for salvation, this position views the unevangelized as definitely lost.

Pessimistic exclusivism: While not completely certain of the fate of the unevangelized, this position views people without Christ as apparently lost. God may perform an extraordinary work of grace apart from the explicit gospel proclamation, but there is no direct scriptural support that he will. Many who hold this position think that if God does such an extraordinary work of grace, it inevitably leads to an encounter with the preached gospel (missionary, evangelist).

Nonrestrictive exclusivism: In the absence of absolute certainty about the fate of the unevangelized, nonrestrictive exclusivists say Scripture gives indications that God can and may reach out to the lost in some extraordinary ways. Some Christians see little difference, however, between this view and inclusivism.

The exact relationship of the gospel proclamation to the unevangelized is a continuing point of discussion within the exclusivist/particularist camp.[26] Some current evangelical exclusivists (nonrestrictivists) argue that while the proclamation of the gospel is necessary, they suggest that the sovereign God is not dependent upon the imperfect efforts of human beings to bring the message of salvation to the unevangelized. They suggest that God can, on rare and special occasions, convey his grace through other extraordinary means (dreams, visions, energized general revelation). Thus they say, those who have never explicitly heard the gospel message are not unduly penalized by the church's failure to achieve the Great Commission.

Other evangelical exclusivists (restrictivists) insist that hearing and responding to the explicit gospel message is both necessary and the only way of partaking of salvation. They argue that Scripture clearly connects the conscious response of faith to the explicit preaching of the gospel. God commands the church to fulfill its universal imperative to preach the gospel to all people, everywhere. They also suggest that the idea of God acting through other extraordinary means is purely anecdotal and without clear or explicit scriptural support.

Exclusivists concur, however, that the church has a divine imperative to preach the gospel to the world, and people must have explicit faith in Christ. This mandate surely includes bringing Christ's Word to those trapped in the erroneous belief systems of the world's religions. Christians have a mandate to seriously reflect upon ways to complete the Great Commission. Sound missionary, evangelistic, and apologetic endeavors deserve full support to take the gospel to unbelievers. Ironically, one of the benefits of a pluralistic and global society is that the unevangelized are increasingly coming to where the gospel is openly preached. Exclusivism demands a commitment to the Great Commission:

> "All authority in heaven and on earth has been given to me. Therefore go and make disciples of all nations, baptizing them in the name of the Father and of

the Son and of the Holy Spirit, and teaching them to obey everything I have commanded you. And surely I am with you always, to the very end of the age." (Matt. 28:18–20)

Discussion Questions

1. How does the historic Christian concept of revelation impact the question of how to view the world's religions?
2. Does a commitment to the unique veracity of Christianity imply that every single feature of non-Christian religions is false?
3. Could God's grace work through other (non-Christian) religious traditions? Why or why not?
4. Is Christian exclusivism arrogant or morally repugnant?
5. What kinds of things can a person do to support the Great Commission?

For Further Study

Anderson, Norman. *Christianity and World Religions*. Downers Grove, IL: InterVarsity, 1984.

Corduan, Winfried. *Neighboring Faiths: A Christian Introduction to World Religions*. Downers Grove, IL: InterVarsity, 1998.

Halverson, Dean C., gen. ed. *The Compact Guide to World Religions*. Minneapolis: Bethany, 1996.

Nash, Ronald H. *Is Jesus the Only Savior?* Grand Rapids: Zondervan, 1994.

Okholm, Dennis L., and Timothy R. Phillips, eds. *More Than One Way? Four Views on Salvation in a Pluralistic World*. Grand Rapids: Zondervan, 1995.

Sanders, John. *No Other Name: An Investigation into the Destiny of the Unevangelized*. Grand Rapids: Eerdmans, 1992.

14

AREN'T CHRISTIANITY
AND SCIENCE ENEMIES?

There is but one thought greater than that of the universe, and that is the thought of its Maker.

—John Henry Newman, *The Idea of a University*

Modern science was conceived, and born, and flourished in the matrix of Christian theism.

—Alvin Plantinga, "Darwin, Mind and Meaning"

British mathematician-philosopher Bertrand Russell once remarked, "I am as firmly convinced that religions do harm as I am that they are untrue."[1] In his popular and controversial work *Why I Am Not a Christian*, Russell leveled the charge that Christianity has been an opponent to all intellectual progress, especially in the area of science.[2] Other outspoken advocates of a purely naturalistic worldview have echoed Russell's claim, asserting that Christianity is incompatible with—even hostile to—the achievements and findings of modern science. Many view Christianity as unscientific at best and antiscientific at worst.

Conflicts between some scientific theories and the Christian faith do exist, but the level of disagreement has been exaggerated. And, Christianity's positive influence upon science is seldom acknowledged.[3]

Historically speaking, science and Christianity have more often been allies than enemies. The time has come to demonstrate how the Christian world-view is uniquely compatible with science, while the naturalistic worldview suffers from serious science-related inadequacies. To discover the mutual support between science and the Christian faith one may begin by reviewing the history of the scientific enterprise.

The Late Emergence of Science

A latecomer on the scene of human history, modern science emerged in Europe around the middle of the seventeenth century. But why didn't it come forth sooner, breaking out all around the globe? The scientific endeavor can take root only in the fertile soil of a particular worldview (a conceptual framework for interpreting reality). And not every culture subscribes to a worldview conducive to science. In fact, the foundational philosophical thinking in many historic cultures clearly inhibited progress toward a scientific outlook.

Though several great civilizations of the ancient world (Mesopotamia, India, China, Egypt, Greece, Rome) developed some significant technological achievements and in small ways contributed to prescientific thinking, these early societies lacked the philosophical framework necessary to birth the experimental enterprise known as today's modern science. Even the ancient Greeks, whose significant accomplishments in mathematics and logic reached their apex at the time of Aristotle (384–322 BC) lacked, among other things, the experimental and testing emphases so central to modern Western science.

Pagan Impediments Cause the Stillbirth of Science

The eminent historian and philosopher of science Stanley Jaki has argued that science was "stillborn" in other great civilizations outside Christian Europe because prevailing ideas not only failed to nourish but also stifled its development.[4] Foundational ideas (what is real, true, and good) made a difference in the birth of science because their philosophical and religious presuppositions deeply influenced the way people viewed physical reality. Pagan beliefs about reality prevented earlier civilizations from developing a self-sustaining form of scientific inquiry.[5] The following presuppositions stood in the way of science's emergence in ancient civilizations.

A Cyclical View of Time

Virtually all ancient civilizations held to a cyclical (constantly repeating) view of time. Unlike a linear (beginning-to-end) view of time, introduced in the West by Augustine (AD 354–430), the cyclical approach to time was deterministic. Thus, it hindered progress, promoted complacency, and provided no adequate basis for exploring or questioning cause-effect relationships. Eastern religious concepts such as karma (cycle of justice) and reincarnation (cycle of rebirths) reflect this cyclic or reoccurring view.

Astrology

Pseudo-scientific explanations for natural phenomena permeated the ancient world. Astrology—the ancient belief that the fate or destiny of individuals as well as nations is determined by the stars—led the way. While astronomy developed from astrology, the latter's fatalism generally suppressed human initiative and stood in the way of genuine scientific inquiry.

Deifying Nature

Metaphysical views that deified nature were common in antiquity. The primitive religious belief called animism taught that parts of nature (mountains, seas, winds, and so forth) were imbued with spirit, while pantheism (literally "all is god") and forms of paganism deified the world corporately or as a whole. Viewing the world as a mysterious and sacred object of worship meant it could not be subjected to independent objective analysis. Hence, no empirical experimentation.

Denying Nature

The religion of Hinduism, which emerged from the Indus Valley civilization of ancient India, relies heavily upon the *Upanishads* (part of the Vedic scriptures), and these teach that the physical world is ultimately an illusion. (This worldview is especially evident in the more philosophical branch of Hinduism.) A distinctive feature of Hinduism is the concept of *maya*, the belief that a person's senses are bombarded with false knowledge. According to Hindu belief, the material world is part of that pseudo-reality. Science cannot be taken seriously when the dominant philosophical views deny the reality of nature itself (idealism). Even the Greek Platonic tradition viewed the physical world (the world of appearance) as less real than the transcendent world of Forms (Plato's conceptual world of ideal essences, the world of reality).

Arbitrary and Whimsical Nature of God(s)

The gods of the ancient civilizations were typically capricious and illogical, as evidenced in their supposed interactions with humanity and the world. According to ancient beliefs, the physical state of the world was left to the unpredictable and unreliable will of the gods (a sort of ancient form of relativism). Science could not take root in a world without order and regularity. Even the advanced state of medieval Islamic culture suffered from belief in the arbitrary nature attributed to the Muslim deity, Allah.

Science in the Womb

Many secularists agree that the superstitions of the ancient world prevented the birth of a self-sustaining scientific inquiry. However, many of these same people consider the Middle Ages (the so-called "age of the church") as "the dark ages," a period inhibitive to scientific progress. Some have suggested that the collective consciousness of the medieval world suffered because people were too heavenly minded to be any earthly good.[6] But this seems an excessively critical assessment.

While the early part of the Middle Ages (ca. AD 500–800) brought an eclipse of Greco-Roman (classical) learning (thus the term "dark" age) and a sharp cultural decline in Western Europe, the rest of the medieval era was not nearly so bleak. In fact, leading specialists on medieval intellectual history have pointed out that the scientific revolution, which came in the sixteenth and seventeenth centuries, took root in the high Middle Ages.[7]

Oxford theologian and scientist Alister McGrath identifies three medieval developments that nurtured the later emergence of the natural sciences. These advancements included: (1) translation of important Greek and Arabic science–related texts into Latin, (2) establishment of the great universities of Western Europe (with courses in the developing scientific disciplines), and (3) university-trained Christian theologians' and philosophers' affirmation of the value and importance of studying the natural world, which was created by God.[8] This intellectual synthesis in the medieval world therefore paved the way for experimental science's later arrival.[9]

In a Christian Cradle

Christianity uniquely and decisively shaped the intellectual climate that gave rise to modern science (roughly three and a half centuries ago).[10] It is even correct to say that modern science was born in the cradle of Christian civilization. Not only were virtually all of the founding fathers of science devout Christians (including Copernicus, Kepler, Galileo, Newton, Boyle, and Pascal),[11] but the Christian worldview provided a basis for modern science to emerge and flourish.

Christian theism affirmed that an infinite, eternal, and personal God created the world *ex nihilo* (literally "out of nothing"). The creation, reflecting the rational nature of its Creator, was therefore orderly and uniform (as well as divinely pronounced "good"). Further, mankind was viewed as "created in God's image" (Gen. 1:26–27), thus capable of observing, reasoning, and ultimately discovering the intelligibility of the created order. In effect, the Christian worldview supported the underlying principles that made scientific inquiry both possible and desirable.

The Bible itself played a role in the development of the scientific method. The principles underlying the scientific method (testability, verification, falsification) are uniquely compatible with the intellectual virtues affirmed in the Judeo-Christian Scriptures. Christian doctrine nurtured the experimental method.[12] Because the Christian founders of modern science believed that the heavens genuinely declare the glory of God (Ps. 19:1), they possessed both the necessary conceptual framework and the spiritual incentive to explore boldly nature's mysteries. According to Christian theism, God has disclosed himself not only in the Bible ("God's Word") but also through the "general revelation" of God (via creative actions) discoverable in nature ("God's world"). (For more on this point, see chapter 3.) Puritan scientists in England and in America viewed the study of science as a sacred attempt to "think God's thoughts after him."

The wisdom literature of the Old Testament consistently exhorts God's people to pursue "wisdom, knowledge, and understanding," all of which are rooted in "the fear of the LORD" (Job 28:28; 34:4; Ps.111:10; Prov. 1:7; 9:10). And the intellectual virtues of discernment, reflection, and testing are biblical mandates (Acts 17:11; Rom. 12:2; 1 Cor. 14:29; Col. 2:8; 1 Thess. 5:21; 1 John. 4:1; Rev. 2:2). These critical principles embraced by the early theological naturalists (early scientists), served as the backdrop for the emerging experimental method.[13]

Necessary Conditions for Science

Scientists are fond of saying that one of science's fundamental features is that it works. However, the operation of science presupposes certain foundational truths not wholly derived from science itself. In order for the experimental venture to work and thrive, certain nonempirical assumptions about the world must be true. In other words, it takes a certain kind of world for science to be possible.[14] The scientific process simply cannot work in every conceivable world. In fact one reason modern science started so late was that the philosophical views (conceptual framework) of earlier cultures were inadequate to justify and sustain the necessary preconditions for scientific advance.

Science was born and nurtured and ultimately flourished within the Christian European civilization because the Christian vision of reality possesses all the necessary presuppositions to undergird the scientific enterprise. The following points[15] reflect how the Christian worldview anticipated, shaped, encouraged, justified, and sustained the general character and presuppositions of modern science.

The Christian worldview undergirds science by its recognition of these ten truths:

1. The physical universe is a distinct, objective reality.

By his incalculable wisdom and awesome power, the God of the Bible created the universe (matter, energy, time, and space) *ex nihilo*. The universe therefore has a distinct existence of its own (apart from the mind and will of the human observer) contingent upon the creative and sustaining power of God. If, as suggested by other cultures and philosophical traditions, the universe were somehow less than an objective reality, science would be superfluous. The transcendent God revealed in Scripture is the necessary causal agent of the contingent universe.

2. The laws of nature exhibit order, patterns, and regularity.

Because a personal God designed the universe to reflect his inherent rationality, the world exhibits elegant order, detectable patterns, and dependable regularity. These teleological (purposeful) qualities are essential to the nature of science, for they make self-consistent scientific theories possible. Since it mirrors the mind of its Creator, the cosmos reflects elegance and coherence. Philosopher of science Del Ratzsch comments: "And given that the cosmos precludes fundamental chaos, we insist on self-consistent theories, and since we expect the patterns to be broad and unified, we expect that theories which are even approximately true will mesh with each other."[16]

3. The laws of nature are uniform throughout the physical universe.

Because of God's providential ordering and governance, the orderliness and regularities of nature hold throughout the entire universe. Critical to the scientific enterprise, the universality of these laws guarantees predictability and the possibility of duplicating scientific outcomes. The uniformity of nature assures the scientist that causal relationships tomorrow will correspond with those of today. The inductive method and inferential reasoning depend upon the uniformity of nature's laws, and that universality corresponds to what would be expected when looking through the lens of the Christian theistic worldview.

4. The physical universe is intelligible.

Since the world reflects the wisdom of its Maker, the order and patterns of the universe are understandable and comprehensible. The physical world can therefore be objectively studied, making science possible. The world's amazing intelligibility led British physicist John Polkinghorne to note: "We are so familiar with the fact that we can understand the world that most of the time we take it for granted. It is what makes science possible. Yet it could have been otherwise. The universe might have been a disorderly chaos rather than an orderly cosmos."[17]

5. The world is good, valuable, and worthy of careful study.

God calls his creation "very good" (Gen. 1:31). The created order testifies to God's existence, power, wisdom, majesty, righteousness, and glory. Therefore, studying nature reveals truth about him. The world is also the place where human beings live out their destiny. The study of nature holds great benefit for mankind (medical, technological, and economical as well as spiritual), and humanity as the crown of creation has a divine imperative to manage the planet's living and nonliving resources (Gen. 1:28).

6. Because the world is not divine and therefore not a proper object of worship, it can be an object of rational study.

The Judeo-Christian Scriptures condemn as idolatrous all belief systems that deify the natural order (for example, animism, pantheism, paganism). As an independent physical reality, the universe is a potential object of rational study (experimentation). Christianity's curbing of superstition regarding nature allowed science to be viewed as an appropriate pursuit of knowledge.

7. Human beings possess the ability to discover the universe's intelligibility.

Because of the *imago Dei*, human beings possess profoundly important rational capacities. God made people specifically capable of knowing and discerning truth. He created them with the cognitive and sensory faculties necessary to observe, reason, and ultimately recognize the intelligible order of the created world. He also gave humans the ability to interact on an intellectual level, thus able to check each others' inferences (making the scientific practice of peer review possible). As the designer of both the world and the human mind, God made possible the congruence between the two. Thus he guaranteed the validity of such truths as mathematics, logic, and language.

Such congruence between the physical universe and the human mind is a powerful witness to the truth of divine design as set forth in historic

Christianity. McGrath explains the significance of this connection: "There is a deep-seated congruence between the rationality present in our minds, and the rationality—the orderedness—which we observe as present in the world. Thus the abstract structures of pure mathematics—a free creation of the human mind—provide important clues to understanding the world."[18]

8. The free agency of the Creator makes the empirical method necessary.

God's creative patterns could have taken a variety of pathways. Since human beings have no prior knowledge of those set patterns, the empirical method with its experimental process is necessary. The creation illustrates that God, among other things, is a playful artist. For example, he makes different varieties within a particular plant or animal species similar to one another, yet different enough from each other to require careful study and inspire curiosity. Roses and poppies differ widely, yet both are flowers. Bats and bears hardly seem comparable, yet both are mammals.

9. God encourages, even propels, science through his imperative to humans to take dominion over nature.

God not only created human beings with the ability to study the natural world, but he also virtually commanded the first human, Adam, to do so. Adam's interaction with the natural world (caring for the garden and naming the animals) involved a certain mastery and classification of nature. God's imperative to man to "subdue" nature certainly warrants and necessitates the scientific enterprise.

10. The intellectual virtues essential to carrying out the scientific enterprise are part of God's moral Law.

Science must be practiced in a particular way in order to flourish and equip Adam's progeny for their God-given task. Good science must involve such intellectual virtues as honesty, integrity, discernment, humility, and courage.[19] These moral qualities are part of God's intended moral law for mankind. Moral principles must be grounded in something objective (see chap. 18 on relativism).

Can Naturalism Justify the Preconditions of Science?

The necessary preconditions of science comport well with Christian theism's truth-claims concerning an infinite, eternal, and personal Creator who carefully ordered the universe and provided man with a mind and sensory system that correspond to the universe's intelligibility. This Christian schema provided the inspiration and the intellectual breeding ground for modern science. But what about naturalism? Can it explain the necessary preconditions of science?

Naturalism is the belief system that regards the natural, material, and physical universe as the only reality. Nature is the whole show. This viewpoint is often characterized by corollary beliefs such as monism (all reality is one), materialism (reality is ultimately matter), antisupernaturalism (all supernatural explanations are to be rejected *a priori*), scientism (only the scientific method yields "truth"), and humanism (humanity is the ultimate outcome, hence "value"). According to naturalism, everything (things, people, and events) can be reduced to "matter in motion." Everything is reducible to, or explained in terms of, certain fundamental natural phenomena (physics, chemistry, and biology). Carl Sagan expressed the position of strong naturalism in a famous statement in his television series *Cosmos*: "The cosmos is all that is, or ever was, or ever will be."

If naturalism is to be accepted as an adequate worldview, then it must possess genuine explanatory power. But some difficult questions emerge to challenge the purported truth of a purely naturalistic worldview.[20]

- How can a world that is the product of blind, purposeless, random natural processes account for and justify the crucial conditions that make the scientific enterprise possible?
- Aren't the order, regularity, and uniformity of nature out of place (unaccounted for and valueless coincidences) in a purely naturalistic world which could as easily have been a purely random and chaotic universe?
- What accounts for the existence of abstract, nonempirical entities such as numbers, propositions, the laws of logic, and inductive inferences in a world that is the product of a mindless accidental process?
- If the sensory organs and cognitive faculties of human beings are the result of chance and accident, how can they be trusted to yield coherent data, much less objective "truth"?[21]
- Since naturalism implies a type of physical determinism (all things are the product of genetic, chemical, and environmental factors), then doesn't that by necessity rule out such things as uncoerced, deliberate thought?
- Since this determinism is incompatible with rational thought, free will, and moral decisions, wouldn't naturalism be self-defeating?

Christian philosopher Greg L. Bahnsen has argued that far from justifying their underlying presuppositions, naturalists illegitimately rest their scientific operation on Christian theistic principles.[22] The naturalist is borrowing Christian philosophical/epistemological capital. Naturalism appears unable to explain the assumptions that make modern science possible. It also seems at odds with the very practice of science. The discipline of science presupposes a biblical-like worldview. Physicist and popular science writer Paul Davies offers this observation:

> In the ensuing three hundred years the theological dimension of science has faded. People take it for granted that the physical world is both ordered and intelligible. The underlying order in nature—the laws of physics—are simply accepted as given, as brute facts. Nobody asks where they came from; at least they do not do so in polite company. However, even the most atheistic scientist accepts as an act of faith that the universe is not absurd, that there is a rational basis to physical existence manifested as lawlike order in nature that is at least part comprehensible to us. So science can proceed only if the scientist adopts an essentially theological worldview.[23]

Could science have arisen if the dominant metaphysical views of the time were naturalistic and materialistic in nature? And would naturalism be able to sustain the scientific enterprise that Christian theism birthed? A rational person can't help but wonder.

Does Christianity Comport with the Prevailing Views of Science?

Clearly Christianity contributed to the launch of modern science. But this question arises frequently today: how do the prevailing scientific views concerning the universe comport with Scripture? A brief consideration of big bang cosmology and the emerging "anthropic principle" (fine-tuning for the benefit of human life) help provide an answer.

The Beginning of the Universe

The cosmologies of all ancient holy books are at odds with the findings of modern science, except one. In accord with well-established conclusions, the Scriptures reveal these things (among others) about the universe:[24]

1. The universe had a singular beginning *ex nihilo* (Gen. 1:1; John 1:3; Rom. 4:17; Col. 1:16–17; Heb. 11:3; Rev. 4:11).

- "In the beginning God created the heavens and the earth" (Gen. 1:1).
- "The God who gives life to the dead and calls things that are not as though they were" (Rom. 4:17).

- "By faith we understand that the universe was formed at God's command, so that what is seen was not made out of what was visible" (Heb. 11:3).

2. The universe is continuously expanding (Job. 9:8; Ps. 104:2).

- "He alone stretches out the heavens and treads on the waves of the sea" (Job 9:8).
- "He wraps himself in light as with a garment; he stretches out the heavens like a tent" (Ps. 104:2).
- "This is what God the Lord says—he who created the heavens and stretched them out" (Isa. 42:5).

3. Matter, energy, space, and time had a specific beginning (John 1:3; Col. 1:16–17; 2 Tim. 1:9; Titus 1:2).

- "Through him all things were made; without him nothing was made that has been made" (John 1:3).
- "For by him all things were created: things in heaven and on earth, visible and invisible, whether thrones or powers or rulers or authorities; all things were created by him and for him. He is before all things, and in him all things hold together" (Col. 1:16–17).
- "This grace was given us in Christ Jesus before the beginning of time" (2 Tim. 1:9).
- "A faith and knowledge resting on the hope of eternal life, which God, who does not lie, promised before the beginning of time" (Titus 1:2).

4. The universe experiences decay (the second law of thermodynamics, Rom. 8:21).

- "The creation itself will be liberated from its bondage to decay" (Rom. 8:21).

5. The universe will come to an end (2 Pet. 3:7, 10, 13; Rev. 21:1).

- "The heavens will disappear with a roar; the elements will be destroyed by fire, and the earth and everything in it will be laid bare" (2 Pet. 3:10).
- "Then I saw a new heaven and a new earth, for the first heaven and the first earth had passed away" (Rev 21:1).

Since the universe had a (singular) beginning, to inquire about its cause makes sense. Logically speaking, everything that begins must have a cause. Gottfried Leibniz's classic question, "Why is there something rather than nothing?" seems even more provocative in light of what is now known about the big bang universe. To believe that the universe came into existence from nothing by nothing, seems far less reasonable than to believe it came into existence from the hand of a transcendental, personal agent.

The Just-Right-for-Human-Life Universe

The Greek word for universe is *kosmos*. This word in the New Testament conveys a world created by God and therefore characterized by order, purpose, and complexity. God crafted the cosmos using infinite knowledge and wisdom. A variety of scriptural passages affirm God's active involvement in its design:

- "By the word of the LORD were the heavens made, their starry host by the breath of his mouth" (Ps. 33:6).
- "How many are your works, O LORD! In wisdom you made them all; the earth is full of your creatures" (Ps. 104:24).
- "By wisdom the LORD laid the earth's foundations, by understanding he set the heavens in place" (Prov. 3:19).
- "You are worthy, our Lord and God, to receive glory and honor and power, for you created all things, and by your will they were created and have their being" (Rev. 4:11).

The anthropic principle (familiar and accepted in the scientific community) refers to the scientific observation that the universe exhibits all the necessary and narrowly drawn qualities and characteristics to make human life possible.[25] The fundamental cosmological constants of nature are conspicuously fine-tuned to allow a universe anywhere and at any time hospitable to human life. These four key constants include the strong nuclear force, weak nuclear force, gravitational force, and electromagnetic force. If the measurable values of these constants ranged slightly larger or smaller, no life would be possible anywhere or ever in the universe.[26] Physicist Paul Davies comments: "The seemingly miraculous concurrence of numerical values that nature has assigned to her fundamental constants must remain the most compelling evidence for an element of cosmic design."[27]

Astronomer and Christian apologist Hugh Ross has catalogued more than three dozen independent cosmic characteristics that must be exquisitely fine-tuned for life to exist at all, and twice that number (or more) of galactic, solar system, and planetary features that require painstaking exactness for life to be possible on Earth.[28] This exquisite and essential fine-tuning of physical characteristics led Nobel Prize–winning physicist Arno Penzias to comment: "Astronomy leads us to a unique event, a universe which was created out of nothing, one with the very delicate balance needed to provide exactly the conditions required to permit life, and one which has an underlying (one might say 'supernatural') plan."[29]

Conclusion

Conflicts between Christianity and some scientific theories have arisen from time to time over the years, and some issues remain in tension today, but clearly the two realms of thought have been strong historic allies. Science owes a special debt to Christianity, for the scientific enterprise was born and nurtured under Christian cultural influences. In fact, the Christian worldview undergirded science by anticipating, shaping, encouraging, justifying, and ultimately sustaining the general character and presuppositions of modern science. Furthermore the frontiers of science support what the Bible generally says about the universe and humanity's place within it.

Science does not invalidate Christianity; nor does Christianity invalidate science. However, some people call Christianity into question not because of something that comes from outside the church (such as science) but because of something from within—hypocrisy. This topic is explored in the next chapter.

Discussion Questions

1. Why was scientific progress stifled in the ancient world?
2. How did Christianity shape and influence the founding of modern science?
3. How do aberrant forms or expressions of Christianity stifle science?
4. In what kind of world does science work?
5. How would you describe Christianity's current relationship to science?

For Further Study

Hummel, Charles E. *The Galileo Connection*. Downers Grove, IL: InterVarsity, 1986.

Jaki, Stanley L. *The Savior of Science*. Grand Rapids: Eerdmans, 2000.

McGrath, Alister E. *Science and Religion*. Oxford: Blackwell, 1999.

Moreland, J. P. *Christianity and the Nature of Science*. Grand Rapids: Baker, 1989.

Moreland, J. P., ed. *The Creation Hypothesis*. Downers Grove, IL: InterVarsity, 1994.

Pearcey, Nancy R., and Charles B. Thaxton. *The Soul of Science*. Wheaton, IL: Crossway, 1994.

Ratzsch, Del. *Science and Its Limits: The Natural Sciences in Christian Perspective*. 2nd ed. Downers Grove, IL: InterVarsity, 2000.

Ross, Hugh. *The Creator and the Cosmos*. Colorado Springs, CO: NavPress, 1993.

Torrance, Thomas F. *Reality and Scientific Theology*. Edinburgh, U.K.: Scottish Academic Press, 1985.

15

DOESN'T HYPOCRISY
INVALIDATE CHRISTIANITY?

In the so-called ages of faith, when men really did believe the Christian religion in all its completeness, there was the Inquisition, with its tortures; there were millions of unfortunate women burned as witches; and there was every kind of cruelty practiced upon all sorts of people in the name of religion.

—Bertrand Russell, *Why I Am Not a Christian*

Christianity is . . . rarely understood by those outside its bounds. In fact, this is probably one of the greatest tasks confronting the apologist—to rescue Christianity from misunderstandings.

—Alister E. McGrath,
Intellectuals Don't Need God and Other Modern Myths

Glaring moral failures of contemporary Christians and injustices committed throughout history in the name of Christ understandably hinder some people from even considering the truth-claims of Jesus of Nazareth. In fact, the so-called hypocrisy excuse may be the most common reason people cite for rejecting Christianity. While the objection takes many forms, its central thrust is that hypocrisy and moral failures in the name of Christ invalidate Christianity. A thorough response to this objection involves four elements: (1) showing the excuse illogical, (2) correcting some common misperceptions about the gospel of Jesus Christ, (3) offering compassion in response to the nonrational (often emotional) issues frequently behind the excuse, and (4) affirming the need for Christian churches to seriously and continually confront flagrant hypocrisy within their own ranks.

The Logic Test

To reject the truth-claims of Christianity because "there are too many hypocrites in the church" or because of "a bad experience with Christian people" is to commit a logical fallacy known as the *trivial objection*. In the study of logic, a trivial objection "focuses critical attention on some point less significant than the main point or basic thrust of the argument."[1] The fallacy is committed when an arguer raises minor (and/or inconsequential) criticism of a given position, then erroneously asserts that such criticism successfully undermines that position.

The term for this type of fallacy certainly doesn't mean that the pain inflicted by Christians (or supposed Christians) is trivial. Hurt can be enormous and significant and must never be trivialized. However, to reject a belief system on the grounds that Christians act hypocritically or inconsistent with their professed values is in logical terms, a case of majoring in the minors.

A Christian's success (or failure) in adhering to biblical principles (ethics) is not the crucial point when it comes to evaluating the truth of Christianity. The central issue is whether the historical, factual, and theological claims of Christianity are true: Was Jesus of Nazareth a real historical person? Was he truly God incarnate, the divine Messiah? Did his death atone for human sin? Did he actually rise from the dead?

Logically, a Christian's ethical inconsistency (while never to be condoned and understandably disconcerting) has little or no bearing on the objective truth-claims of Christianity. To put it more directly—the negative, sinful, or evil actions of individual Christians (real or so-called) do not falsify the historic claims about Christ—his perfect life, sacrificial death, and bodily resurrection. Because some Christians act in a hypocritical manner, it does not follow that Jesus ceases to be the Son of God and the Savior of the world.

Flagrant hypocrisy among Christians is certainly offensive to God (see Matthew 23) as well as to fellow humans. Unfortunately, inconsistent actions undermine trust and make it much harder for the nonbeliever to accept Christian testimony concerning the truth of the faith. In effect, hypocrisy drains legitimate apologetic arguments of their potency. But this problem does not logically invalidate the objective truth-claims of Christianity. As Christian apologist John Warwick Montgomery once quipped, "If Albert Einstein were arrested for shoplifting, would that make $E = mc^2$ wrong?" A message or teaching can still be true even if the messenger is morally flawed.

Getting the Gospel Right

Widespread confusion about the true nature of the Christian faith exacerbates the hypocrisy objection. Many people see Christianity as a system of ethics. In their thinking, to be "Christian" is to follow certain ethical principles that inevitably result in the individual's becoming a "better person." This concept represents a serious distortion. Christianity is centrally about Jesus Christ: who he is (God incarnate; see chap. 9) and what he accomplished (the atonement; see chap. 11).

British theologian Alister E. McGrath succinctly describes Christianity's christological core: "If Christianity has a center, it is Jesus Christ. It is impossible for the Christian to talk about God, salvation, or worship without bringing Jesus into the discussion, whether explicitly or implicitly. For New Testament writers, Jesus is a window onto the nature, character, and purposes of God."[2] Historic Christianity is first and foremost about what Jesus Christ has done, not about what his followers have or have not done morally—though it is certainly true that moral values appropriately and necessarily flow from a redemptive relationship with Christ. Understanding this point is critical for non-Christians.

Two misconceptions tend to take the focus off Jesus Christ and tempt people to think of Christianity as merely a list of moral rules. These misimpressions are widely held and treacherously off-base.

Misconception #1: Sin is merely a bad behavior or habit.

A serious misunderstanding of the nature and effects of sin undoubtedly generates much of the deep disdain nonbelievers express when confronted with the moral inconsistencies of believers. Sin, broadly defined from a biblical perspective, is anything contrary to (or less than) the holy character and perfect law of God (see chap. 11). Although many people view "sin" as just a bad deed or habit, the Bible describes sin as a debilitating force that permeates the core of every human being (Ps. 51:5; 58:3; Prov. 20:9). In fact, humans are not sinners simply because they happen to sin. Rather the problem is much deeper. Human beings sin because they are sinners by nature.

According to Scripture, all human beings suffer from original sin, having inherited a sin nature from their progenitor, Adam (Rom. 5:12, 18–19). This inherited sin nature resides at the very heart (inner being) of mankind (Jer. 17:9; Matt. 15:19), and thus affects the entire person—including the mind, will, affections, and body (Eph. 2:3; 4:17–19). The result is that all people personally sin and are therefore morally accountable to God (Rom. 3:23).

However, Jesus Christ offers the solution to man's sin problem. The gospel offers news of divine forgiveness—received through personal repentance of sin and faith exercised in Jesus Christ as Lord and Savior (Rom. 5:1; 6:23;

see chap. 11). Through faith, a believer's sins are forgiven and Jesus Christ's perfect righteousness is credited to him or her (2 Cor. 5:21). Thus Christians become righteous in God's eyes.

Upon regeneration (spiritual rebirth, John 3:3), the Holy Spirit implants a new righteous nature in the justified-by-faith sinner. However, a person's original sin nature remains even after conversion, thus Christians still sin (1 John 1:8–10). Conversion is the beginning—not the end—of a long process of transformation called sanctification (being set apart to do God's will). Biblically speaking, moral and ethical perfection is not instantaneous, nor even attainable, in this life (1 Kings 8:46; 1 John 1:8). So a certain level of immaturity and imperfection, including some hypocrisy (though always regrettable) can be expected of believers (James 3:2).

Christians spend a lifetime struggling to gain freedom not from sin's penalty (which Christ accomplished through the cross) but from its power over their attitudes, intentions, and actions. The ultimate transformation, which is glorification into the expressed image of Christ, awaits the Christian only in the eternal age to come. Evangelical theologian John Jefferson Davis offers a balanced biblical view of the process of sanctification: "The state of holiness begins with regeneration and conversion, and is to grow throughout the believer's life through the ministry of the Word and Spirit and through personal faith and obedience."[3]

The common Christian bumper sticker, "Christians aren't perfect, just forgiven," has real theological meaning. Christians have been judicially declared righteous through faith in Christ by divine justification (Rom. 3:28; 5:1) which removes the guilt of sin. And they are progressively being made righteous through the Spirit-led process of sanctification (2 Cor. 7:1; 1 Thess. 5:23), which begins to remove the moral pollution of sin.

Misconception #2: Christianity is essentially about moral rules.

Unfortunately, too many Christians themselves promote and reinforce the mistaken idea that Christianity is principally a system of ethics. They often do this by placing an unhealthy emphasis upon behavioral rules. The message conveyed is often something like the following: "To be a Christian means that one doesn't drink, smoke, dance, go to movies, or listen to rock music." Rules-oriented Christianity comes across to the nonbeliever as a repugnant "holier-than-thou" attitude.

The problem with this rules emphasis is threefold: First, such prohibitions are attached to debatable matters of conscience and/or choice, certainly not cardinal Christian virtues. Second, even when the rules apply to more substantive matters, Jesus is not first and foremost the Christian's inspiring moral example; rather, he is a believer's Lord and Savior. Righteous behavior is a manifestation of his grace at work. Third, as fallen creatures, even though redeemed in Christ, people simply cannot perfectly and consistently emulate the moral example of Jesus Christ (though God motivates and encourages a person's attempt). In recent years many Christians have been urged to ask, in trying situations, "What Would Jesus Do?" But this noble desire and goal represents a standard seriously beyond human moral ability. Better to ask, "What would Jesus have me do given what he did for me at the cross and in the tomb?" "What would he have me do in light of the power of his resurrection and the new life generated within me by his Holy Spirit?" Believers are called and commanded to grow in godliness and maturity, but behavioral injunctions should take into account that Christians still struggle with a sin nature even after receiving salvation.

Admittedly, commitment to the Lordship of Jesus Christ demands submission to God's commands, but at times Christians confuse and overestimate their "righteous" abilities. They then misrepresent Christianity as a religion of "self help" (clean up your act through rigid discipline), rather than as a religion of true "divine rescue" (Jesus Christ has rescued believers from the penalty of their sins through his life, death, and resurrection).

McGrath provides some helpful clarification: "Christianity is a strongly ethical faith. This does not, however, mean that Christianity is about a set of rules, in which Christians mechanically conform to a set of instructions. Rather, it is about a set of values which arises from being redeemed."[4] Christians don't achieve redemption or good standing with God by "being moral." Rather, because they have been redeemed (forgiven and reconciled to God) by God's grace through faith in Christ, they desire and strive to conform their lives to divinely revealed moral values (Eph. 2:8–10; Titus 3:5, 7). Grace, the unmerited favor of God, is the source and cause of believers' salvation and of their progress in sanctification (Titus 2:11–14).

Theological naiveté among Christians can and does hurt their desired impact on nonbelievers. Two things will strengthen their testimony and make the hypocrisy issue less of a problem. First, Christians can be careful to present the truth about Christ as the essence of the Christian faith. Second, they can strive to become more biblically knowledgeable about how personal choices and behavior relate to the truth of the gospel (for example, understanding how justification relates to sanctification).

What about All the Evil Done in the Name of Christ?

Closely related to the charge of personal hypocrisy is the more complex and grievous objection concerning all the evil committed throughout history in the name of Christianity (the Crusades, the Inquisitions, and the Catholic–Protestant wars, among others). Isn't it justifiable to evaluate a religion based upon the ethical fruit it produces? Does Christianity's collective fruit contain more poison than nourishment?

While Christians must accept the fact that their history has a dark side, to say that all who performed evil in the name of Christ were truly Christians or that they followed Christ's teachings is false. The actions of evildoers represent the very antithesis of God's expressed will. Christian philosopher Thomas V. Morris remarks, "Certainly organizations calling themselves 'Christian' have often had deleterious and even disastrous effects on human society. But such movements have clearly diverged at least as far from the gospel of Christ as they have from the restraints of common morality. Sheep ought not to be judged by the actions of wolves who wear wool."[5]

Religion in general, and Christianity in particular, can clearly attract the unscrupulous who prey upon and exploit the sincere and trusting souls who belong to the community of faith. Counterfeit sheep (wolves) often inflict great damage within the church, and sully the church's reputation among nonbelievers.

To blame so-called religious wars exclusively on religion and specifically on Christianity is to commit the fallacy of the oversimplified cause. It is, in a word, naive. Throughout the history of Western civilization the relationship between political and ecclesiastical powers has been a complex affair. Religious wars of the past and present arise as much from economic, political, and social conflict as from religion per se. This is certainly true of both the medieval Crusades and the European wars following the Reformation, and it remains true of contemporary conflicts including those in Northern Ireland and in the Middle East. Simply because Christianity held sway during historical periods of atrocious events doesn't mean that the political or ecclesiastical powers of the time operated according to Christian moral or ethical principles.

Ironically, when Christians violate biblical moral principles, their own worldview provides the basis for moral judgment and correction. Hypocrisy among Christians is often easy to detect and condemn because of the superlative nature, clarity, and coherence of Christian ethics as a whole. Christian ethical principles are objective, universal, unchanging, and absolute in nature and can therefore readily identify and correct breaches in morality. Informed nonbelievers know that the dark side of Christianity stands at odds with the specific teachings of its founder.

By contrast, non-Christian philosophies have no secure grounds for correcting injustices. What basis, for example, did the secular-led French revolution or the atheistic philosophies of Soviet and Chinese communism have for judging moral behavior? How indeed can moral values be justified without appealing to a transcendent source of moral absolutes? (This important question is addressed in chapter 18.)

If Christianity is to be judged according to the moral and ethical fruit it produces, all of the benevolence for which Christianity has been responsible over the past two millennia must also be considered. The fact is that contemporary views of social justice are deeply rooted in the Judeo-Christian tradition.[6] For example, the view that all people are endowed with inherent and equal dignity and moral worth is grounded in the timeless biblical truth that human beings are created in the image of almighty God (Gen. 1:26–27).

Such moral injunctions as "the strong should help the weak" and "the rich should help the poor" and "treat others as you would like to be treated" are also grounded in the Christian vision of reality.[7] Recognition of all humans' intrinsic worth and value is central to the Bible, and has seldom been affirmed or practiced by other cultures and religions in history.[8] It is not surprising, therefore, that religious groups (especially Christian ones) have started the vast majority of the world's charitable organizations. In contrast, relatively few are initiated by atheist societies.

Judging a religion or belief system based upon the ethical fruit it produces does have some secondary validity. However, to be fair, that evaluation must take into account the religion's broad influence, both good and bad, and whether the religion is being lived out authentically. Cult leaders Jim Jones and David Koresh produced horrific results with a deadly impact in the name of Christ, but they were wolves. Their beliefs, motives, and intentions ran counter to those of Scripture and historic Christianity. They were *not* authentic Christians.

The primary consideration remains: the good ethical fruit of a religion only corroborates what is already well supported as truth. The question of whether a belief or belief system is factually and objectively true must supercede in importance the question of whether the belief produces good and beneficial effects. Whether Christianity works (ethically) represents an important question, but that question is not nearly as important as whether Christianity's truth-claims are real and true. What is ethically good cannot be separated from what is metaphysically real and epistemologically true. Workability must be evaluated in terms of what is first shown to be real and true.

Responding to Emotional Factors

A discussion of logic (and illogic) along with clarification of what being a Christian does and does not mean may be important steps along the way to discovering—and discussing—a person's deeper, often emotionally charged reasons for rejecting Christianity. Here a person must proceed with care and compassion, as though treating a life-threatening injury. An emotional arrow or sword may need to be pulled out, but not without anesthetic, antiseptic, bandaging, and follow-up. Christians who personify love and integrity can, and often do, help bind up emotional wounds and lead people to faith in Christ.

The messenger of salvation in Christ must be sufficiently credible—an important component of evangelism in light of the way some people consider the claims of Christianity. Believers who demonstrate strong moral and intellectual virtue make it easier for skeptics to consider the claims of Christ. And the reality is that most Christians are not flagrant hypocrites who feign virtue and religiosity. All Christians struggle to face and overcome their moral inconsistencies, but most are sincere, not two-faced, duplicitous actors.

People may *embrace* or *reject* Christianity based upon both rational and nonrational factors. Unethical behavior by some Christians does not constitute rational grounds for rejecting Christianity, but many people do formulate their beliefs based upon personal experiences. Knowing this, God calls Christians to live transparent, exemplary lives, repenting from sin and being motivated by hearts full of gratitude to God for his loving kindness toward them (Rom. 12:2; Titus 2:1–15). Because of God's grace Christians can admit their hypocrisy both to God and to fellow humans.

When confronted with the objection that there are too many hypocrites in the church, the following question seems an appropriate response: What better place for hypocrites to be than in church where the transforming power of God through the gospel can continually convict, forgive, and renew them day by day? The best medicine for hypocrisy is to be confronted with the authentic gospel of Jesus Christ.

Policing the Ranks through Appropriate Church Discipline

Leaders or shepherds within the Christian church have the spiritual and moral responsibility to watch over their flock. Their obligation is to protect, teach, guide, nurture, and, if need be, lovingly discipline their people. These same leaders must be careful to live in a way that avoids moral reproach (1 Tim. 3:1–10; Titus 1:5–9). The congregants within the church also have responsibilities, including election or appointment of mature godly leaders and submitting to scriptural guidance, including appropriate church discipline. The church, then, both leaders and members, must work together to police its ranks and to guard its moral reputation before an unbelieving world.

When Christian churches are confronted with flagrant and/or criminal moral violations such as sexual abuse or financial impropriety (whether among clergy or laity), circumspect church leaders must act justly, fairly, and decisively to protect the innocent and to see that the guilty are brought to justice. Only diligent church officials can effectively address such issues so as to protect their people and instill confidence in the church's moral judgment and responsibility. Sadly, in too many congregations church membership, if it is subscribed to at all, means very little and church discipline is lax. Many church leaders and members skirt church discipline and simply move on. Thus people avoid any real personal accountability and important opportunities for growth. When the church corporately fails to discharge biblically directed spiritual and moral responsibilities, it pours fuel on the hypocrisy fire.

Focusing on the Real Issue

No one can rightfully judge God based upon the actions of those who call themselves his followers. To reject Christianity because of hypocrisy among Christians is to engage in a logically flawed form of thinking. The real test for the validity of the Christian faith centers on the truth-claims by and about Jesus Christ. They focus upon Christ's person and work. The logically pertinent questions are: Was Jesus of Nazareth a real historical person? Was he truly the divine Messiah? Did his death atone for human sin? Did he actually rise from the dead?

As Jesus himself stated: "I am the way and the truth and the life." Because this wonderful truth—that Jesus, not human effort to be good— offers sinful humans the gift of forgiveness and righteousness, some believers take an extremely lax view of moral behavior, by underemphasizing the importance of submission to God's moral law. The next chapter addresses the question of freedom to do as "I" please.

Key Scriptural Passages

Regarding sin: Psalm 51:5; 58:3; Proverbs 20:9; Jeremiah 17:9; Romans 3:23; Ephesians 2:3; 1 John 1:8

Regarding justification by grace alone, through faith alone, on the account of Christ alone: Luke 18:14; Acts 13:39; Romans 3:23–24, 28; 5:1; Ephesians 2:8–10; Galatians 2:16; 3:24; Titus 3:5, 7

Discussion Questions

1. From a Christian point of view, how is being a sinner different from being a hypocrite?
2. How can believers help nonbelievers to better understand the core issues of Christianity?
3. How should a Christian deal with hypocrisy in his or her own life?
4. Why do questions of truth supercede questions of practical results?
5. How can Christian churches and individuals build greater spiritual and moral accountability?

For Further Study

Corduan, Winfried. *No Doubt about It: The Case For Christianity*. Nashville: Broadman & Holman, 1997.

Evans, C. Stephen. *Why Believe? Reason and Mystery as Pointers to God*. Grand Rapids: Eerdmans, 1996.

Hoekema, Anthony A. *Saved By Grace*. Grand Rapids: Eerdmans, 1989.

McGrath, Alister E. *Introduction to Christianity*. Cambridge, MA: Blackwell Publishers, 1997.

Shelley, Bruce L. *Church History In Plain Language*. 2nd ed. Dallas: Word, 1995.

16

DON'T I HAVE A RIGHT TO DO WHAT I WANT WITH MY OWN BODY?

Do you not know that your body is a temple of the Holy Spirit, who is in you, whom you have received from God? You are not your own; you were bought at a price. Therefore honor God with your body.

—1 Corinthians 6:19–20

I will neither give a deadly drug to anyone if asked for, nor will I make a suggestion to this effect. Similarly I will not give to a woman an abortive remedy.

—Oath of Hippocrates

Liberty, freedom, and individual independence seem fundamental to being human, especially for those born and raised in the democracies of the West. As long as it doesn't hurt anyone else, why can't "I" do things my way? Even among Christians there is sometimes an antinomian (against all law) attitude that "since Jesus has already paid the penalty for my sin, I can do whatever I want."

But can this claim to self-determination be pushed too far? Aren't there appropriate limits to human autonomy? The American zeitgeist or "spirit of the age" (the general intellectual, moral, and cultural climate) reflects an increasing secularization. Many people view themselves as being utterly independent, absolutely self-governing, and as totally free agents.

This new spirit of radical human autonomy exceeds more traditionally accepted standards of human freedom and liberty. Today, autonomy often includes independence from other human beings and even independence from God. This self-proclaimed freedom is clearly visible in popular culture's libertarian[1] response to such ethical and social issues as abortion, infanticide, homosexuality, physician-assisted suicide, euthanasia, drug and alcohol abuse, prostitution, and virtually all manner of sexual behavior. This autonomy claim is often expressed in the mantra: *"As long as my actions do not harm anyone else, I am free to do as I please with my own body."*

Though this thinking permeates Western culture, many Christians admit being at a loss as to how to respond to this bold claim. While Christianity certainly teaches that people make authentic choices, bear real responsibilities, and enjoy a certain level of personal liberty, this radical autonomy claim is incompatible with Christian truth and values. In fact, it is inconsistent with reality, especially with the harm factor.

An effective critique of this autonomy claim from a classical Christian viewpoint must address the assertion that people are free to do as they please with their own bodies. For this autonomy claim has increasingly impacted society worldwide through such controversial practices as abortion and euthanasia and more recently, homosexuality and cohabitation. A brief discussion of the biblical worldview, especially concerning mankind's relationship to God, is the place to begin that needed critique.

Man's Relationship to God

According to the Bible, human beings are created in the image of an infinite, eternal, just, wise, holy, loving, and gracious God (Gen. 1:26–27). As the crown of creation, the image of God (*imago Dei*) is reflected in mankind's rational, volitional, relational, and spiritual capacities, and in his unique ability to exercise dominion over the plant and animal kingdoms.

The Genesis creation account reveals human beings as distinct in *kind* from the animal kingdom, not merely distinct in *degree*. And while human beings are as similar to God as any finite creature could possibly be (neither the animals nor the angels are said to bear the divine image), they remain mere creatures clearly distinct from their infinite Creator. In Christian theology, this difference is known as "the Creator/creature distinction."

The Bible uniquely presents human beings as "created persons."[2] This anthropological viewpoint accepts a paradox. For creatures (humans) are by their very nature absolutely dependent upon God. Yet, persons, on the other hand, possess a relative independence (autonomy) from God. Persons are not mere puppets. Scripture, however, without explanation, nevertheless sets man's *creatureliness* (unlike God) and *personhood* (like God) side by side as compatible truths. In this regard, the Bible's anthropology stands apart from all other philosophical and religious views of mankind.

Scripture also reveals that the first human beings misused their God-given freedom and willfully chose to rebel against God and go their own autonomous way. Adam and Eve chose to pursue knowledge, beauty, and pleasure outside of God and his specific commands. They trusted the word of the serpent and followed their own interests. This rejection of God's authority and command on the part of his creatures is what the Bible calls "sin." Biblically speaking, sin is anything short of or contrary to God's nature and will. While Scripture repeatedly speaks of sin as the breaking of God's law (Rom. 8:7–8; James 2:9–11; 1 John 3:4), this state of rebellion resulted (through original sin[3]) in all of mankind being justly condemned before God and his holy law. God, however, in his infinite kindness has provided redemption[4] for repentant sinners through the life, death, and resurrection of the God-man, Jesus Christ (see The atonement, chap. 11).

From a Christian perspective, therefore, mankind is utterly dependent upon God from at least three critical points of view: First, mankind's very existence as a physical, intellectual, and spiritual being comes from God's work as the transcendent Creator of the universe. Genesis 2:7 powerfully depicts God's special creation of man: "And the LORD God formed man from the dust of the ground and breathed into his nostrils the breath of life, and man became a living being." To be made in the image of God means that human beings possess body, mind, and soul.

Second, mankind's continued existence (which includes the need for gravity, oxygen, food, shelter, clothing, and so forth) is made possible by God's work as the providential Sustainer of the universe. Human beings depend moment by moment upon God's faithful provision and protection. The apostle Paul specifically appealed to God's unique providential care for humankind when he preached on Mars Hill to the first-century Greek philosophers: "And he [God] is not served by human hands, as if he needed anything, because he himself gives all men life and breath and everything else" (Acts 17:25).

Third, the salvation of the believer is from first to last a work of God's grace in and through the work of the divine Savior, Jesus Christ. Salvation is exclusively a gift of divine grace, through faith alone, and solely on the account of Christ. The apostle Paul testifies to God's sovereign and gracious act of redemption in these words: "But because of his great love for us, God, who is rich in mercy, made us alive with Christ even when we were dead in transgressions—it is by grace you have been saved" (Eph. 2:4–5).

The believer's recognition of his utter dependence upon God as Creator, Sustainer, and Savior appropriately leads to a life of gratitude, obedience, and worship. For the Christian, the ultimate context of life itself is the reality of, and a relationship with, the sovereign Lord and Savior of the cosmos.

A Christian Response

From a biblical viewpoint, the claim that people are radically free to do what they want with their own body is both alien and presumptuous. Worldview considerations reveal a stark contrast between secular and biblical anthropologies. Three responses address different elements of the autonomy position.

1. When people assert they can do as they please so long as they don't harm *anyone else*, Christians can appropriately ask two Socratic-like questions: "Does the '*anyone else*' about whom you speak include God? Are you so certain about ultimate reality that you can safely exclude God?"

The appeal to autonomy ignores the Christian's ultimate context of life. If the biblical God does actually exist as an objective reality (see God's existence, chap. 1), then this claim of radical human autonomy is a destructive distortion with disastrous repercussions both in this life and in the next. Christian philosopher Thomas V. Morris elaborates:

> The question about the existence of God, likewise, is not just a question about whether one more thing exists in the inventory of reality. It is a question about the ultimate context for everything else. The theist and the atheist should see *everything* differently. In the same way, the question about whether there is life after death should not be just a question about whether we are to expect one more segment of existence, however long, after bodily death. It should be viewed as a question about the overall context for all our actions in this life. Will we live forever or not? That should make a difference not just for the future but for the present. And those who believe in an afterlife do not, by virtue of their belief, devalue this life. Rather, they embrace a larger context that infuses much greater value into the small things of this life.[5]

Philosophical reflection is an inevitable part of human life. Asking probing questions concerning what is ultimately real (metaphysics), true (epistemology), and good (ethics) is a critical part of living a rational and contemplative life. If only for personal expediency, a person would do well to reflect upon ultimate questions such as the possibility of God and of human immortality. And if certain answers to these ultimate questions are not contrary to reason, would a person not also be prudent to ask how his or her choices and actions in this life might relate to what is ultimately real?

Doing as one pleases with one's own body may bring harm, even irreparable harm, to that body in this life and, to the soul in the next. The risk of a person's individual choices may be greater than what he or she initially thinks. As creatures limited in knowledge and in perspective, to proceed cautiously with regard to choices that may extend beyond a person's immediate ability to perceive seems sensible.

2. When people assert that they are free to do what they want so long as they *do not harm anyone else*, the Christian can again ask two questions: "How can you be certain that your actions will harm no one else—now and in the future? If it's wrong to hurt other people, why isn't it just as wrong to hurt the self (such as in the case of active euthanasia or drug or alcohol abuse)?"

According to Christianity, God has created an interconnected community of humanity. "No man is an island," author John Donne reminds. The disciplines of science, sociology, psychology, and political science testify to humanity's complex interdependence. Attempting to predict just how the consequences of an individual's actions will affect others is a very tricky business. So-called victimless crimes (for example, prostitution, drug abuse) are seldom, if ever, truly victimless. When people engage in reckless personal behavior under the assumption that their behavior affects only themselves, others (family, society) usually suffer and end up trying to pick up the broken pieces that result from these narcissistic choices.

Christianity asserts that since human beings have been created in the image of God, all human life is sacred (given by God, worthy of reverence or respect, valuable, unrepeatable). Therefore, just as it is morally wrong to murder or ruin the life of others because they bear God's image (Gen. 9:6; James 3:9), it is also morally wrong to murder or ruin a person's own life. Suicide, for example, is self-murder. Christians should ask those who embrace the autonomy claim to explain on what basis they can assert that it is wrong to harm others, but acceptable to harm one's self. Wouldn't legal and moral prohibitions against harming others also logically apply to one's self?

3. When people assert, "It's *my body*," the Christian can once more ask two probing questions: "Just what kind of ownership do you actually have over your body? Since you had no say in your body's coming into being, what makes you think you have absolute say about what happens to it now?" Christians can inquire on what basis people think they are the masters of their own fate.

Evangelical theologian John Jefferson Davis notes that while many people see themselves as lord of their own life, "the Christian sees human life as a gift from God, to be held in trusteeship throughout man's life on earth."[6] According to Scripture, all people owe their lives to God. The New Testament underscores the point that Christians belong, body and soul, to God. The apostle Paul makes this message very clear:

- "For none of us lives to himself alone and none of us dies to himself alone. If we live, we live to the Lord; and if we die, we die to the Lord. So, whether we live or die, we belong to the Lord" (Rom. 14:7–8).
- "Do you not know that your body is a temple of the Holy Spirit, who is in you, whom you have received from God? You are not your own; you were bought at a price. Therefore honor God with your body" (1 Cor. 6:19–20).

Everything a person possesses belongs ultimately to the Lord, even the body, which is made to be God's temple (whether or not the person invites God in). Ultimately, claims to human autonomy are a direct affront to God, for it is God who numbers the very days of all human beings' lives. Sobering words reflect God's sovereignty over the human life span:

- "Man's days are determined; you have decreed the number of his months and have set limits he cannot exceed" (Job 14:5).
- "All the days ordained for me were written in your book before one of them came to be" (Ps. 139:16).

These passages don't remove the reality of authentic human choices and of genuine responsibility (especially concerning one's body). However, from a biblical perspective, human choices ultimately conform perfectly to God's sovereign ends. The issue of God's sovereignty and human responsibility may be an inscrutable problem for the finite human mind to comprehend, but Scripture nevertheless teaches both truths as critical to life.[7]

A Powerful Impact

A biblical perspective on the inherent worth of human life and on the body's inherent dignity can powerfully impact any society. Someone once said that a culture should be judged in terms of how it treats its most vulnerable members. The world in the twenty-first century must not forget what happened under Hitler and Stalin in the West or under Mao Tse-tung and Saddam Hussein in the East and Middle East. A cavalier view of fragile human life in its earliest and latest moments continues to this day—"a Dixie Cup" approach (use and throw away). A Christian response to the radical autonomy claim provides an important context for critical ethical issues: abortion, sexual relationships, and euthanasia.

On Abortion

The pro-choice position on abortion is based upon an appeal to physical autonomy, and defenders of abortion on demand routinely employ the "physical dependence" argument.[8] This argument asserts that the unborn is merely an extension of the mother's body, and since the mother has a right to do what she wants with her own body, then she has a natural right to abortion. Three significant criticisms show that flaws lurk within this reasoning.

First, the unborn baby is not a mere extension of the mother's body. Very early in development, the fetus possesses its own individual identity. This identity is evidenced in the baby's having its own distinct fingerprint, as well as its own blood type and sex (and about half of all babies have a different blood type and sex from their mother's).[9] The genetic makeup of the unborn child is also unique from the start, and not identical to that of the parents.

Second, the mother doesn't have a right to do *anything* she wants with her body. Moral and civil laws constrain her actions. And because the unborn baby is a distinct human being, the mother's choices as to how she uses her body must respect the rights of other distinct human life growing in her womb. The fact that a child grows in the woman's body doesn't make him or her less human, just more vulnerable. Sound moral reasoning reveals that the right of the unborn human to live must outweigh the mother's arbitrary right to take away that life, privately or otherwise. It is self-evident that matters of life and death take priority over matters of personal (or social) privacy and convenience.

Third, the morally superior action on the part of the pregnant woman who feels she cannot raise her child would be to bring the baby to term and allow the child to be adopted. By doing so she would indeed achieve her goal of avoiding parental responsibility. She would also preserve the life of another human being and give another family the opportunity to raise a precious child. In this case, the mother would be acting in a morally magnanimous fashion, putting the child's welfare above her own circumstances. The vast majority of abortions are obtained by young women for reasons of convenience (birth control), not for rare matters relating to the mother's health, or the rarer case of conception through rape or incest. (Ironically, the number of requests for adoption each year in the United States roughly equals the number of abortions. And, generally speaking, adopted children fare just as well in life as children raised by their biological parents.) Adoption is a real moral alternative to the plague of abortion.

On Sexuality

From a traditional Christian viewpoint, as well as from numerous sociological, psychological, anthropological, historical, and medical studies, adhering to biblically based virtues on sexuality and family relationships is the healthiest way to live. According to Scripture, God created human sexuality ("male and female," Gen. 1:27; 5:2). God made human bodies and ordained that sex take place within the proper context of the marriage covenant.

Scripture reveals that sexual intimacy between a husband and wife is actually an allegory of the love relationship between God and his people (God/Israel, Christ/church; see, for example, the Song of Songs). The physical nature and pleasures of sex should never be separated from such critical accompanying issues as love, commitment (marriage), personal intimacy, and possible procreation. Because sex is a symbol of a greater spiritual intimacy between God and mankind, and because it is the means of procreation, sex should never be practiced casually or outside its proper covenantal context.

Biblical prohibitions against fornication, adultery, homosexuality, and bestiality (Exod. 20:14; Eph. 5:3; 1 Thess. 4:3–4) not only instruct people as to what is and is not acceptable sexual behavior in the eyes of God but serve to protect people from the devastating physical, psychological, social, and spiritual consequences that tend to accompany a sexually "free" lifestyle. Such "freedom" fails to deliver its advertised results. Just as abortion has failed to decrease child abuse, cohabitation and sexual intimacy prior to marriage has failed to reduce divorce and abuse rates. Homosexuality may seem to yield greater happiness for some; but suicide, drug abuse, alcoholism, and disease rates among active homosexuals soar far above average rates for the whole populace.

Following the biblical mandate regarding sex and marriage would go a long way toward reducing both personal and societal problems—and costs. Further, God's moral precepts pay dividends to the obedient both in this life and in the next. A sensible and virtuous approach to sexuality accompanied with an appreciation for self-sacrifice (as distinct from asceticism) would benefit—immeasurably—any society.

On Euthanasia

The term *euthanasia* literally means "good death" or "happy death." It is further defined as the "taking of a human life for some good purpose, such as to relieve suffering or pain."[10] It is therefore sometimes referred to as "mercy killing." Forms of euthanasia may be considered when people are nearing death or suffering from terminal illness. Ethicists have identified two basic types of euthanasia: *active* and *passive*.[11]

1. Active euthanasia (including suicide and assisted suicide): To intentionally and/or actively take the life of a terminally ill patient, either by the patient himself (suicide) or by the assistance of another (possibly a physician, family member, or friend). Active euthanasia actually produces or causes death. This means that the patient's death results not from the terminal illness itself but from the specific act of euthanasia (lethal dose of medication, gunshot, etc.).

2. Passive euthanasia: To allow a terminally ill patient to die naturally without intervening, usually by withholding or withdrawing life-sustaining (artificial) treatment. Passive euthanasia permits death to take its natural course but does not actually cause death itself.

The traditional Christian view: Most theologians and ethicists who hold a traditional or historic Christian viewpoint accept the active-versus-passive distinction logically and morally. However, they would view active euthanasia as morally offensive and unacceptable. Such action violates the scriptural principle that prohibits suicide and homicide—the intentional taking of "innocent" human life (see Exod. 20:13 and Deut. 5:17). Many Christian ethicists believe that given the state of human sinfulness (original sin, total depravity: Ps. 51:5; 58:3; Prov. 20:9), active euthanasia weakens respect for human life and sets a dangerous precedent.[12]

Passive euthanasia, on the other hand, has been generally accepted by traditional Christian theologians and ethicists but with some careful qualifications. Passive euthanasia can be acceptable if natural life-sustaining measures (air, water, food) are not deprived (though artificial measures may not be necessitated). Further conditions cited to justify passive euthanasia are when the physical condition of the patient is irreversible, death is imminent, and further treatment can only lead to a burdensome prolongation of death.

A biblical alternative: Some, if not many people support active euthanasia because they believe a person should be allowed to end life rather than remain alive and suffer great physical pain. However, this reasoning misrepresents the medical facts concerning terminal illness. According to the American Medical Association, the physical pain of most patients suffering from a life-threatening illness can be successfully managed through medication. Advances in drugs and medical technology have allowed physicians to help control the physical suffering of most patients. But someone may ask: "What about the few whose pain can't be so managed?" There is indeed a moral and practical recourse for them and their families (preferable to suicide)—the age-old practice of hospice.

Hospice, which has Christian roots (see Acts 6:1–7), consists of caring for the special needs of the dying. Terminally ill patients cannot be cured of their illness, but can be cared for and comforted (palliative care: "from cure to care").[13] In contrast to conventional medical care which emphasizes the "extension of life," hospice focuses upon the "quality of life" for those facing death. Patients are kept as pain-free and comfortable as possible and are allowed to die with dignity. Hospice care often involves a team of caregivers, including physicians, nurses, social workers, home health aides, pastors, church volunteers, family members, and friends. When people know they will be loved and cared for during the difficult process of dying, even with *some* physical pain, active euthanasia loses much of its perceived appeal. For most people, the anguish of having no one to love and care for them is much worse than the physical pain of their illness. Hospice is a moral alternative to dealing with the needs of the dying.

The ethical principles derived from Scripture provide real solutions to difficult societal problems—but they have to be implemented.

Finding Freedom in Body and Soul

The rational and volitional abilities that human beings possess are a direct product of being made in God's image. However, mankind misused its God-given freedom and consequently became enslaved by sin. True liberty must come in redemption from sin, and that redemption comes uniquely in the saving work of Jesus Christ. Only in Christ are human beings free from the devastating consequences of sin and thus free to obey God rather than their sinful nature.

In answer to the question, "Can't I do as I please with my own body?" the enduring wisdom of centuries past provides the superlative answer. The Heidelberg Catechism (a Reformed statement of faith published in 1563) asks and states:

> What is your only comfort in life and in death?
> That I am not my own, but belong—body and soul, in life and in death—to my faithful Savior Jesus Christ . . .[14]

For the Christian, the ultimate context of life and death is found in the reality of, and in relationship with, the sovereign Lord and Savior of humanity.

But isn't that view intolerant of others? The next chapter about the "exclusive" truth-claims of Christianity addresses this challenge.

Discussion Questions

1. What are the theological implications of man as a "created person"?
2. How is man dependent upon God?
3. What are the implications of the ultimate context principle for the Christian?
4. How is adoption a meaningful and practical response to the abortion controversy?
5. How is hospice a meaningful and practical response to the euthanasia controversy?

For Further Study

Beckwith, Francis. *Politically Correct Death*. Grand Rapids: Baker, 1993.

Beckwith, Francis J., and Norman L. Geisler. *Matters of Life and Death*. Grand Rapids: Baker, 1991.

Davis, John Jefferson. *Evangelical Ethics*. Phillipsburg, NJ: Presbyterian and Reformed, 1985.

Moreland, J. P., and Norman L. Geisler. *The Life and Death Debate*. New York: Praeger, 1990.

Rae, Scott B. *Moral Choices: An Introduction to Ethics*. Grand Rapids: Zondervan, 1995.

17

DOESN'T CHRISTIANITY PROMOTE INTOLERANCE?

The classical rule of tolerance is still a good guideline: Tolerate persons in all circumstances by according them respect and courtesy. Tolerate (allow) behavior that is moral and consistent with the common good, and tolerate (accept) ideas that are sound.

—Gregory Koukl, *Relativism*

Do not conform any longer to the pattern of this world, but be transformed by the renewing of your mind. Then you will be able to test and approve what God's will is—his good, pleasing and perfect will.

—Apostle Paul (Rom. 12:2)

An impassioned rabbi on the television program *Larry King Live* charged that Christians exhibit the "height of intolerance" when they assert that individual Jews will face divine judgment if they do not accept Jesus of Nazareth as their Messiah.[1] Such accusations are not rare. Increasingly in popular culture, evangelical Christians are judged guilty of intolerance because they claim that Christianity is the one true religion (for a discussion of religious exclusivism,[2] see chap. 13).

According to the New Testament, Jesus Christ made exclusive and unprecedented claims: He said, "I am the way and the truth and the life. No one comes to the Father except through me" (John 14:6). "I told you that

222

you would die in your sins; if you do not believe that I am the one I claim to be, you will indeed die in your sins" (John 8:24). Does Jesus' statement represent conceited intolerance or might the popular understanding of "tolerance" be seriously flawed?

Because of past prejudices and injustices against certain religious and ethnic groups, many people in today's culture have embraced tolerance as an indispensable moral virtue. And in the United States—a nation of diverse racial, cultural, and religious groups—tolerance is a core value. However, a convoluted idea of tolerance causes many people to vilify individuals or groups who express any form of intolerance—except their own.

The tolerance issue as it relates to Christian truth-claims raises important cultural apologetic questions. How can Christians respond to the charge that the exclusivism of their faith promotes social intolerance? And what is the relationship between tolerance and truth?

How Should Evangelical Christians View "Tolerance"?

The word *tolerance* suffers from both ambiguity (multiple meanings) and vagueness (imprecision) in current usage, but the *American Heritage Dictionary of the English Language* defines it as the practice of "respecting the nature, beliefs, or behavior of others."[3] While over the centuries there has been strong disagreement among Christians as to how the church should relate to or tolerate secular or worldly society, many or most evangelical Christians would accept the following three points.

1. According to the Bible all people are created in the image of God (Gen. 1:26–27; 9:5–6; James 3:9–10). Therefore, each human person deserves respect. Because of the *imago Dei* all people possess inherent dignity and moral worth regardless of their culture, race, sex, or social class (Ps. 8:3–6). Christian philosopher Richard Purtill points out that the foundation for most contemporary views concerning social justice are deeply rooted in the Judeo-Christian religious traditions.[4] Valuing the life and dignity of each individual person is a core Christian virtue.

2. The individual right of others to think as they please and believe what they will, even if particular beliefs are irrational, morally wrong, and/or contrary to Christian teaching, also warrant respect. Judicial systems restrict human behavior, not thought (though some ideological positions fail to appreciate this important distinction).[5] Christianity teaches respect for human personhood, individual volition, and personal moral responsibility. This respect, however, leaves room for appropriate use of persuasion to convince others of truth, especially the ultimate truth of Jesus Christ as Lord and Savior of mankind.

3. In a diverse society, Christians rightfully tolerate the practices (religious and otherwise) of others, so long as those practices are legal, moral, and generally promote the common good. Common decency affords all people the same societal rights and privileges. This last point is doubtless the most controversial of the three, for the practices of others can be tolerated only within reasonable limits. In a democratic form of government, the views of the majority usually prevail.

In summary, evangelical Christians can and do demonstrate appropriate tolerance by being respectful of the personhood and practices of others in society. The promotion of human rights and dignity are integral to the Christian theistic system of ethics (moral absolutism; see chap. 18).

Further points of clarification concerning the issue of tolerance are in order.[6] First, intolerance does not mean mere disagreement with a position taken by another. Tolerance presupposes disagreement. A person does not tolerate those with whom he or she agrees, only those with whom there is disagreement. Tolerance and disagreement, therefore, go hand in hand.

Second, when it comes to tolerance careful differentiation must be made between ideas and the person who holds them. While all people should be treated with respect and welcomed in the marketplace of ideas, that doesn't mean all ideas or arguments are of equal merit, validity, or truth. Objective standards of logic evaluate the validity of an argument and logic is by its very nature intellectually "intolerant." Criticizing ideas and arguments is necessary and perfectly appropriate. Christian apologist Gregory Koukl concludes, "To argue that some views are false, immoral, or just plain silly does not violate any meaningful standard of tolerance."[7]

And third, tolerance can only be a virtue if there are moral absolutes (which themselves mandate tolerance). A universal principle requiring tolerance is inconsistent with moral relativism. Ironically, many people pushing so-called standards of tolerance in defense of their politically correct ideology hold to moral relativism.

Is It "Intolerant" to Claim That Jesus Christ Is the Only Path to God?

Logical truth-claims are by nature inherently intolerant. Why? Because truth-claims are by definition either true or false. The formal laws of logic[8] make it impossible for all religious truth-claims to be true at the same time and in the same respect. For instance, Jesus Christ cannot be both God incarnate (the Christian view) and not be God incarnate (the Jewish[9] and Muslim view) at the same time and in the same respect. The two statements about Jesus cannot be true at the same time and in the exact same way, without violating the law of noncontradiction (A cannot equal A and also equal non-

A). In addition, Jesus Christ must either be God incarnate or not be God incarnate, for the law of excluded middle (either A or non-A) proves that no middle position is logically possible.

In light of this necessary reasoning, certain conclusions must be drawn about Jesus of Nazareth. Because Jews, Christians, and Muslims all identify him in different ways (Jews view Jesus as a human teacher or blasphemer, Christians view him as God incarnate, Muslims view Jesus as a human prophet), logically speaking, these religious perspectives simply can't all be correct. To put it another way, somebody must be wrong. There is just no getting around this logical conclusion.

To develop the reasoning further, it is conceivably possible that all three positions on Jesus' identity are wrong (for instance, if Jesus never existed, though in actuality this is a historically untenable position), but they certainly can't all be true.

Yet, popular culture says that to declare or imply that any religious belief is wrong is intolerant, arrogant, and even bigoted. But how can it be religiously intolerant to state what is logically necessary and obvious? Don't cold hard logical conclusions have to trump contemporary society's purely subjective standards concerning tolerance? Calling people nasty names (such as bigot) just because they draw or infer proper logical conclusions concerning religious truth-claims is itself absurd, morally offensive, and genuinely intolerant.

In stark contrast to extreme advocates of religious tolerance who demand acceptance of all religious views as equally true, the laws of logic insist on a rigid intolerance when it comes to the quagmire of contradictory religious truth-claims. A contradiction in logic reflects a specific relationship. When two statements are contradictory they have opposite truth value (exactly one is true and exactly one is false). Therefore whenever the claims of one religion directly contradict (negate or deny) the claims of another religion, then both claims cannot be true.[10]

When evangelical Christians claim that Jesus Christ is God incarnate (John 1:1, 14, 18; 20:28; Rom. 9:5; Titus 2:13; Heb. 1:8; 2 Pet. 1:1) and therefore the exclusive way of salvation (John 14:6; Acts 4:12), they are not being any more intolerant than Jews and Muslims who assert that Jesus Christ is not God incarnate. Opposite truth-claims inherently conflict. Exclusivism and a proper form of intellectual intolerance are logically inescapable when it comes to truth-claims. Many who speak of tolerance in religious matters fail to recognize that a person can be personally and socially tolerant while simultaneously being (appropriately) intellectually intolerant. The latter stance makes the necessary distinction between persons and ideas or arguments. In fact, exclusivism is unavoidable in matters of religious truth for even the religious pluralist affirms an exclusivist belief that all religions are true.

Exclusivism is the historic position of the Christian church when it comes to the question of the truth of other religions. Evangelical exclusivists are therefore simply being true to their tradition and to what they believe Scripture plainly teaches. Historic Christianity is an exclusive religion by its very nature. To fail to proclaim Christ's exclusive claims to the world in order to conform to contemporary standards of tolerance would be to compromise the faith.

Christianity clearly and emphatically affirms social tolerance. But, when the American zeitgeist (spirit of the age) pressures evangelical Christians to adopt an intellectually tolerant, inclusivistic, and/or pluralistic view of truth, it is really asking Christians to betray the core convictions of their faith. How tolerant (respectful) is that?

The Christian's conviction of ultimate truth must supercede arbitrary societal standards of tolerance. Tolerance is an important Christian virtue, but only as long as it doesn't compromise truth. Without truth, tolerance is meaningless.

The charge that the exclusive truth-claims of Christianity lead to intolerance is often made by those who themselves doubt or reject the concept of ultimate truth. They either deny the reality of objective truth by accepting some form of "hard multiculturalism" (belief that all cultures have their own truth),[11] or they believe that no one really knows ultimate truth, thus embracing some form of skepticism. Yet historic Christianity affirms that ultimate truth exists and that truth has been revealed in Jesus Christ.

For those who take the Bible seriously as a revelation from God, the issue of excessive religious tolerance becomes especially difficult. In a real sense, Christianity is unlike any other religion, because religions tend to be man's pursuit of the divine or of spiritual reality. Human-derived religion can afford to be tolerant and pluralistic, for it is groping in its pursuit of the truth. Christianity, on the other hand, is a belief system that claims to be directly revealed by God himself, who came historically in human flesh (John 1:14; Phil. 2:6–8; Col. 2:9). Those who affirm historic Christianity are not in doubt as to God's mission, message, and intent for humanity. If God indeed historically revealed himself in actions, events, and words, then beliefs that contradict his revelation must be considered false. In essence, Christians have a hard time with religious pluralism and excessive views of tolerance because their faith teaches them that ultimate Truth came in person and revealed himself specifically to humanity. It was not Christians but rather God incarnate who declared, "I am the way and the truth and the life. No one comes to the Father except through me" (John 14:6).

What's a Proper Response to the Challenge of Tolerance?

Christians can do five important things in response to tolerance. First, they can point out that truth exists and really does matter.[12] Love and tolerance must never be divorced from truth, especially from the concept of ultimate truth. All denials of objective truth are self-defeating.[13]

Second, Christians can point out that sound logic requires that contradictory religious truth-claims cannot be simultaneously true. Therefore the dictates of reason do not constitute a violation of acceptable standards of tolerance.

Third, Christians can graciously present their specific apologetic case for the truthfulness of Christianity. They can offer persuasive arguments for the truth of the gospel of Jesus Christ (1 Pet. 3:15; Jude 3) and point out difficulties in alternative, non-Christian belief systems (2 Cor. 10:5) without expressing arrogance or other obnoxious attitudes.

Fourth, Christians can freely admit that Western society has at times promoted or permitted the unacceptable form of intolerance (for example, twentieth-century European anti-Semitism). Christians are justified sinners and should personally and corporately admit their struggle with sin (see chap. 15). They can, however, point out that Christianity affirms genuine social tolerance as a virtue, acknowledging each individual's right to believe as he or she chooses and to exercise beliefs within the boundaries of moral and civil law.

Fifth, Christians are called to witness to the truth of the gospel of Jesus Christ with both their words (preaching) and their lives (exemplary conduct). The world needs to see the power of lived truth. This witness can be accomplished when Christians are personally and socially tolerant while simultaneously being intellectually intolerant of conflicting truth-claims.

At the heart of the Christian faith is the conviction that "Jesus Christ is Lord" (Mark 12:35–37; John 20:28; Rom. 10:9–13; 1 Cor. 8:5–6; 12:3; Phil. 2:11). This exclusive claim is no more popular or palatable today than it was two thousand years ago in the ancient Roman Empire. Not only does this declaration make acceptance of conflicting truth-claims impossible, but it also carries great significance with respect to morality. The next chapter addresses this subject.

Discussion Questions

1. In what way can tolerance be a Christian virtue?
2. Why isn't it intolerant to say Jesus is the only way to God?
3. How can one be socially tolerant and intellectually intolerant?
4. How has genuine religious intolerance contributed to the current tolerance movement?
5. How are the truth-claims of Christianity logically intolerant by necessity?

For Further Study

Adler, Mortimer J. *Truth in Religion*. New York: Macmillan, 1990.

Beckwith, Francis. *Politically Correct Death*. Grand Rapids: Baker, 1993.

Beckwith, Francis J., and Michael Bauman, eds. *Are You Politically Correct? Debating America's Cultural Standards*. Buffalo: Prometheus, 1993.

Beckwith, Francis J., and Gregory Koukl. *Relativism: Feet Firmly Planted in Mid-Air*. Grand Rapids: Baker, 1998.

Corduan, Winfried. *No Doubt about It: The Case For Christianity*. Nashville: Broadman & Holman, 1997.

Green, Michael. *"But Don't All Religions Lead To God?"* Grand Rapids: Baker, 2002.

Kreeft, Peter, and Ronald K. Tacelli. *Handbook of Christian Apologetics*. Downers Grove, IL: InterVarsity, 1994.

Nash, Ronald H. *Is Jesus the Only Savior?* Grand Rapids: Zondervan, 1994.

18

ISN'T MORALITY
SIMPLY IN THE EYE
OF THE BEHOLDER?

Ethics, although it contains an element of human creativity and inventiveness, is even more clearly a discovery, something which is not of our own making

— Louis P. Pojman, *Ethics*

It is extremely difficult to be a normal human being and not think that some actions are wrong and some are right.

— Alvin Plantinga, *Great Thinkers on Great Questions*

Many familiar expressions capture the essence of today's relativism—the denial of absolute or objective truth and morality: "Different strokes for different folks." "That's true for you but not for me." "Morality, like beauty, is in the eye of the beholder."

Relativistic thinking permeates the marketplace of ideas in America today and in many other parts of the Western world. Culturally, it comes in various forms. Relativistic judgments can be detected in such contemporary trends as religious pluralism, multiculturalism, politica! correctness, and so-called tolerance (see chap. 12 on religious pluralism, and chap. 17 on tolerance). This distinctly relativistic and skeptical mind-set with regard to what is real, true, and good serves as the underpinning for the phenomenon called postmodernism.

Relativism, in terms of both truth and ethics, directly challenges—in fact, contradicts—the historic Christian faith. Understanding the problems of ethical relativism through a brief critique of both its subjective and conventional forms can help Christians stand strong when the winds of changing mores blow. Developing a case for moral absolutes, one that emphasizes their compatibility with biblical revelation, can set people on a path toward the broader Christian worldview.

Ethical Subjectivism

While ethical relativism comes in a number of forms,[1] the two most popular varieties are individual (ethical subjectivism) and cultural (ethical conventionalism), respectively. Ethical subjectivism asserts that the criteria for judging moral right and wrong are "the individual's perceptions, opinions, experiences, inclinations, and desires."[2] Moral truth is therefore relative to the individual. Absolute, unchanging, universal moral standards don't exist. In contrast, ethical values are considered private, personal, individual, and subjective in nature. Moral statements such as "Whatever a person thinks is right is right"[3] reflect no more than the subjective thinking or feelings of the speaker.

Ethical subjectivism appeals powerfully to human nature;[4] however, it simply cannot withstand the rigorous logical analysis any formal ethical theory warrants. In fact, the problems with ethical subjectivism are insurmountable. The following six criticisms illustrate this ethical theory's bankruptcy.

Six Reasons for Rejecting Ethical Subjectivism

1. If ethical subjectivism were true, then no one can be wrong about his or her moral views. As philosopher Ed Miller points out: "If the individual is the basis of moral truth then none of us could ever be mistaken in our moral opinions, for whatever we believe must be true."[5] But if right is what each person thinks is right, then nothing can be wrong.

Is it reasonable to conclude that the institution of slavery is simultaneously appropriate and reprehensible? Is it coherent to conclude that Martin Luther King, Jr. and the Ku Klux Klan were both correct about civil rights? Can an ethical theory that supports everyone's view of the holocaust as right, including Adolf Hitler's, be accepted? Is abusing children okay simply because the abuser thinks it is? If some people are just plain wrong in their ethical thinking (which seems intuitively obvious), then ethical subjectivism must be false.

2. A crucial flaw in ethical subjectivism is its failure to make the necessary distinction between a person's opinions and speculations about morality and actual morality itself.[6] Some may object that this criticism seems to beg the question. However, this important distinction is a necessary part of all moral deliberation. To perform authentic ethical thinking and adjudicate between alternative points of view, an individual must make distinctions between his or her opinions about morality and moral truth itself, or else no such thing as ethical deliberation even exists.

3. Ethical subjectivism reduces morality and moral deliberation to personal tastes—thus eliminating any possibility of rational argument in support of a moral judgment. Moral philosopher Louis P. Pojman explains: "This form of moral subjectivism has a sorry consequence: It makes morality a useless concept, for, on its premises, little or no interpersonal criticism or judgment is logically possible."[7] If morality is synonymous with a person's feelings, likes, or dislikes, then rational considerations have no proper application. Therefore, since ethical subjectivism offers no place for logical analysis and argument, a supporter of ethical subjectivism could never argue in favor of his or her so-called moral point of view.

4. Ethical subjectivism undermines the very concept of morality by removing its normative or prescriptive nature. Morality involves such concepts as "should" and "ought." Ethical subjectivism reduces morality to merely personal preferences. Rather than being prescriptive, ethical subjectivism is a descriptive statement of morality. As more than one moral philosopher has noted, there seems to be a logical contradiction between ethical subjectivism and the very idea of morality itself.[8]

5. Ethical subjectivism fails to distinguish between virtue and vice. According to this theory, Nazi Führer Adolf Hitler was just as moral as Mother Teresa. Each did what he or she thought right. The specific individual actions of these two persons (and inevitable consequences) are an irrelevant consideration for the ethical subjectivist. Can anyone, or any civilization, survive a theory that makes all moral positions equivalent?

6. Ethical subjectivism is unlivable. To affirm ethical subjectivism means that the moral decisions and actions of others can never be condemned. But people do condemn. To some extent everyone imposes his or her morality on others.[9] Moral judgments and evaluations are constantly imposed. For example, to discriminate against another person based purely on race is just wrong. But according to ethical subjectivism, no one has the right to condemn such actions. It is therefore virtually impossible to live consistently with the affirmation of ethical subjectivism.

Ethical subjectivism is a shallow and incoherent approach to moral values. This individualistic type of relativism leads to the logical and moral quagmire that no human is better (more virtuous) than another, and no moral code is better than another. All ethical choices are equally good.[10] Given the importance of morality, no one can afford to settle for deficient ideas about it. This individualistic form of moral relativism is logically incoherent and morally bankrupt.

Ethical Conventionalism

Ethical conventionalism is the view that ethical truth is relative, not to the individual person, but rather to the overall culture or the society.[11] Moral values, therefore, are rooted in the given beliefs, practices, preferences, and ideals of a specific cultural group. Ethical conventionalism asserts that people ought to obey the moral rules of their given culture or society, yet those moral rules may differ from one culture to another. Therefore like ethical subjectivism, ethical conventionalism denies the existence of absolute, unchanging, universal moral standards. A statement typical of the ethical conventionalist position would be: "Whatever a person's culture says is right is right."

Ethical conventionalism suffers from some of the same problems as ethical subjectivism. Yet because the conventionalist position is typically seen as being a more substantive relativistic theory than its more individualistic counterpart, four statements in its favor are listed and critiqued. Four positive reasons for rejecting ethical conventionalism as an inadequate moral theory are then explained.

In Favor of Ethical Conventionalism

A culturally defined moral relativism is supported by the fact that all people learn their basic moral principles from their cultural environment (family, school, peers, church, and so forth).

Response: Culture can serve as the instrument or vehicle by which people come to know their moral obligations without being the foundation, source, or justification of those values.[12] An individual learns many things through his or her culture, but the truth of those things is not necessarily dependent upon culture. Universal logical and mathematical truths can be learned through an educational institution, but the truths of logic and mathematics themselves are clearly independent of that institution. Parents teach their children that $5 + 7 = 12$, and yet the truth of arithmetic is not dependent upon the parents themselves.

The founding fathers of the United States of America recognized that moral values need a ground and justification beyond mere culture. According to the Declaration of Independence, individual rights are grounded in the divine Creator who transcends culture.

A culturally defined moral relativism is supported by the existence of diverse moral opinions and practices among the various cultures of the world.

Response: The fact that people disagree over an issue doesn't mean that there isn't an objectively true or correct position on that issue (for example, people used to vigorously disagree about whether the universe had a beginning or not). Ethical differences may result from the difficult application of moral values rather than from real differences in core values.[13] Christian thinker C. S. Lewis has argued persuasively that general agreement on moral issues has existed among various historical civilizations and cultures.[14]

A culturally defined moral relativism should be the preferred viewpoint because it successfully promotes the important virtue of tolerance.

Response: Tolerance is a genuine virtue only so long as it doesn't stand in the way of truth, reality, and moral goodness (see chap. 17). Transcultural or objective values may curb the excesses of ethnocentrism (cultural superiority) far better than a culturally defined relativism. Yet if ethical conventionalism is true, why is ethnocentrism a problem at all? As Louis Pojman appropriately asks, "If [as relativism says] no moral principles are universally valid, how can tolerance be universally valid?"[15] Logic says those who extol the virtues of cultural diversity and tolerance must be willing to tolerate the intolerance of other cultures.

Doesn't democracy itself require a form of cultural relativistic thinking?

Response: Differences of opinion or perspective, which reflect an individual's basic freedoms, can be tolerated without losing the reality of objective truth. Often the superior form of moral persuasion comes through the free exchange of ideas. Truth can be discovered through the democratic process of inquiry, dialogue, and debate that goes on in the marketplace of ideas.[16]

Against Ethical Conventionalism

The four following points clearly show ethical conventionalism to be logically and morally unacceptable.

1. The acceptance of ethical conventionalism ("whatever a person's culture says is right is right") means one culture cannot criticize the moral actions of another culture. But if this concept is true (depending upon how culture and/or society are defined) then Americans could never condemn the treatment of Afghani women by the Taliban or the genocidal acts performed by Nazi Germany against the Jews in the Holocaust during World War II. Yet how can one accept a so-called system of morality that makes it impossible to bring ruthless people, such as the Nazis, to the bar of justice?

This form of cultural relativism would indeed have made the Nuremberg Trials an impossibility. Ethical conventionalism would also have excused the actions of Nazi Rudolf Höss, the commandant of Auschwitz concentration camp, who admitted exterminating more than two million people. Höss could have made a good case that he was simply following the moral consensus of his culture. Ironically Hitler's second in command, Hermann Göring, insisted at the Nuremberg Trials (1945–1946) that the Allies had no moral right to judge the actions of the greater German culture.[17] To judge the awful tyrants of history requires objective and absolute moral values.

2. Ethical conventionalism leaves no possibility for the moral reform of a culture. If what a particular culture thinks is right is right, then that culture need never correct or revise its moral point of view. This conclusion also runs contrary to the facts of history. Culture has frequently been shown to need moral reform (slavery, women's rights, segregation). The ethical conventionalist position would completely rule out the need for such moral reformers as Moses, Wilberforce, Gandhi, and King. Changing society and its unjust laws through appropriate deliberation and civil disobedience would be utterly unnecessary.

3. Ethical conventionalism suffers from a serious practical dilemma. Culture and society are difficult concepts to define, especially in today's so-called pluralistic society.[18] An individual may belong to more than one group, culture, or subculture simultaneously. So how can people identify their moral obligations if they belong to multiple groups with contradictory moral viewpoints? A registered Democrat in America today who is affiliated with a women's rights group, but was raised in a traditional Roman Catholic family is pulled in contradictory moral directions when it comes to the issue of abortion. Which group defines his or her moral viewpoint?

4. From a historic Christian perspective, ethical conventionalism ignores the transcultural Law of God written on the hearts of all human beings (natural law: Rom 2:14–15). According to Scripture, all people know that certain actions are wrong regardless of what a particular culture says. "Thou shalt not murder" is a transcultural moral imperative. The moral views of a person's culture can seriously conflict with his or her intuitive moral awareness or personal conscience.

Morality—Invented or Discovered?

Both forms of ethical relativism (subjectivism and conventionalism) depend on the untenable position that virtue is invented, rather than discovered. If morality is merely a human convention, it lacks an objective foundation and cannot truly be understood as prescriptive. If morality is invented, there really is no ultimate right or wrong. Acting in an expedient or convenient or pragmatic way does not equate with prescriptive morality. It is important, especially for secularists, to understand that while self-interest and prescriptive morality may overlap, they are not exactly the same. Ethics based on conventional wisdom provide no compelling reason for people to be moral. In a world truly without objective values, a person might choose to live like Gandhi rather than like Saddam Hussein, but that decision would be totally personal and value-free, much like choosing Coke instead of Pepsi.[19] In fact, in a world of invented ethics, it would be just as acceptable to model one's life after Hussein.

Other forms of moral relativism suffer from similar criticisms. With moral relativism being intellectually and morally unacceptable, moral absolutism with its biblical basis becomes a beneficial, reasonable, and workable alternative.

Moral Absolutism

Though some philosophers distinguish between moral objectivism and moral absolutism,[20] this study simply defends the position of moral absolutism. It asserts that objective, universal, and unchanging moral standards exist—values that offer "abiding and fixed reality common to all."[21] Absolutism affirms that these values are distinct from, and independent of, the human mind and will. Therefore, objective moral values are discovered, not invented. Further, ethical absolutism does not necessarily imply that humans either completely understand or properly apply these absolute values. This position even grants that moral awareness may indeed develop over time, yet the core values themselves remain the same.

Reasons for Supporting Moral Absolutism

1. Either ethical principles are relative in nature or they are not (there is no third alternative: law of excluded middle).[22] Therefore, if ethical (moral) relativism is false (which it clearly appears to be), then ethical objectivism or ethical absolutism must be true.

2. The denial of absolute moral values leads to an irrational position and moral disintegration. The particular examples addressed under ethical subjectivism clarify this point.

3. Absolute moral values represent a necessary and expected part of a certain worldview (for example, theism). A person could even argue that a rational and well supported worldview is itself evidence of moral absolutes.

4. Moral intuitions (immediate and direct moral awareness and sense of "oughtness") testify to the truth of objective moral values. Generally speaking, humans are intuitively aware of their objective moral obligations. At the core of their being, people recognize that certain things *should* or *ought* to be done, and other things *should not* or *ought not* be done. These moral obligations reflect not the way people behave (descriptive), but rather the way

people should behave (prescriptive). People can deny, ignore, or rationalize their moral obligations, but they are nevertheless a real and necessary part of human experience and existence. People can and do choose to violate their moral intuitions, but from a biblical perspective this choice reflects the sinful human condition (see chap. 11).

Objective Moral Obligations

The following are three examples of absolute moral intuition:

- "It is wrong for everyone, at all times, everywhere to torture children."
- "It is wrong for everyone, at all times, everywhere to deliberately and intentionally kill innocent human beings."
- "It is right to be truthful, honest, just, and courageous."

How can the existence of these objective moral values be explained? Where did they come from? What guarantees their validity? What do they convey about the nature of reality? The existence of objective moral obligations requires a source or foundation. Ethical principles cannot exist in a metaphysical or epistemological vacuum; they need a ground or foundation that can justify them. What is good (ethics) cannot be separated from what is real (metaphysics) and what is true (epistemology).

The Foundation for Ethical Absolutes

Ethical absolutes are incompatible with a naturalistic worldview: Objective moral values seem clearly incompatible with metaphysical naturalism, materialism, and atheistic evolutionary theory for at least five reasons.[23]

1. If everything is reducible to, or explainable in terms of, physical matter, no basis exists for abstract, nonphysical, universal, invariant realities such as objective moral principles. Moral absolutes have no place in a world of physicalism.

2. If mankind is reducible to "matter in motion," that is, to matter and its physical properties (physical, chemical, and biological processes), a person cannot escape some type of physical determinism. He or she cannot be capable of deliberate, intentional moral choice. Moral deliberation is incompatible with genetically imprinted behavior patterns (evolutionary physicalism).

3. The existence of objective moral absolutes is at odds with the idea that mankind is the result of blind, purposeless, undirected evolutionary processes. Ethical absolutes are meaningless in a purposeless world.

4. The evolutionary given of "survival instincts" (promotion of human flourishing through natural selection) doesn't equate with prescriptive morality. Acting according to self-interest or in a convenient or pragmatic way

does not equate with prescriptive morality. Based upon evolutionary theory, a person might choose to follow the Golden Rule hoping it promotes survival, but he could just as well choose murder hoping to promote the same. Evolution offers no foundation for objective morality and no compelling reason to act in an ethical fashion. Heroic (altruistic) acts are inexplicable in an evolutionary framework.

5. In an atheistic, materialistic, evolutionary world, how can moral principles be anything other than invented, conventional, and subjective? Yet subjective, relativistic ethics are incoherent and incompatible with the reality of moral obligation.

Ethical absolutes are incompatible with the worldview of pantheism: Objective moral obligations (absolutes) are not compatible with an impersonal, amoral transcendental reality. Moral principles necessitate the existence of a personal being (someone with a mind and will). In some Eastern religions God (or ultimate reality) is impersonal and therefore beyond such concepts as "good and evil."

Ethical absolutes are compatible with the worldview of Christian theism: Objective moral obligations are compatible with the existence of an infinite, eternal, personal, holy, loving, and just God as the following points from a biblical perspective demonstrate:

1. Absolute moral values are grounded in the existence of the transcendent Creator of the universe, who is also the Incarnate Redeemer of sinful mankind.

2. Moral values flow from God's moral character. God neither arbitrarily creates ethical principles nor are these values above God's being.

3. God is a morally perfect Being, fully and perfectly possessing such moral attributes as holiness, love, wisdom, mercy, goodness, righteousness, truthfulness, and justice.

4. God has revealed his moral principles through both the human conscience and explicit historical statements (the Ten Commandments, the Golden Rule, and the Sermon on the Mount).

5. The Bible reveals moral principles as being objective, universal, and unchanging (absolutes).

Conclusion

The reality of human moral obligation is incompatible with all forms of ethical relativism (including ethical subjectivism and ethical conventionalism). Ethical relativism is incoherent as a system and thus fails as a foundation for any moral values. Subjectivist ethics also fail to account for mankind's conscious awareness of moral obligation. Careful reflection on these moral obligations indicates that they are certainly more than mere transitory or

culturally imposed impulses. Ultimately, the subjectivist approach to morality collapses because it lacks an adequate metaphysical basis (a transcendent
and morally perfect one, such as the God of the Bible).

Unlike secular explanations for ethics, Christianity grounds ethics in the
holy, just, righteous, and loving nature of God. The Christian worldview thus
provides a foundation and justification for absolute moral values. One of
the strongest evidences that Christianity is true is its ability to explain and
justify the meaningful realities of life. And nothing is more central to human
existence than absolute moral values.

But what about the problem of evil? How can a holy and just God allow
horrific acts of human malice beyond comprehension? This topic is addressed
in the next chapter.

Discussion Questions

1. Why do many philosophers consider ethical subjectivism incoherent?
2. What problems arise when one asserts that moral principles are
   solely derived and justified from culture?
3. If one learns one's moral obligations from culture, doesn't that mean
   morals are culturally relative?
4. Why are evolutionism's ethical standards at odds with prescriptive
   morality?
5. According to historic Christianity, what is God's relationship to
   absolute moral values?

For Further Study

Beckwith, Francis J., and Gregory Koukl. *Relativism: Feet Firmly Planted in Mid-Air.*
   Grand Rapids: Baker, 1998.

Corduan, Winfried. *No Doubt about It: The Case For Christianity.* Nashville: Broadman & Holman, 1997.

Lutzer, Erwin. *The Necessity of Ethical Absolutes.* Grand Rapids: Zondervan, 1981.

Pojman, Louis P. *Ethics: Discovering Right and Wrong.* Belmont, CA: Wadsworth,
   1990.

Purtill, Richard L. *Thinking about Ethics.* Englewood Cliffs, NJ: Prentice Hall, 1976.

Rae, Scott B. *Moral Choices: An Introduction to Ethics.* Grand Rapids: Zondervan,
   1995.

19

HOW CAN A GOOD
AND ALL-POWERFUL GOD
ALLOW EVIL?

Is he [God] willing to prevent evil, but not able? Then is he impotent. Is he able, but not willing? Then is he malevolent. Is he both able and willing? Whence then is evil?

—David Hume, *Dialogues Concerning Natural Religion*

Where then is evil? What is its origin? How did it steal into the world?. . .Where then does evil come from, if God made all things and, because he is good, made them good too?

—Augustine of Hippo, *Confessions*

A mother drowns her five children. Mass graves are found in Iraq. A sniper lies in wait, holding a community hostage. If God is benevolent and almighty, how can he allow such atrocities? Does he close his eyes? Is he nowhere to be found? Are some things beyond his control?

Perhaps the greatest challenge to the truth of Christianity lies with the perennial problem of evil. The dilemma of evil raises questions about whether the Christian concept of God is even coherent. Many people cite the existence of evil and suffering as their number one reason for rejecting belief in the Christian God. This challenge therefore deserves careful reflection.

Much could and should be said about this topic. Entire books are written on it. But even briefly examining non-Christian viewpoints and exploring the nature and purposes of evil can develop a basic Christian response to this important apologetic challenge. While the issue of evil and suffering raises difficult questions, historic Christianity supplies unique and powerful answers to them.

Is There Really Evil in the World?

Some people today deny that real evil exists in the world. Some mental health professionals think evil is an outdated and misguided concept. They claim people are basically good, or at worst, neutral; therefore, negative or violent behavior results from physiological or environmental factors. Many psychologists and psychiatrists assert that the heinous crimes committed in society are not committed by evil people, but rather by mentally sick people. In their view, violent crime has a basic pathological cause, not a moral one.

Secular psychology and psychiatry for the most part rejected the idea that sin and moral evil actively influence human nature. However, while questioning the existence of evil, these same people are forced to believe in human suffering, for it is evident all around them.

Some forms of Eastern religion consider evil to be a mere illusion. The more philosophic strand of Hinduism[1] embraces monism, idealism, and pantheism. *Monism* is the perspective that all reality is one, whereas *idealism* asserts that the one reality is mind, idea, or spirit. According to the Hindu writings known as the *Upanishads*, the physical world is an illusion and all reality is ultimately spirit or god. Thus, they teach pantheism—"all is god and god is all."

According to Hindu thought, once a person achieves the right state of mystical consciousness, evil is absent. Ultimate reality is not only beyond the appearance of the physical but is also beyond the rational and moral categories of good and evil. In Hinduism, this belief is part of the broader principle called *maya* in which mere appearance and illusion stand in the way of apprehending the deeper reality or truth.

Mind science groups such as Christian Science and Religious Science as well as popular New Age spirituality embrace a similar view. Hindu thinking has influenced all three of these Western groups; the principal problem of human beings is ignorance or lack of enlightenment, not sin or moral evil.

Evil, however, cannot be so easily dismissed or sidestepped. One of the reasons for rejecting the conclusions of much of modern secular psychology as well as Eastern mysticism is that their views about human nature do not comport with most people's experiences in the world. Evil and suffering are stark realities of life. They can neither be reduced to, nor explained away as either pathological or mystical occurrences. Too often modern psychological theories undermine the truth that each person has a basic moral responsibility.[2] And Hinduism's concept of *maya* fails to explain where the so-called illusion originated or why evil remains a powerful and universal human experience. *Maya*, under logical scrutiny, reduces to absurdity.[3]

The history of the twentieth century alone illustrates the harsh reality of evil and suffering. The totalitarian regimes of Adolf Hitler, Josef Stalin, and Mao Tse-tung provide ample objective evidence that unadulterated evil exists, as demonstrated in the Nazi death camps, the Soviet gulags, and the Chinese cultural revolution. It should be noted that of the approximate six million Jews systematically exterminated by the Nazis during World War II, one and a half million of these people were children. The number of people murdered in Stalin's purges in the Soviet Union is estimated in the tens of millions. A similar number of Chinese people (or more) were slain by order of Chairman Mao. World War II, with its resulting fifty to sixty million deaths, has been called the greatest catastrophe in history.[4] The world wars of the twentieth century make the view that evil is an illusion impossible to take seriously. Dismissing evil as an illusion is itself a serious departure from reality.

Evil is real. It's ugly. It's painful. And its resulting consequences devastating.

The reality of evil in the world and specifically in human beings raises serious questions about its relationship to the Christian vision of an infinitely loving and powerful God. Some people argue that evil and the Christian God cannot logically coexist. They suggest that the existence of evil inevitably leads to a denial of God's existence.

Is God's Existence Incompatible with Evil?

To disprove God is an extremely difficult epistemological task, for there are definite limits to disproof. However, logically incoherent *concepts* of God may be considered false. For whatever is genuinely incoherent (irrational) cannot be true (for example, a circle can't be square). Some skeptics and atheists believe that the problem of evil creates a problem of coherence for the Christian concept of God. Eighteenth-century Scottish skeptic David Hume's questions illustrate the dilemma of many: "Is he willing to prevent evil, but not able? Then is he impotent. Is he able, but not willing? Then is he malevolent. Is he both able and willing? Whence then is evil?"[5]

Hume raised what some skeptics call "the inconsistent triad." Christians believe, based upon Scripture, that God is omnibenevolent (perfectly good) and omnipotent (completely powerful). Yet these two divine attributes combined with the reality of evil, result in an alleged logical incompatibility. The reasoning often follows this pattern:

- An omnibenevolent God *would want* to eliminate evil.
- An omnipotent God *would be able* to eliminate evil.
- Yet evil conspicuously *still* exists.

The logical tension is clear. How could evil exist in the world when God has both the desire and the power to eliminate it? This alleged inconsistent triad makes the following conclusions seem reasonable:

1. God is willing to eliminate evil but not able. Therefore God is impotent (lacking power).

2. God is able to eliminate evil but not willing. Therefore God is malevolent (lacking goodness).

3. An omnibenevolent and omnipotent God must not exist.

This reasoning leads some skeptics and atheists to accept the following argumentative flow: Since omnibenevolence, omnipotence, and evil are logically incompatible, and since all three must be affirmed in order to accept the Christian God, then the Christian concept of God is logically incoherent and therefore cannot be true.

This so-called problem of evil has been used as a powerful weapon in the atheistic arsenal against Christian theism over the last several centuries. Yet, very few people have been willing to accept the option that God is actually malevolent. In direct response to this argument, however, some religious philosophers have acquiesced and adopted a limited view of God—the notion that he is willing to eliminate evil but not totally capable of doing so. He requires the support of human beings. This position has been given various names (finite godism, limited theism), but its defining characteristic is that God is finite (limited), especially in terms of his power. This ideology was embraced roughly a century ago by such distinguished philosophers as John Stuart Mill, William James, and Edgar Brightman. A similar position is reflected today in the popular book *When Bad Things Happen to Good People* by Rabbi Harold Kushner.

At least three major problems emerge from finite godism and similar viewpoints.[6] First, it provides no guarantee that evil will ever be defeated. If this god doesn't have the ability to overcome evil and must rely upon the help of human beings, then the world is in a hopeless mess. Second, this finite god created a world he cannot control. He is neither omnipotent nor omniscient and therefore seems an unlikely candidate for human worship. Third, there is no compelling need to adopt a finite view of God in the first place because the so-called inconsistent triad is logically resolvable.

A Consistent Triad

No insurmountable logic problem exists within the three points raised by skeptics concerning the theistic God's attributes and the existence of evil.

- An omnibenevolent God *would want* to eliminate evil.
- An omnipotent God *would be able* to eliminate evil.
- Yet evil conspicuously *still* exists.

The three statements do not form a logical contradiction. The following brief response to this argument against the God of Christian theism explains.

The truth and reasonableness of the first two statements is very much open to question. First, if evil and suffering can potentially yield a greater good, it seems reasonable to conclude that an omnibenevolent God might not necessarily desire to eliminate all evil and suffering, at least not immediately. Christian philosopher Richard Swinburne thinks that this greater-good theory is the key to answering the problem of evil. He explains: "The basic solution is that all the evils we find around us are logically necessary conditions of greater goods, that is to say that greater good couldn't come about without the evil or at any rate the natural possibility of evil."[7]

By way of analogy, conscientious human parents often allow their children to undergo difficulties and pain. Even though the parents could shield against some predicaments, they allow problems because the experience produces greater good within their children—independence, perseverance, strength, courage, wisdom, and maturity. An infinitely wise, just, and loving God may similarly allow evil and suffering to exist because they serve a greater purpose for human beings and the universe, and ultimately lead to the greater glory of God himself. The existence of evil and ultimate divine goodness are not then necessarily incompatible. God may simply have a good reason for allowing evil and suffering for a time.

Second, an omnipotent God who has created morally responsible creatures may have chosen to eliminate evil through a careful process that initially allows it. Omnipotence, in a biblical context, doesn't mean that God can literally do anything (for example he cannot sin or perform the absurd). Rather, omnipotence means that God can do all things consistent with his rational and moral nature. Creating persons who are at least capable of some degree of independence may logically limit God's options. To quote Christian philosopher Alvin Plantinga: "To create creatures capable of moral good, therefore, he [God] must create creatures capable of moral evil."[8] A reasonable conclusion is that if God created human beings with free agency, then eliminating depravity would likely have to be done through a process that involves evil and suffering. Eliminating wickedness, even for God, may not be an immediate and painless task. Evil and suffering may be necessary for the greater good of humanity and may lead to the greater glory of God.

Alvin Plantinga has suggested something like the following line of reasoning in response to the problem of evil:[9]

- God is omnibenevolent and omnipotent.
- God created a world which contains evil and had a good reason for doing so (for purposes of a greater good).
- Therefore, the world contains evil, but evil is consistent with the Christian view of God.

Another approach may reflect how God will act over time concerning the problem of evil:

- An omnibenevolent God *would want* to eliminate evil.
- An omnipotent God *would be able* to eliminate evil.
- Though evil exists now, God will eliminate it in the future.

While these responses certainly don't solve all the problems connected with God's relationship to evil,[10] the reasoning of Swinburne, Plantinga, and other Christian philosophers has been successful in showing that evil is not necessarily inconsistent with the Christian view of God. Thus the argument against God's existence or omnipotence from the standpoint of evil isn't logically compelling. The distinguished philosopher of religion, William Rowe, a self-professed atheist, agrees: "Some philosophers have contended that the existence of evil is *logically inconsistent* with the existence of the theistic God. No one, I think, has succeeded in establishing such an extravagant claim."[11]

Since some atheists, as many other people, feel a sense of outrage in the face of evil, an atheistic solution to the problem of evil deserves consideration. Can evil be overcome in an atheistic world? Or is there really any evil at all in a godless universe?

Does Atheism Offer a Coherent Explanation?

Real evil in a godless world is difficult to imagine. If the atheist affirms a naturalistic materialistic worldview, then he must accept human beings as just an amazing cosmic fluke—mere "matter in motion." As products of a blind and purposeless evolutionary process, no compelling reason exists to believe that human beings possess genuine inherent dignity and objective moral worth. Yet if the worth of human beings is at best questionable, then what judgment can a person pronounce upon acts of genocide, ethnic cleansing, and infanticide? From an atheistic perspective, one can hardly argue with the comment of Dostoevsky's Ivan Karamazov: "If God doesn't exist, everything is permissible."[12]

While a particular atheist may find these things personally objectionable, another atheist might readily agree with them. But one viewpoint is no better than the other, for both would be purely subjective and arbitrary within their worldview. Things happen in a godless, merely physical world, but who's to say that any of it is "bad"?

For evil to exist requires an objective moral judgment. But in a godless world morals can only be arbitrary, subjective, and relativistic in nature. They lack an objective metaphysical foundation (see Relativism, chap. 18). Therefore without God and absolutes, there may be obstacles, inconveniences, and unpleasantries in conjunction with an individual's subjective desires and needs, but these cannot be called evil. Atheists may choose to act in an expedient or convenient or pragmatic way, but such action cannot be considered prescriptively moral (having anything to do with "should" or "ought"). Indeed prescriptive morality is necessary to the concept of evil.

Most atheists do, nonetheless, express belief that some things or actions in the world are indeed evil. They may recognize something is morally amiss in the universe. This "amiss," or incongruity elicits their objection against God. Many atheists fail to acknowledge that when they object to evil they must appeal beyond their godless world to an objective standard of goodness. Something can only be nefarious if it has transgressed the good. By its very nature moral injustice implies a standard of right and wrong, good and evil. As Gerard J. Hughes notes: "The problem of evil cannot even be stated unless it is assumed that it is proper to speak of moral truth; and it cannot be stated with much force unless it is assumed that moral does not simply depend on human conventions which could well have been quite different."[13]

All these moral considerations raise serious difficulties for the atheist. Logic forces them to reasonably account for the "problem of good." Ironically, the problem of evil may serve as powerful evidence for God's existence; for an objective standard of goodness needs an adequate metaphysical foundation. The existence of a theistic God explains both the existence of goodness as well as its opposite, evil.

Some Christian philosophers have pointed out that when atheists are indignant about evil and God's relationship to it, they are actually borrowing from the Christian theistic worldview.[14] Their own worldview provides no adequate basis upon which to make such moral claims. This assessment of the unbeliever's moral confusion in light of his indebtedness to God's inherent moral Law is clearly spoken of in Scripture (Rom. 1:18–2:16). Biblically speaking, the incongruent scenario has been played out by various secular thinkers in their moral complaint against God concerning evil. The atheist, in effect, depends upon the objective moral system of Christianity in order to raise moral objections against the Christian God. As Christian philosopher Greg L. Bahnsen succinctly puts it, "Antitheism presupposes theism to make its case."[15]

Atheism offers no adequate explanation for evil and suffering. Atheists cannot even speak about evil without relying upon borrowed moral capital, nor can they account for the concept of good. Since atheism's argument about the problem of evil fails to make a case against God, it is necessary to consider why God, specifically the God of Christianity, chooses to allow evil and suffering.

A Historic Christian Response to Evil

Christian revelation does not provide a complete and comprehensive explanation for the problem of evil and suffering. God, for reasons known only to himself, has not chosen to reveal or explain all the details of his cosmic plan. The Creator is the sovereign King of the universe, and as Scripture proclaims: "The secret things belong to the LORD our God" (Deut. 29:29). Undoubtedly, many mysteries will remain until the dawning of the eternal age to come, and the purposes behind evil and suffering perhaps top the mystery list. Yet Christianity provides many unique and satisfying responses to the questions that evil and suffering raise. Some of these distinct Christian responses follow in summary form.

Is Evil a "Stuff"?

One of historic Christianity's greatest thinkers, North African church father Augustine of Hippo[16] (AD 354–430), gave considerable reflection to the problem of evil. It was one of the central issues that kept him from embracing Christianity earlier in life.[17] His thinking led him to the conclusion that evil, though genuinely real, is not a thing or substance or stuff.[18] Rather, evil is a "privation" (Latin: privatio), that is, a lack or absence of something.

For Augustine, evil is specifically the lack of something that should be present in a person or thing. Evil is therefore defined in the negative (Latin: negatio). Analogously, a person acknowledges blindness not as a physical thing, but rather as the absence of sight. Similarly, a cavity is not so much a thing, as it is a lack (a hole), namely a lack of enamel in a tooth. Yet like evil, blindness and cavities are not things, but they are realities of life. It must be underscored that Augustine did not deny the reality of evil.

Augustine asserted that evil is specifically a privation of being and goodness. To be precise, evil is the absence of goodness that should be there in the will of the creature. He asserted, "What are called vices in the soul are nothing but privations of natural good."[19] Evil is therefore properly defined (according to Augustine) as a deficiency or corruption of the good—a type of ontological parasite on goodness.[20] In Augustine's words, "What is that which we call evil but the absence of good?"[21]

An important apologetic upshot springs from Augustine's line of reasoning concerning evil. If evil is not a positive substance or stuff, then God did not create evil as he did all other substances. The source of evil is found rather in the corruption of the good that God originally made.

Augustine's approach to defining evil as a privation of being or goodness has not been universally accepted among Christian philosophers and theologians, let alone non-Christian thinkers. It finds greater acceptance among those who are at least generally sympathetic to a Platonic theory of metaphysics (the nature of reality). It may also be fairly stated that Augustine's definition of evil fails to account fully for the dynamic and fluid nature of evil implied in the Bible's depiction of sin. Thus, this definition of evil has been characterized by some as incomplete.

Nevertheless, Augustine brought forth two profound apologetic insights concerning the nature of evil. First, his conclusion that evil is in some sense parasitically dependent upon goodness provides a powerful argument that the problem of evil presupposes the prior existence of goodness. As he pointed out: "There can be no evil where there is no good."[22] In response to those who seek to deny God's existence on the basis of evil, one can say that evil, by its very nature, is dependent upon goodness.

Second, he recognized that evil is not a stuff or a thing. Rather evil is, in one sense, thought of as a nonphysical, conceptual moral judgment (a violation of the presumed good). But critical conceptual realities such as moral judgments (as well as mathematical and logical constructs) must be accounted for in the world of human beings. These abstract realities comport well with Augustine's Christian theistic worldview, but they seem foreign and unaccounted for in a godless, naturalistic worldview.

Whence Comes Evil?

Scripture is clear that the choices of God's creatures have resulted in evil. The misuse of freedom on the part of those whom God created yielded two distinct rebellions. First, the angel named Lucifer, though possessing a high position in the order of God's angelic creatures (Ezek. 28:12–19), in an attempt to usurp God's authority led a revolt in the angelic ranks (Isa. 14:12–20). Lucifer, now known as Satan or the devil (along with his rebel cohorts, demons), directly opposes the moral goodness of God. He is an agent of evil. The Bible mentions in numerous places Satan's diabolical influence on the world of humankind (John 12:31; 2 Cor. 4:4; Eph. 2:2; 1 John 5:19).

But how could a finite being who was made good and who lacked any external evil to influence him possibly choose evil? Augustine again provided a provocative explanation.[23] He proposed that Lucifer's sin was actually one of idolatry. Lucifer didn't directly choose evil. Rather he chose a good thing—himself—but subsequently exalted himself above (substituted himself for) the ultimate good, which is God. Lucifer was overcome with pride, the first expression of sin (1 Tim. 3:6).

A similar rebellion took place among human beings (Genesis 3). Adam and Eve, the first humans, misused their freedom to rebel against God's sovereign authority. Tempted by Satan, they chose to exalt their own choice above God's command. Their disobedience resulted in immediate alienation from God—manifested in spiritual and (later) physical death. Yet because Adam represented all humanity before God, the sinful actions and state of the first humans have passed to all subsequent human beings (original sin, Rom. 5:12–21). Consequently, all people are pervasively sinful and capable of evil (Ps. 51:5; 58:3; Jer. 17:9; Matt. 15:19).

It can reasonably be argued that most evil and suffering tearing at the world stems directly from the will of the creature. This truth explains much about evil.

What about God's Sovereignty?

The Bible reveals that God is not only the transcendent Creator of all things (Gen. 1:1), but he is also the providential Sustainer of all things (Acts 17:25–27; Col. 1:17; Heb. 1:3). Nothing happens outside of God's sovereign direction and control, for he "works out everything in conformity with the purpose of his will" (Eph. 1:11). Even evil, calamity, and suffering are under God's unique sustaining and controlling power (Exod. 4:11; Isa. 45:7; Lam. 3:38). Yet while the Bible reveals God's sovereignty (Prov. 21:1; Rom. 9:21), it also reveals human beings' moral culpability for wrongdoing (Matt. 16:27; Rev. 22:12).

These paradoxical truths[24] are both taught in Scripture, sometimes in the very same verse (Luke 22:22; Acts 2:23). The Bible nowhere explains how God can be the cause of all events and actions and also rightly hold human beings accountable for their choices and actions. God's sovereignty and human responsibility are compatible truths, but how God works them out is known only to him. Those in the Augustinian-Reformed tradition would say that the answer to this great mystery lies in God's infinite wisdom and power. As Scripture reveals, God is capable of things far beyond the comprehension of mere mortals (Rom. 9:14–23; 11:30–36).

So while God's cosmic plan involves evil, calamity, and suffering, the Scriptures never indicate that God directly performs evil himself nor does he coerce his creatures to engage in evil and commit sin (James 1:13).[25] And though God's sovereign governing power makes every event an actuality—even evil—the Scriptures indicate that God is not the author of evil, and he is just in holding his creatures accountable for their sin. The clear message of Scripture is that God is directing all things toward his ultimate righteous and just ends (Dan. 4:35; Rom. 11:36). Reformed theologian Louis Berkhof remarks about God's sovereignty and the reality of sin:

> The decree of God is His eternal plan or purpose, in which He has foreordained all things that come to pass. . . . It covers all the works of God in creation and redemption, and also embraces the actions of men, not excluding their sinful deeds. But while it rendered the entrance of sin into the world certain, it does not make God responsible for our sinful deeds. His decree with respect to sin is a permissive decree. . . . It may be said, however, that the decree merely makes God the author of free moral beings, who are themselves the authors of sin. Sin is made certain by the decree, but God does not Himself produce it by His direct action. At the same time it must be admitted that the problem of God's relation to sin remains a mystery which we cannot fully solve.[26]

Evil and suffering under the direct control of the sovereign God lead a person to wonder why God allows dreadful things to happen.

Why Does God Allow Evil and Suffering?

Christians must avoid presumption and glibness concerning the causes of evil and suffering because this question remains a deep mystery. Attempting to explain why there is evil in a world made by a good God is called *theodicy* (justifying the ways of God). While much more could be said regarding the issue of theodicy, three broad points come to bear on this difficult question.

1. God has a morally adequate, but not yet fully revealed, reason for allowing evil and suffering.

God assures his people that his decrees and actions are righteous and holy. The Scriptures are replete in declaring God's moral perfection and his dealings with mankind just. The patriarch Abraham declares in Genesis 18:25: "Will not the Judge of all the earth do right?" And the psalmist pronounces in Psalm 89:14: "Righteousness and justice are the foundation of your throne." But while God has a morally justifiable reason for all he does, as the sovereign ruler of the universe he seldom chooses to explain himself to his creatures.[27]

Nor is God, in his decisions, subject to the critique of finite and imperfect human beings. Even if God were to explain in detail his ultimate purposes to human beings, there is no realistic reason to think that mere creatures could fully understand his majestic ways. God's classic discussion with Job concerning the problem of evil and suffering subsequently reveals God's inscrutable wisdom and Job's limited comprehension of the Creator's purposes in creation and redemption (Job 38:1–11; see also Isa. 55:8–9). The apostle Paul declares:

> Oh, the depth of the riches of the wisdom and knowledge of God! How unsearchable his judgments, and his paths beyond tracing out! Who has known the mind of the Lord? Or who has been his counselor? Who has ever given to God, that God should repay him? For from him and through him and to him are all things. To him be the glory forever! Amen. (Rom. 11:33–36)

2. God's sovereignty and glory will be displayed by his ultimate prevailing over evil.

The Westminster Shorter Catechism[28] (a Reformation statement of faith from 1647) begins with the reflective question: "What is the chief end of man?" The answer: "Man's chief end is to glorify God, and to enjoy him for ever." All of God's great works (creation and redemption) are intended to display God's sovereignty and glory. However, God's final prevailing over evil and sin will all the more exhibit his splendor and dominion.

This prevailing has already begun with the life, death, and resurrection of the divine Messiah, Jesus Christ. God's plan to deal with evil is prepared for in creation but executed in redemption. Satan and his forces are already defeated foes with Christ's first coming as Savior (Heb. 2:14–15), and all evil and human sin will forever be vanquished at Christ's second coming as Judge and King (Revelation 21).[29] After these cataclysmic eschatological events, God will bring forth the new creation, forever free from evil and its consequences.

Revelation 21:1–3 speaks of God's creating a new heaven and a new Earth along with the Holy City—the New Jerusalem. At that glorious time, all sin, suffering, and sorrow will be forever eliminated. God will have eradicated the problem of evil. The apostle John provides a prophetic glimpse of this glorious eternal age to come in the book of Revelation:

> They will be his people, and God himself will be with them and be their God. He will wipe every tear from their eyes. There will be no more death or mourning or crying or pain, for the old order of things has passed away. (Rev. 21:4)

3. God allows evil and suffering because of the greater good that results from it.

According to Scripture, the greatest good for humanity came out of the greatest act of evil. Jesus Christ, none other than God in human flesh, came to reveal God's love to humanity. Though he was perfectly holy and blameless, he was rejected by both the religious and political authorities, falsely accused, convicted, and subsequently beaten and executed as a common criminal. Jesus suffered the agony of Roman capital punishment—crucifixion. However, God had planned this incredible miscarriage of justice from all eternity (Acts 2:22–23). Out of this horrible incident of malice and agony came divine redemption for sinners. God brought the greatest good out of the greatest evil.

Augustine's words explain: "For the Almighty God, who, as even the heathen acknowledge, has supreme power over all things, being Himself supremely good, would never permit the existence of anything evil among His works, if He were not so omnipotent and good that He can bring good even out of evil."[30]

God's Purposes for Evil and Suffering

While Christians should be cautious about claiming to identify God's purposes behind specific incidents of injustice and suffering, the Bible does reveal some insight to how God uses evil and suffering for good.

1. God may use evil and suffering to get an unbeliever's attention and ultimately draw that person to himself (Zech. 13:7–9; Luke 13:1–5; John 9).

Christian apologist Walter R. Martin used to say that some people will not look up until they are flat on their back. Evil and suffering can shock people out of their lives of diversion and indifference to spiritual things. And, sometimes out of their false sense of control. In this way problems may be used by God's grace to bring a person to faith. As C. S. Lewis so eloquently put it: "God whispers to us in our pleasures, speaks in our conscience, but shouts in our pains: it is his megaphone to rouse a deaf world."[31]

2. God may use evil and suffering to build the moral and spiritual character of his people or to express fatherly discipline (Rom. 5:3; Heb. 10:36; 12:4–11).

Courage is forged only through facing one's fears. Steel must be refined by fire. For faith to grow, it often has to be tested by trial. God expresses more concern for his children's character than their comfort. Therefore God uses evil and suffering to facilitate the believer's moral and spiritual maturity. The apostle Paul, who endured much evil and suffering, explains the causal relationship between suffering and character: "But we also rejoice in our sufferings, because we know that suffering produces perseverance; perseverance, character; and character, hope" (Rom. 5:3).

A loving earthly father disciplines his children. Though unpleasant at the time, discipline is crucial to a child's growth as a responsible person. God similarly allows evil and suffering to bring about discipline in the life of his children. As the writer of Hebrews declares: "Endure hardship as discipline; God is treating you as sons" (Heb. 12:7). The assuring guarantee for the Christian, however, is that God does not allow evil and suffering to come into a believer's life without producing a greater good for that person. The apostle Paul sets forth that divine promise in Romans 8:28:

> And we know that in all things God works for the good of those who love him, who have been called according to his purpose.

However, facing evil and suffering is never easy, even if a person knows that God is ultimately in control. There are some practical things Christians can keep in mind during difficult times.

An Assurance for Christians

Three critical comforts can help Christians when confronted with evil and suffering. First, believers can know they never suffer alone. God is acquainted with suffering for God has suffered in Christ. Jesus came into the world as a man, suffering with human beings and for them. God himself entered into the painful, ugly mix of evil. Of all the world's religions, only Christianity reveals the God who suffers with humanity and for humanity! His suffering in earthly life and relationships—and on the cross—can transform his people's experience of suffering.[32]

Even now Jesus serves as the great High Priest interceding for believers during their trials and difficulties. Jesus is not aloof or indifferent to human anguish, for he suffered as a real man. The author of Hebrews describes Christ's role as a sympathetic High Priest:

> Therefore, since we have a great high priest who has gone through the heavens, Jesus the Son of God, let us hold firmly to the faith we profess. For we do not have a high priest who is unable to sympathize with our weaknesses, but we have one who has been tempted in every way, just as we are—yet was without sin. Let us then approach the throne of grace with confidence, so that we may receive mercy and find grace to help us in our time of need. (Heb. 4:14–16)

Second, God calls all his children to live a life of faith (confidence and trust) in the goodness and sovereignty of God despite the presence of evil and suffering. Scripture points to the powerful examples of Abraham, Moses, Job, and Paul. In the words of a familiar song, believers don't know what the future holds, but they do know who holds the future. Faith is trusting in the character of God when circumstances are painful and confusing. Christians can trust God in the midst of suffering because they are aware of his character and his promises. The apostle Paul assures the church through asking and answering a probing question:

> Who shall separate us from the love of Christ? Shall trouble or hardship or persecution or famine or nakedness or danger or sword? . . . No, in all these things we are more than conquerors through him who loved us. (Rom. 8:35, 37)

Third, evil and suffering go beyond a logical or philosophical problem. They are deeply personal and human problems. When people face suffering they need comfort and reassurance. Christians can confront evil and suffering in a powerfully practical way by comforting those afflicted by evil and by easing the suffering of people around them.

The historic Christian answer to the problem of evil and suffering is found in the example, as well as the identity of Jesus Christ. God came in the flesh to heal his children's suffering to comfort as well as to teach, and ultimately to destroy the power of evil. The suffering of God in Christ is the solution to the problem of evil for human beings.

Questions such as the problem of evil (and the others in this book) concern believers and nonbelievers alike. How Christians can be better prepared to answer them is the topic of the next chapter.

Discussion Questions

1. Why is the problem of evil the number one reason given for not believing in God?
2. Why is viewing evil as an illusion such an inadequate response?
3. If God has good reasons for allowing evil, what might some of those reasons be?
4. How does the philosophical problem of evil differ from the psychological problem of evil?
5. How is Jesus Christ the ultimate answer to the problem of evil and suffering?

For Further Study

A. Philosophical problem of evil and suffering:

Frame, John M. *Apologetics to the Glory of God.* Phillipsburg, NJ: Presbyterian and Reformed, 1994. See chapters 6–7.

Geisler, Norman L. *The Roots of Evil.* Grand Rapids: Zondervan, 1978.

Lewis, C. S. *The Problem of Pain.* New York: Macmillan, 1962.

Nash, Ronald H. *Faith and Reason: Searching for a Rational Faith.* Grand Rapids: Zondervan, 1988. See chapters 13–15.

Peterson, Michael. *Evil and the Christian God.* Grand Rapids: Baker, 1982.

B. Psychological problem of evil and suffering:

Plantinga, Alvin C. *God, Freedom, and Evil.* Grand Rapids: Eerdmans, 1974.

Eareckson Tada, Joni, and Steve Estes. *A Step Further.* Grand Rapids: Zondervan, 1978.

Kreeft, Peter. *Making Sense Out of Suffering.* Ann Arbor, MI: Servant, 1986.

Lewis, C. S. *A Grief Observed.* London: Faber, 1961. Reprint, San Francisco: Harper San Francisco, 2001.

Yancey, Philip. *Where Is God When It Hurts?* Rev. and expanded ed. Grand Rapids: Zondervan, 1997.

20

HOW SHOULD A CHRISTIAN PREPARE
TO GIVE REASONS FOR FAITH?

But in your hearts set apart Christ as Lord. Always be prepared to give an answer to everyone who asks you to give the reason for the hope that you have. But do this with gentleness and respect.

—1 Peter 3:15

We demolish arguments and every pretension that sets itself up against the knowledge of God, and we take captive every thought to make it obedient to Christ.

—2 Corinthians 10:5

Giving reasons for faith or defending the truth of the faith is called apologetics (from the Greek *apologia*). Throughout the centuries Christian thinkers have engaged in a fourfold defense that includes: (1) presenting and clarifying the central truth-claims of Christianity, (2) offering clear and compelling positive evidence for accepting Christian truth, (3) answering people's questions and objections concerning the faith, and (4) providing a penetrating critique and refutation of alternative non-Christian systems of thought.[1]

Apologetic endeavors have played a critical role in the first two millennia of Christianity. The apostles themselves used thoughtful argumentation to guard the gospel message against the doctrinal deviations of the early Gnostics

(1 John 4) and the Judaizers (Galatians 1), as well as the speculative philosophies of the Greco-Roman world (Acts 16–17). Given our postmodern and "politically correct" culture, apologetic ventures remain as important today as at anytime in the past.

Preparing for Apologetic Engagement

For those who desire to engage in this exciting and essential enterprise, three personal challenges almost ensure effective dialogue:

1. Cultivate the life of the mind to the glory of God.

"A mind is a terrible thing to waste." The United Negro College Fund motto captures what is at stake for the Christian. A human mind, part of the image and likeness of an infinite, eternal, and personal God (Gen. 1:26–27), is *a fortiori* (Latin: "with greater force," "all the more") a terrible thing to waste. Because the human soul survives death, cultivating the life of the mind to the glory of God takes on an eternal dimension. The scriptural imperative to love the Lord your God with all of your being (Matt. 22:37) includes using and developing God's incredible gift of the mind.

Mankind's intellectual abilities reflect his status as the crown of God's creation. It is the *imago Dei* (image of God) that distinguishes mankind from the animals, and it is this same image that makes the life of the mind important. Only human beings pursue, discover, and reflect upon the truths of logic, mathematics, science, technology, philosophy, morality, the arts, and a religious worldview. Human beings alone are time, truth, and reality conscious. Only humans recollect the past, recognize the present, anticipate the future, and can philosophize about them.

Christians tend to emphasize the moral virtues mentioned in the Bible, but sometimes neglect the intellectual virtues mentioned therein. Believers are called to pursue "wisdom, knowledge, and understanding," all of which are rooted in the fear of the Lord (Job 28:28; 34:4; Ps. 111:10; Prov. 1:7; 9:10). Discernment, reflection, testing, and intellectual renewal are all biblical mandates (Acts 17:11; Rom. 12:2; 1 Cor. 14:29; Col. 2:8; 1 Thess. 5:21). Of all people, the Christian who understands the meaning of the *imago Dei* has reason—and motivation—to value, cultivate, and pursue the "life of the mind." Simply stated, the Christian's pursuit of the mind is really the pursuit of the infinite and eternal God who made it and everything else in creation.

Apologetics has been popularly called "the head side of evangelism." Certainly only a well-prepared mind, one deeply grounded in Christian truth, can give objective reasons for faith and provide satisfying answers when the nonbeliever asks questions.

2. Offer thoughtful and winsome answers to people's questions.

The asking and answering of questions is an essential part of a sound learning process. Important and penetrating questions drive people to pursue answers that are well-grounded, well-reasoned, well-supported, and therefore true and logically compelling. The great Greek philosopher Socrates developed an approach to ultimate questions called the "Socratic method." Socrates sought precision in crafting incisive queries. He also searched for insightful and enduring answers.

Christianity claims to have answers to life's ultimate questions. When people ask honest questions about the truth of the faith, those inquiries must be taken seriously. They deserve thought and attention. By answering questions about their faith, Christians engage in two important tasks. They actively participate in apologetic evangelism (a divine imperative: 1 Pet. 3:15). They also seize an opportunity to grow in greater understanding of their own beliefs. The ancient Christian thinker Augustine (AD 354–430) called this activity "faith seeking understanding."

Perplexing questions force Christians to research, reflect, and stretch their understanding. Perhaps God granted his children the privilege of preaching and defending the gospel (as the means to his sovereign ends) because apologetic evangelism greatly benefits them.

When answering objections to the faith, a Christian finds guidance in the apostle Peter's careful instruction. His or her thinking should be grounded in, and a reflection of, personal commitment to Jesus Christ as Lord and Savior. An individual should reason in a way consistent with the principles found in God's revealed truth. In discussions with non-Christians, ultimately apologetic arguments should draw attention to, and support, the truth-claims of Jesus Christ, particularly his unique claims of Lordship.

Scripture exhorts Christians to be ready always to give reasons for their hope. This endeavor requires diligent study and reflection concerning Christian truth-claims. What has not been carefully studied cannot be defended. For Christians, the cultivation and use of the mind is crucial to fulfilling God's apologetic commission. It also requires a confidence and boldness to speak about beliefs even when confronted with indifference or hostility. Courageous fortitude is a critically important virtue to the apologist, along with humility.

Christians must always demonstrate an attitude of gentleness and respect. Apologists must resist the temptation to quarrel with people or engage in *ad hominem* (Latin: "against the man") and emotive attacks. Instead their arguments should reflect sound reasoning and their lives resonate with moral integrity. Non-Christians are quick to point out when the lives of Christians do not match their words. It is a deep misunderstanding to think that Christians will be perfect, devoid of all hypocrisy and inconsistency (see chap. 15), but apologists who avoid separating their arguments from everyday living are more effective evangelists. Both a person's arguments and his or her life are being examined by the nonbeliever. Integrity applies to both arguments and lifestyle.

3. *Focus study on the best sources for consistent, truthful, and solidly biblical answers.*

To be an effective apologist today takes diligent and diverse intellectual preparation. As a significant part of this preparation, four specific disciplines can enhance a person's ability to defend the Christian faith:

First, the Christian's apologetic strategy should be informed by familiarity with Scripture and a sound biblical theology. In order to defend the faith, a person must first have a clear idea what the faith is all about. It is vitally important that Christians trained (professionally or avocationally) in such disciplines as philosophy, literature, history, science, and law invest the necessary time and effort to become doctrinally and theologically sophisticated. To first decide on an apologetic strategy and only then fit theology in the back door seems a misguided approach.

A familiarity with the classical categories of systematic theology—Scripture, God, Christ, sin, salvation, and so forth—can help the apologist think about Christianity in a logical and comprehensive way. An awareness of the different branches of theology (biblical, philosophical, and historical) rounds out and buttresses an apologist's given area of specialization. While no one can be an expert in every area, a good general understanding of Christian theology goes a long way in apologetic preparation.

Second, an important and useful tool in the apologetic task, worthy of time and attention, is "worldview thinking." A worldview may be defined as a conceptual framework for interpreting reality.[2] Developing a worldview involves an attempt to arrange basic beliefs into a consistent system or pattern so that a person can evaluate and correctly interpret reality. Those beliefs would include one's views of God, ultimate reality, knowledge, ethics, human nature, and human destiny. Worldview thinking allows the apologist to think comprehensively about various belief systems and evaluate their coherence, correspondence to established truths, explanatory power, simplicity, existential livability, pragmatic consequences, and necessary presuppositions.

Third, an apologist greatly benefits from a thorough familiarization with the laws of logic and the formal rules of argumentation (including deductive, inductive, and abductive reasoning). A rigorous study of logic can help the apologist to order his or her own thinking as well as to detect fallacious forms of reasoning in the arguments of others. Being exposed to the basic principles of moral, analogical, legal, and scientific reasoning revolutionizes and energizes a person's intellectual life.

Fourth, rhetorical skill, the persuasive use of language, is a valuable asset for the Christian apologist. Learning to speak clearly, concisely, graciously, and in a logical organized way pays dividends, especially when communicating via various media outlets. Studying the art of public speaking and debating can enhance the presentation of Christian truth.

A Worthy Endeavor

God calls his people to be ambassadors for the faith, and the church needs effective advocates in every age and generation. As Christians cultivate the mind, learn to give intelligent responses, and focus their study on key areas, they will dramatically increase their effectiveness in apologetic ministry. This is true for both apologetic beginners and experts. While these areas require diligence and reflection, they equip believers to defend the faith (2 Cor. 10:5; 1 Pet. 3:15; Jude 3) by giving answers that not only assure the heart, but satisfy the mind.

Discussion Questions

1. What is apologetics?
2. What specific tasks does the apologetic enterprise encompass?
3. Why should a Christian cultivate the life of the mind?
4. What personal qualities need to accompany any apologetic encounter?
5. Why is the process of asking and answering questions so important?

For Further Study

Bahnsen, Greg L. *Always Ready: Directions For Defending the Faith*. Texarkana, AR: Covenant Media Foundation, 1996.

Boa, Kenneth D., and Robert M. Bowman Jr. *Faith Has Its Reasons: An Integrative Approach to Defending Christianity*. Colorado Springs: NavPress, 2001.

Craig, William Lane. *Reasonable Faith: Christian Truth and Apologetics*. Wheaton, IL: Crossway, 1994.

Dulles, Avery. *A History of Apologetics*. Eugene, OR: Wipf and Stock, 1999.

Frame, John M. *Apologetics to the Glory of God: An Introduction*. Phillipsburg, NJ: Presbyterian and Reformed, 1994.

Nash, Ronald H. *Faith and Reason: Searching for a Rational Faith*. Grand Rapids: Zondervan, 1988.

NOTES

Introduction

1. For a discussion of Augustine's apologetic views, see Avery Dulles, *A History of Apologetics* (Eugene, OR: Wipf and Stock, 1999), 59–69; also see Kenneth D. Boa and Robert M. Bowman Jr., *Faith Has Its Reasons* (Colorado Springs: NavPress, 2001), 30–32.

Chapter 1: How Can Anyone Know That God Exists?

1. Christian apologist William Lane Craig argues for God's existence as the best explanation for life's realities. Some of my arguments in this chapter were influenced by Craig's arguments in his debate with atheist Corey G. Washington. See "The Craig-Washington Debate: Does God Exist?" (debate, University of Washington, Seattle, WA, February 9, 1995), http://www.leaderu.com/offices/billcraig/docs/washdeba-craig1.html (accessed May 7, 2003).

2. Ed L. Miller, *God and Reason: An Invitation to Philosophical Theology* (Upper Saddle River, NJ: Prentice Hall, 1995), 52–54.

3. For an explanation and defense of big bang cosmology, see Hugh Ross, *The Creator and the Cosmos: How the Greatest Scientific Discoveries of the Century Reveal God*, 3rd ed. (Colorado Springs: NavPress, 2001).

4. Miller, *God and Reason*, 52. For a detailed scientific discussion of this topic, see John D. Barrow and Frank J. Tipler, *The Anthropic Cosmological Principle* (New York: Oxford University Press, 1986), 166–73, 401–3.

5. Gottfried Wilhelm Leibniz, *The Principles of Nature and of Grace, Based on Reason*, in *Philosophic Classics: Bacon to Kant*, ed. Walter Kaufmann (Englewood Cliffs, NJ: Prentice Hall, 1961), sec. 7, 256.

6. Peter Kreeft and Ronald K. Tacelli, *Handbook of Christian Apologetics: Hundreds of Answers to Crucial Questions* (Downers Grove, IL: InterVarsity, 1994), 58. For discussion of the *Kalam* cosmological argument, see Moreland, *Scaling the Secular City*, 18–42; and William Lane Craig, *The Existence of God and the Beginning of the Universe* (San Bernardino, CA: Here's Life, 1979).

7. See Dean C. Halverson, gen. ed., *The Compact Guide to World Religions* (Minneapolis: Bethany, 1996).

8. Terry L. Miethe and Gary R. Habermas, *Why Believe? God Exists! Rethinking the Case for God and Christianity* (Joplin, MO: College Press, 1993), 74.

9. Ross, *The Creator and the Cosmos*, 171–74.

10. To consider the coherence of certain Eastern views of God, see Richard Purtill, *Thinking about Religion: A Philosophical Introduction to Religion* (Englewood Cliffs, NJ: Prentice Hall, 1978), 95–109; and Mortimer J. Adler, *Truth in Religion: The Plurality of Religions and the Unity of Truth* (New York: Macmillan, 1990), 69–92.

11. For a discussion of the anthropic principle, see Patrick Glynn, *God, The Evidence: The Reconciliation of Faith and Reason in a Postsecular World* (Rocklin, CA: Prima, 1997), 21–55; and Ross, *The Creator and the Cosmos*, 145–67.

12. For the figures on the probabilities of the fine-tuning necessary for life in the universe, see appendixes A, B, and C in Hugh Ross, Kenneth Samples, and Mark Clark, *Lights in the Sky and Little Green Men: A Rational Christian Look at UFOs and Extraterrestrials* (Colorado Springs: NavPress, 2002).

13. Richard Taylor, *Metaphysics*, 4th ed. (Englewood Cliffs, NJ: Prentice Hall, 1974), 110–16.

14. Moreland, *Scaling the Secular City*, 80–82.

15. Ibid., chapter 3.

16. Kenneth Richard Samples, "Augustine of Hippo: Rightly Dividing the Truth," pt. 2 *Facts For Faith*, no. 6 (Quarter 2 2001): 34–39, http://www.augustinefellowship.org (accessed June 1, 2003).

17. Concerning the laws of logic, see Peter A. Angeles, *The HarperCollins Dictionary of Philosophy*, 2nd ed. (New York: HarperCollins, 1992), s.v. "laws of thought, the three"; and Ronald H. Nash, *Life's Ultimate Questions: An Introduction to Philosophy* (Grand Rapids: Zondervan, 1999), 193–208.

18. See lecture notes by Alvin Plantinga, "Two Dozen (or So) Theistic Arguments," available from http://www.homestead.com/philofreligion/files/Theisticarguments.html (accessed April 23, 2003).

19. For discussion of the moral argument, see Miller, *God and Reason*, 89–106; and C. S. Lewis, *The Abolition of Man* (New York: Macmillan, 1955).

20. For a Christian assessment of existentialism, see C. Stephen Evans, *Existentialism: The Philosophy of Despair and the Quest for Hope* (Grand Rapids: Zondervan, 1984).

21. C. S. Lewis, *Mere Christianity* (New York: Macmillan, 1952), 45–46.

22. See Ron Rhodes, *Christ before the Manger: The Life and Times of the Preincarnate Christ* (Grand Rapids: Baker, 1992), 233–37; and Josh McDowell, *Evidence that Demands a Verdict: Historical Evidences for the Christian Faith* (San Bernardino, CA: Here's Life, 1979), 141–77.

23. For a defense of miracles from a Christian perspective, see Douglas Geivett and Gary R. Habermas, eds., *In Defense of Miracles: A Comprehensive Case for God's Action in History* (Downers Grove, IL: InterVarsity, 1997).

Chapter 2: How Can I Believe in a God I Can't See?

1. J. P. Moreland, *Scaling the Secular City: A Defense of Christianity* (Grand Rapids: Baker, 1987), 226–28. Moreland presents six different arguments for rejecting this visibility criticism of God. Four of his arguments are utilized in this chapter.

2. For an introductory discussion of empiricism as an epistemological theory, see Ed L. Miller, *Questions That Matter: An Invitation to Philosophy*, 4th ed. (New York: McGraw-Hill, 1996), 233–58.

3. Moreland, *Scaling the Secular City*, 226.

4. Cited by Christian theist William Lane Craig in his debate with atheist Michael Tooley on the existence of God. See "A Classic Debate on the Existence of God" (debate, University of Colorado, Boulder, CO, November 1994), http://www.leaderu.com/offices/

billcraig/docs/craig tooley0.html (accessed January 12, 2003).

5. Attempts to reduce the mind to mere brain states result in a form of physical determinism, a self-referentially absurd theory (see Moreland, *Scaling the Secular City*, 77–103).

6. For a clear and insightful discussion of the formal laws of logic, see Ronald H. Nash, *The Word of God and the Mind of Man: The Crisis of Revealed Truth in Contemporary Theology* (Grand Rapids: Zondervan, 1982), 103–12; and Miller, *Questions That Matter*, 31–54.

7. Christian theist Greg Bahnsen made this point in his recorded debate with atheist Edward Tabash (see Covenant Media Foundation, 4425 Jefferson Ave., Texarkana, AR 71854).

8. Greg L. Bahnsen, *Always Ready: Directions for Defending the Faith*, ed. Robert R. Booth (Texarkana, AR: Covenant Media Foundation, 1996), 188.

9. For a summary of the problems associated with the naturalistic worldview, see Ronald H. Nash, *Worldviews in Conflict: Choosing Christianity in the World of Ideas* (Grand Rapids: Zondervan, 1992), 116–29. For a detailed philosophical critique of naturalism from a theistic perspective, see William Lane Craig and J. P. Moreland, eds., *Naturalism: A Critical Analysis* (London: Routledge, 2000).

10. Hugh Ross, *The Creator and the Cosmos: How the Greatest Scientific Discoveries of the Century Reveal God*, 3rd ed. (Colorado Springs: NavPress, 2001).

11. Moreland, *Scaling the Secular City*, 227.

12. Richard Swinburne, *Is There a God?* (Oxford: Oxford University Press, 1996), 2. For an advanced philosophical discussion of how God serves as an adequate explanation for reality, see Richard Swinburne, *The Existence of God* (Oxford: Clarendon, 1979).

13. Craig Blomberg, *The Historical Reliability of the Gospels* (Downers Grove, IL: InterVarsity, 1989), 11.

14. C. S. Lewis, *The Joyful Christian* (New York: Macmillan, 1977), 51.

Chapter 3: How Has God Revealed Himself?

1. Millard J. Erickson, *Christian Theology* (Grand Rapids: Baker, 1998), 178.

2. Ibid., 178–99.

3. Bruce A. Demarest, "Revelation, General," in *Evangelical Dictionary of Theology*, ed. Walter A. Elwell (Grand Rapids: Baker, 1984), 944–45.

4. General revelation texts: "nature" (Job 36:25; 38:1–39:30; Pss. 19:1–4; 104:1–35; 148:1–14; Dan. 3:59–63; Acts 14:15–17; 17:24–31), "history" (Job

12:23; Pss. 47:7–8; 66:7; Isa. 10:5–13; Dan. 2:21; Acts 17:26), "conscience" (Gen. 1:26–27; John 1:9; Rom. 2:11–16).

5. Special revelation texts: among many, John 20:31; 2 Timothy 3:15–17; Hebrews 1:1–4.

6. Christian theologian and apologist Robert M. Bowman Jr. suggests a slightly different but insightful way of analyzing special revelation. Through personal correspondence in 2000 with the author, he stated: "I would suggest speaking of special revelation as taking two forms. First, that of the living Word who acted on Israel's behalf in the Old Testament and became incarnate in Jesus Christ. Second, that of the verbal Word, which was spoken through prophets and apostles and written down in Scripture."

7. Carl F. H. Henry, "Revelation, Special," in *Evangelical Dictionary of Theology* (see note 3), 946.

8. Robert Saucy communicated this information in a personal conversation with the author (La Mirada, CA, 1999).

9. Belgic Confession (Art. 2), in *Ecumenical Creeds and Reformed Confessions* (Grand Rapids: CRC Publications, 1988), 79.

10. Demarest, "Revelation, General," 945.

11. Ibid.

12. Ibid.

13. Ibid.

14. Ibid.

15. Erickson, *Christian Theology*, 191–94.

16. Demarest, "Revelation, General," 945.

17. John Jefferson Davis, *Handbook of Basic Bible Texts* (Grand Rapids: Zondervan, 1984), 22.

18. Erickson, *Christian Theology*, 198–99.

19. John Calvin, *Institutes of the Christian Religion* 1.3.1, ed. John T. McNeill, trans. Ford Lewis Battles, Library of Christian Classics (Philadelphia: Westminster Press, 1960), 1:43.

20. Richard A. Muller, *Dictionary of Latin and Greek Theological Terms* (Grand Rapids: Baker, 1985), s.v. "*sensus divinitatis.*"

21. Contemporary Christian philosopher Alvin Plantinga has presented a philosophical argument that builds upon Calvin's idea. He delivered a lecture on this topic at Biola University, La Miranda, CA, February 26, 1999.

22. John Frame, *Apologetics to the Glory of God* (Phillipsburg, NJ: Presbyterian and Reformed, 1994), 22–26.

23. The science of biblical interpretation is called hermeneutics. For a popular hermeneutics text, see R. C. Sproul, *Knowing Scripture* (Downers Grove, IL: InterVarsity Press, 1977); for a more technical work see Bernard Ramm, *Protestant Biblical Interpretation* (Grand Rapids: Baker, 1970).

24. For a defense of the Protestant principle of *sola Scriptura*, see Kenneth R. Samples, "Does the Bible Teach Sola Scriptura?", *Christian Research*

Journal (Fall 1989): 31; see also Kenneth Samples, Catholic/Protestant dialogue with Fr. Mitchell Pacwa on the question of religious authority (audiotapes available through St. Joseph Communications, Inc. P.O. Box 720, W. Covina, CA 91793, 1-818-331-3549).

25. The precise nature and extent of general revelation is debated among Christian theologians. Some assert that general revelation is synonymous with all of the facts of the world or of nature. Others distinguish the facts of nature from the truths of general revelation (i.e., God's existence and attributes, and man's moral accountability to God).

26. Robert Saucy suggests that general revelation provides data that must then be assembled in logical propositions (interpreted); whereas special revelation comes directly as logical propositions (as inspired interpretation).

27. Henry, "Revelation, Special," 946.

Chapter 4: Aren't the Creeds a Thing of the Past?

1. Alister E. McGrath, *I Believe: Understanding and Applying the Apostles' Creed* (Grand Rapids: Zondervan, 1991), 10. For those unfamiliar with the creeds of Christendom, McGrath's book is an excellent introduction to the topic, especially to the Apostles' Creed. Some of McGrath's insightful points are reflected in this chapter.

2. A detailed and scholarly treatment of the creeds can be found in J. N. D. Kelly, *Early Christian Creeds* (London: Harlow, 1972). Various informative articles on the creeds can be found in *New Dictionary of Theology*, ed. Sinclair B. Ferguson, J. I. Packer, and David F. Wright (Downers Grove, IL: InterVarsity, 1988); *Evangelical Dictionary of Theology*, 2nd ed., ed. Walter A. Elwell (Grand Rapids: Baker, 2001); and *The Dictionary of Historical Theology*, ed. Trevor A. Hart (Grand Rapids: Eerdmans, 2000).

3. Geoffrey W. Bromiley, "Creed, Creeds," in *Evangelical Dictionary of Theology*, ed. Walter A. Elwell (Grand Rapids: Baker, 1984), 283–84.

4. Not every usage of the word "Lord" in application to Jesus implies deity; however, the context of the four scriptural references cited above clearly do. See F. F. Bruce, *Jesus: Lord and Savior* (Downers Grove, IL: InterVarsity Press, 1986), 203.

5. O. Guy Oliver, Jr., "Apostles' Creed," in *Evangelical Dictionary of Theology* (see note 3), 72–73.

6. See Robert M. Bowman Jr., *Orthodoxy and Heresy: A Biblical Guide to Doctrinal Discernment* (Grand Rapids: Baker, 1992), 65–66.

7. McGrath, *I Believe*, 15.

8. Ibid., 14.

9. Colin Duriez, ed., *The C. S. Lewis Encyclopedia: A Complete Guide to His Life, Thought, and Writings* (Edison, NJ: Inspiration Press, 2000), s. v. "chronological snobbery," 45.

10. *Ecumenical Creeds and Reformed Confessions* (Grand Rapids: CRC Publications, 1988), 7.

11. Ibid., 8.

12. Ibid., 9–10.

13. Alister E. McGrath, *Introduction to Christianity* (Cambridge, MA: Blackwell, 1997), 131–32.

Chapter 5: How Can God Be Three and One?

1. *Should You Believe in the Trinity?* (Brooklyn: Watchtower Bible and Tract Society, 1989), 31.

2. The Koran, trans., N. J. Dawood (New York: Penguin, 1993), 87, Surah 5:70.

3. Thomas Jefferson to Timothy Pickering, February 27, 1821, in *The Writings of Thomas Jefferson*, vol. 15, ed. Albert Ellery Bergh (Washington, D.C.: Thomas Jefferson Memorial Association, 1907), 323.

4. Athanasian Creed, in *Ecumenical Creeds and Reformed Confessions* (Grand Rapids: CRC Publications, 1988), 9–10.

5. For a discussion of the attributes of God, see John Jefferson Davis, *Handbook of Basic Bible Texts* (Grand Rapids: Zondervan, 1984), 23–39; Louis Berkhof, *Systematic Theology*, new ed. (originally published in two volumes, 1932 and 1938; Grand Rapids: Eerdmans, 1996), 29–81; and Wayne Grudem, *Systematic Theology* (Grand Rapids: Zondervan, 1994), 156–225.

6. These points were influenced by Robert M. Bowman Jr., *Why You Should Believe in the Trinity* (Grand Rapids: Baker, 1989); Millard J. Erickson, *Christian Theology* (Grand Rapids: Baker, 1998), 321–42; Richard A. Muller, *Dictionary of Latin and Greek Theological Terms* (Grand Rapids: Baker, 1985), s.v. "*trinitas*," 306–10; and Wayne Grudem, *Systematic Theology*, 226–61.

7. Tertullian, "On Modesty," chap. 21, *Tertullian, Part Fourth; Minucius Felix; Commodian; Origen, Parts First and Second*, vol. 4 of *Ante-Nicene Fathers*, eds. Alexander Roberts and James Donaldson (1885; repr., Peabody, MA: Hendrickson, 1994), 9.

8. See Robert M. Bowman Jr., "The Biblical Basis of the Doctrine of the Trinity: An Outline Study" (Pasadena, CA: Apologetics.com, 2002), http://www.apologetics.com/default.jsp?bodycontent=/articles/doctrinal_apologetics/bowman-trinity.html (accessed June 13, 2003).

9. Alister E. McGrath, *Introduction to Christianity* (Cambridge, MA: Blackwell, 1997), 193–94.

10. Ron Rhodes, *Christ before the Manger: The Life and Times of the Preincarnate Christ* (Grand Rapids: Baker, 1999), 19–34.

11. Gerald Bray, *The Doctrine of God* (Downers Grove, IL: InterVarsity, 1993), 138–51.

12. D. A. Carson, "Matthew," in *The Expositor's Bible Commentary*, gen. ed. Frank E. Gaebelein (Grand Rapids: Zondervan, 1984), 8:597–98; Erickson, *Christian Theology*, 329.

13. Carson, "Matthew," 598; Bray, *Doctrine of God*, 146.

14. Erickson, *Christian Theology*, 332.

15. See the evangelical critique of a contemporary form of Arianism in Robert M. Bowman Jr., *Jehovah's Witnesses* (Grand Rapids: Zondervan, 1995), 20–30.

16. See the evangelical critique of a contemporary form of modalism in Gregory A. Boyd, *Oneness Pentecostals and the Trinity* (Grand Rapids: Baker, 1992).

17. See the evangelical critique of a contemporary form of polytheism in Kurt Van Gorden, *Mormonism* (Grand Rapids: Zondervan, 1995), 31–47.

18. See the evangelical critique of Unitarianism in Alan W. Gomes, *Unitarian Universalism* (Grand Rapids: Zondervan, 1998).

19. Bowman, *Why You Should Believe in the Trinity*, 16–17.

20. C. S. Lewis, *Mere Christianity* (New York: Simon & Schuster, 1952), 145.

21. For a clear and insightful discussion of the formal laws of logic, see Ronald H. Nash, *The Word of God and the Mind of Man* (Grand Rapids: Zondervan, 1982), 103–12; and Ed L. Miller, *Questions That Matter*, 4th ed. (New York: McGraw-Hill, 1996), 32–33.

22. See Thomas D. Senor's helpful discussion of this philosophical distinction in *Reason for the Hope Within*, ed. Michael J. Murray (Grand Rapids: Eerdmans, 1999), 239–40.

23. Geoffrey W. Bromiley, "Trinity," in *Evangelical Dictionary of Theology*, ed. Walter A. Elwell (Grand Rapids: Baker, 1984), 1112.

24. Bruce Milne, *Know The Truth* (Downers Grove, IL: InterVarsity, 1982), 62.

25. Norman L. Geisler, "Trinity," in *Baker Encyclopedia of Christian Apologetics* (Grand Rapids: Baker, 1999), 736.

26. Athanasian Creed in *Ecumenical Creeds*, 9–10.

Chapter 6: Why Should I Gamble on Faith?

1. Good introductory articles on the life and thought of Pascal are found in *The New Encyclopaedia Britannica* (Chicago: Encyclopaedia Britannica, 1986), s.v. "Pascal," 25:452–54; and *The Cambridge*

Dictionary of Philosophy, ed. Robert Audi (Cambridge: Cambridge University Press, 1995), s.v. "Blaise Pascal," 562–63.

2. An excellent analysis of Pascal's mathematical and scientific achievements can be found in two of Richard H. Popkin's articles in *The Encyclopedia of Philosophy*, ed. Paul Edwards (New York: Macmillan, 1972), s.v. "Blaise Pascal," 6:51–55; and *Great Thinkers of the Western World*, ed. Ian P. McGreal (New York: Harper Collins, 1992), s.v. "Blaise Pascal," 209–12.

3. Two excellent works by contemporary Christian philosophers that have taken Pascalian themes and developed them into book-length apologetic treatments are Thomas V. Morris, *Making Sense of It All: Pascal and the Meaning of Life* (Grand Rapids: Eerdmans, 1992); and Peter Kreeft, *Christianity for Modern Pagans: Pascal's Pensées; Edited, Outlined and Explained* (San Francisco: Ignatius, 1993).

4. Frederick Copleston, *A History of Philosophy* (New York: Image Books–Doubleday, 1994), 4:154–55.

5. *Cambridge Dictionary of Philosophy*, section 4, 562.

6. *Great Thinkers of the Western World*, 210.

7. Ibid.

8. Ibid.

9. Ibid.

10. Kreeft, *Christianity for Modern Pagans*, 9.

11. Blaise Pascal, "The Memorial," *Pensées*, rev. ed., trans. A. J. Krailsheimer (New York: Penguin, 1995), 285–86.

12. Copleston, *History of Philosophy*, 4:155.

13. Ibid.

14. Morris, *Making Sense of It All*, 2.

15. Pascal, *Pensées*, 131/434. The *Pensées* have been translated into two basic versions. The numbering of the sections from both translations is provided.

16. Ibid., 192/527.

17. Ibid., 417/548.

18. Fideism can be defined in more positive terms as the view that recognizes the limits of human reason and emphasizes the importance of faith. If Pascal is a fideist, his fideism is quite moderate and balanced. See William J. Wainwright, *Philosophy of Religion* (Belmont, CA: Wadsworth, 1988), 132–36; C. Stephen Evans, *Faith Beyond Reason: A Kierkegaardian Account*, Reason and Religion (Grand Rapids: Eerdmans, 1998), 49–52; and Kenneth D. Boa and Robert M. Bowman Jr., *Faith Has Its Reasons: An Integrative Approach to Defending Christianity* (Colorado Springs: NavPress, 2001), 367–70.

19. Pascal, *Pensées*, 12/187.

20. Ibid., 377/280.

21. Wainwright, *Philosophy of Religion*, 132–33.

22. Pascal, *Pensées*, 423/277.

23. Ibid., 424/278.

24. Copleston, *History of Philosophy*, 4:165.

25. Ibid., 165–66.

26. Keith Devlin, *Goodbye Descartes: The End of Logic and the Search for a New Cosmology of the Mind* (New York: John Wiley, 1997), 183.

27. For an excellent analysis of the strengths and weaknesses of Pascal's Wager, see Stephen T. Davis, *God, Reason and Theistic Proofs* (Grand Rapids: Eerdmans, 1997), 156–66.

28. Pascal, *Pensées*, 429/229.

29. Ibid., 418/233.

30. Ibid.

31. Copleston, *History of Philosophy*, 4:169–71.

32. Ibid., 156.

33. For an interesting philosophical exchange between an atheist and a Christian concerning Pascal's Wager, see: Alan Carter, "On Pascal's Wager; Or Why All Bets Are Off," *Philosophia Christi*, series 2, 3 (2001): 511–16; Douglas Groothuis, "Are All Bets Off? A Defense of Pascal's Wager," *Philosophia Christi* (2001): 517–23; Alan Carter, "Is the Wager Back On? A Response to Douglas Groothuis" *Philosophia Christi* (2002): 493–500; and Douglas Groothuis, "An Unwarranted Farewell to Pascal's Wager: A Reply to Alan Carter," *Philosophia Christi* (2002): 501–8.

34. Morris, *Making Sense of It All*, 119.

35. Davis, *God, Reason and Theistic Proofs*, 164–66.

Chapter 7: Are the Gospels Trustworthy Accounts of Jesus' Life?

1. My six arguments were influenced by Gary R. Habermas's excellent apologetic outline concerning the trustworthiness of the New Testament, in Gary R. Habermas, *The Historical Jesus: Ancient Evidence for the Life of Christ* (Joplin, MO: College Press, 1996), 275–79.

2. J. P. Moreland, *Scaling the Secular City: A Defense of Christianity* (Grand Rapids: Baker, 1987), 135.

3. Habermas, *Historical Jesus*, 54–56.

4. Bruce Manning Metzger, *The Text of the New Testament: Its Transmission, Corruption, and Restoration*, 2nd ed. (New York: Oxford, 1968), 36. Metzger's book contains a wealth of information concerning the New Testament text.

5. Ibid., 67–86.

6. Ibid., 86–92.

7. Habermas, *Historical Jesus*, 54.

8. Moreland, *Scaling the Secular City*, 135.

9. Habermas, *Historical Jesus*, 55.

10. Metzger, *Text of the New Testament*, 38–39.

11. Ibid., 39.

12. Ibid.

13. Ibid.

14. Ibid., 39–42.

15. Ibid., 37–38.

16. Ibid., 42–51.

17. Ibid.; Norman Geisler, *Christian Apologetics* (Grand Rapids: Baker, 1976), 306.

18. Metzger, *Text of the New Testament*, 42–61.

19. Sir Frederic Kenyon, *The Bible and Archaeology* (New York: Harper & Brothers, 1940), 288–89.

20. Habermas, *Historical Jesus*, 187–228; Geisler, *Christian Apologetics*, 322–25; R. T. France, *The Evidence for Jesus* (Downers Grove, IL: InterVarsity, 1986), 19–58.

21. Ibid.

22. See Edwin M. Yamauchi, "Jesus Outside the New Testament: What Is the Evidence?" in *Jesus Under Fire*, gen. eds. Michael J. Wilkins and J. P. Moreland (Grand Rapids: Zondervan, 1995), 207–22.

23. See Donald Guthrie, *New Testament Introduction* (Downers Grove, IL: InterVarsity, 1986), 33–44, 69–72, 98–109, 241–71; Bruce, *New Testament Documents*, 29–61; Craig L. Blomberg, "Where Do We Start Studying Jesus?" in *Jesus Under Fire*, 28–30.

24. Guthrie, *New Testament Introduction*, 33–44; Leon Morris, *The Gospel According to Matthew* (Grand Rapids: Eerdmans, 1992), 12–15.

25. Guthrie, *New Testament Introduction*, 69–72.

26. Guthrie, *New Testament Introduction*, 69; Bruce, *New Testament Documents*, 36–37.

27. Bruce, *New Testament Documents*, 36.

28. Guthrie, *New Testament Introduction*, 98–115.

29. Bruce, *New Testament Documents*, 42–44.

30. Guthrie, *New Testament Introduction*, 241–71; Bruce, *New Testament Documents*, 49–55.

31. See Guthrie's treatment of the authorship of the four Gospels (as cited above).

32. See Craig L. Blomberg, "The Historical Reliability of the New Testament" in William Lane Craig, *Reasonable Faith: Christian Truth and Apologetics* (Wheaton, IL: Crossway, 1994), 214–21.

33. Moreland, *Scaling the Secular City*, 151–54; Norman L. Geisler, "New Testament, Dating of," *Baker Encyclopedia of Christian Apologetics* (Grand Rapids: Baker, 1999), 528.

34. Craig Blomberg, *The Historical Reliability of the Gospels* (Downers Grove, IL: InterVarsity, 1987), 18.

35. Richard Purtill, *Thinking about Religion* (Englewood Cliffs, NJ: Prentice Hall, 1978), 81–93.

36. A. N. Sherwin-White, *Roman Society and Roman Law in the New Testament* (Grand Rapids: Baker, 1978), 186–93.

37. See Craig, *Reasonable Faith*, 284–85.

38. Bruce, *New Testament Documents*, 45–46.

39. Blomberg, *Historical Reliability of the Gospels*, 81–84.

40. Peter Kreeft, *Between Heaven and Hell* (Downers Grove, IL: InterVarsity, 1982), 74.

Chapter 8: Is Jesus a Man, Myth, Madman, Menace, Mystic, Martian, or the Messiah?

1. John Hick, "A Pluralist View," in *More Than One Way? Four Views on Salvation in a Pluralistic World*, eds. Dennis L. Okholm and Timothy R. Phillips (Grand Rapids: Zondervan, 1995), 54–55.

2. John R. W. Stott, *Basic Christianity* (Downers Grove, IL: InterVarsity, 1980), 21–34. Some of Stott's descriptive statements about Jesus (e.g., see p. 27) have been set forth in this work and his scriptural analysis has been expanded.

3. D. A. Carson, *The Gospel According to John* (Grand Rapids: Eerdmans, 1991), 358.

4. Ibid., 394–95.

5. See Stott, *Basic Christianity*, 29–32.

6. See Robert L. Reymond, *Jesus, Divine Messiah: The New Testament Witness* (Phillipsburg, NJ: Presbyterian and Reformed, 1990).

7. Louis P. Pojman, *Philosophy: The Quest for Truth*, 5th ed. (Oxford: Oxford University Press, 2002), 34–37.

8. Two very good books that generally take an abductive approach to the assassination of President Kennedy are William Manchester, *The Death of a President* (New York: Harper & Row, 1967); and Gerald Posner, *Case Closed* (New York: Random House, 1993).

9. Pojman, *Philosophy*, 36. See also my logical tests for worldviews in Hugh Ross, Kenneth Samples, and Mark Clark, *Lights in the Sky and Little Green Men* (Colorado Springs, CO: NavPress, 2002), 156–58.

10. T. Edward Damer, *Attacking Faulty Reasoning*, 4th ed. (Belmont, CA: Wadsworth, 2001), 115.

11. See Josh McDowell, *Evidence that Demands a Verdict: Historical Evidences for the Christian Faith* (San Bernardino, CA: Here's Life, 1979), 103–9. In McDowell's defense, he addresses other possible alternatives in other parts of the book.

12. A. N. Sherwin-White, *Roman Society and Roman Law in the New Testament* (Grand Rapids: Baker, 1978), 186–93.

13. See chapter 7 in this book; see also Gary R. Habermas, *The Historical Jesus: Ancient Evidence for the Life of Christ* (Joplin, MO: College Press, 1996), 107–14.

14. John Warwick Montgomery, *History and Christianity* (Minneapolis: Bethany, 1965), 66–72.

15. R. T. France, *The Evidence for Jesus* (Downers Grove, IL: InterVarsity, 1986), 19–58; Habermas, *Historical Jesus*, 187–228.

16. Stott, *Basic Christianity*, 23–26.

17. C. S. Lewis, *Mere Christianity* (New York: Macmillan, 1952), 55–56.

18. Montgomery, *History and Christianity*, 62–63.

19. Ronald H. Nash, *Worldviews in Conflict* (Grand Rapids: Zondervan, 1992), 153.

20. Montgomery, *History and Christianity*, 64.

21. For an assessment of Father Divine, see Walter Martin, *The Kingdom of the Cults* (Minneapolis: Bethany, 1977), 213–21. For an assessment of David Koresh, see Kenneth Samples, et al., *Prophets of the Apocalypse: David Koresh and Other American Messiahs* (Grand Rapids: Baker, 1994). For an assessment of Jim Jones see Walter Martin's audiotape "Jonestown, the Death of a Cult," available at http://waltermartin.org.

22. Huston Smith, *The World's Religions: Our Great Wisdom Traditions* (San Francisco: HarperCollins, 1991), 143–44.

23. Ibid.

24. James T. Fisher and Lowell S. Hawley, *A Few Buttons Missing* (Philadelphia: Lippincott, 1951), 273.

25. For evangelical Christian assessments of the New Age movement, see Douglas R. Groothuis, *Unmasking the New Age Movement* (Downers Grove, IL: InterVarsity, 1986); Elliot Miller, *A Crash Course on the New Age Movement* (Grand Rapids: Baker, 1989); and John P. Newport, *The New Age Movement and the Biblical Worldview* (Grand Rapids: Eerdmans, 1998).

26. For an evangelical Christian assessment of the "lost years of Jesus" claim, see Ron Rhodes, *The Counterfeit Christ of the New Age Movement* (Grand Rapids: Baker, 1990), 27–56; and Douglas Groothuis, *Revealing the New Age Jesus* (Downers Grove, IL: InterVarsity, 1990), 147–73.

27. Rhodes, *Counterfeit Christ*, 48.

28. Ibid., 44–46.

29. Ibid., 51.

30. Ibid., 47.

31. Ross, Samples, and Clark, *Lights in the Sky*, 147–58.

32. Ibid., 162–63.

33. Ibid., 164.

34. Ibid., 157–58.

Chapter 9: How Can Jesus Christ Be Both God and Man?

1. *Should You Believe in the Trinity?* (New York: Watch Tower Bible and Tract Society, 1989), 16.

2. John Hick, "A Pluralist View," in *More Than One Way? Four Views on Salvation in a Pluralistic World*, ed. Dennis L. Okholm and Timothy R. Phillips (Grand Rapids: Zondervan, 1995), 55.

3. See the Chalcedonian formulation in Alister E. McGrath, *Introduction to Christianity* (Cambridge, MA: Blackwell, 1997), 131–32.

4. Craig A. Blaising, "Hypostatic Union," *Evangelical Dictionary of Theology*, ed. Walter A. Elwell (Grand Rapids: Baker, 1984), 540.

5. For a discussion of the principle of kenosis, see Bruce Milne, *Know the Truth* (Downers Grove, IL: InterVarsity Press, 1982), 146–47; and Wayne Grudem, *Systematic Theology* (Grand Rapids: Zondervan, 1994), 549–52.

6. Milne, *Know the Truth*, 147.

7. Ibid.

8. These points were influenced by Richard A. Muller, *Dictionary of Latin and Greek Theological Terms* (Grand Rapids: Baker, 1985), s.v. "*incarnatio*," "*persona Christi*," and "*unio personalis*"; Grudem, *Systematic Theology*, 529–67; Charles Hodge, *Systematic Theology* (1952; repr., Grand Rapids: Eerdmans, 1986), 2:387–89; Louis Berkhof, *Systematic Theology* (Grand Rapids: Eerdmans, 1938), 321–30.

9. See Murray J. Harris, *Jesus as God: The New Testament Use of Theos in Reference to Jesus* (Grand Rapids: Baker, 1992).

10. For a thorough and substantive treatment of the scriptural support for the incarnation (especially the deity of Christ), see Harris, *Jesus as God*; and Robert L. Reymond, *Jesus, Divine Messiah: The New Testament Witness* (Phillipsburg, NJ: Presbyterian and Reformed, 1990). For a detailed theological exploration of the doctrine of the incarnation, see Benjamin B. Warfield, *The Person and Work of Christ* (Philadelphia: Presbyterian and Reformed, 1950); and Millard J. Erickson, *The Word Became Flesh* (Grand Rapids: Baker, 1991).

11. The outline material in support of the deity of Jesus Christ was partially derived from Harris, *Jesus as God*, 315–17; and John Jefferson Davis, *Handbook of Basic Bible Texts* (Grand Rapids: Zondervan, 1984), 68–74.

12. All of these titles in their appropriate scriptural context support the notion that Jesus Christ is a divine person. See McGrath, *Introduction to Christianity*, 108–15; and Reymond, *Jesus, Divine Messiah*, 44–126.

13. The outline material in support of the humanity of Jesus Christ was partially derived from Milne, *Know the Truth*, 125.

14. D. A. Carson, *The Gospel According to John* (Grand Rapids: Eerdmans, 1991), 126–27.

15. Ron Rhodes, *Christ before the Manger: The Life and Times of the Preincarnate Christ* (Grand Rapids: Baker, 1992), 249–53; Robert M. Bowman Jr., *Why You Should Believe in the Trinity* (Grand Rapids: Baker, 1989), 78–88.

16. Milne, *Know the Truth*, 125–32.

17. The eight ancient christological heresies listed here are taken from H. Wayne House, *Charts of Christian Theology and Doctrine* (Grand Rapids: Zondervan, 1992), 55–56; Milne, *Know the Truth*, 142–45.

18. Norman L. Geisler, "Logic," in *Baker Encyclopedia of Christian Apologetics* (Grand Rapids: Baker, 1999), 427–29.

19. Blaising, "Hypostatic Union," 540.

20. John Calvin, *Institutes of the Christian Religion* 2.13.4, ed. John T. McNeill, trans. Ford Lewis Battles, Library of Christian Classics (Philadelphia: Westminster Press, 1960), 1:481.

Chapter 10: Did Jesus Christ Actually Rise from the Dead?

1. These points were influenced by Wayne Grudem, *Systematic Theology* (Grand Rapids: Zondervan, 1994), 608–23; Charles Hodge, *Systematic Theology* (1952; repr., Grand Rapids: Eerdmans, 1986), 626–30; and Louis Berkhof, *Systematic Theology*, new ed. (originally published in two volumes, 1932 and 1938; Grand Rapids: Eerdmans, 1996), 346–49.

2. For a detailed harmonization of the material from the Gospels relating to the resurrection, see George E. Ladd, *I Believe in the Resurrection of Jesus* (Grand Rapids: Eerdmans, 1975), 79–103; and John Wenham, *Easter Enigma: Do the Resurrection Accounts Contradict One Another?*, 2nd ed. (Grand Rapids: Baker, 1993).

3. For apologetic evidence of the resurrection of Jesus as well as critiques of alternative naturalistic theories, see William Lane Craig, *Knowing the Truth about the Resurrection* (Ann Arbor, MI: Servant, 1988); William Lane Craig, *Reasonable Faith* (Wheaton IL: Crossway Books, 1994), 255–98; William Lane Craig, *Assessing the New Testament Evidence for the Historicity of the Resurrection of Jesus* (Lewiston, NY: Edwin Mellen, 1989); Norman L. Geisler, *The Battle For The Resurrection* (Nashville: Thomas Nelson, 1992); J. P. Moreland, *Scaling the Secular City* (Grand Rapids: Baker, 1987), 159–83; and Peter Kreeft and Ronald K. Tacelli, *Handbook of Christian Apologetics* (Downers Grove, IL: InterVarsity, 1994), 175–98.

4. Sabbatarians of course dispute this claim, but it is a reasonable inference from Scripture; see D. A. Carson, ed., *From Sabbath to Lord's Day* (Grand Rapids: Zondervan, 1982).

5. Moreland, *Scaling the Secular City*, 151–54. Jesus' prophecy of the fall of Jerusalem is reported in the Synoptic Gospels (Mark 13 and parallels), but the author makes no comment indicating that the event had occurred by his time.

6. Craig Blomberg, *The Historical Reliability of the Gospels* (Downers Grove, IL: InterVarsity, 1987), 18.

7. Richard Purtill, *Thinking about Religion* (Englewood Cliffs, NJ: Prentice Hall, 1978), 81–93.

8. A. N. Sherwin-White, *Roman Society and Roman Law in the New Testament* (Grand Rapids: Baker, 1978), 186–93.

9. See Craig, *Reasonable Faith*, 284–85.

10. Blomberg, *Historical Reliability of the Gospels*, 81–84.

11. Edwin M. Yamauchi, "Easter: Myth, Hallucination, or History?", http://www.leaderu.com/everystudent/easter/articles/yama.html (accessed August 23, 2001). Online version was originally published in Edwin M. Yamauchi, "Easter: Myth, Hallucination, or History?", pt. 1, *Christianity Today* 18, no. 12 (March 15, 1974), 4–7; and Edwin M. Yamauchi, "Easter: Myth, Hallucination, or History?", pt. 2, *Christianity Today* 18, no. 13 (March 29, 1974), 12–16.

12. Kreeft and Tacelli, *Handbook of Christian Apologetics*, 185.

13. See Yamauchi, "Easter."

14. This explanatory hypothesis was publicly debated by philosophers Greg Cavin (advocated) and William Lane Craig (critiqued). Available from http://www.leaderu.com/offices/billcraig (accessed January 8, 2002).

15. Craig, *Knowing the Truth*, 110.

Chapter 11: Why Did Jesus Christ Have to Die?

1. The discussion of sin in this chapter was influenced by the following sources: Alister E. McGrath, *Intellectuals Don't Need God and Other Modern Myths* (Grand Rapids: Zondervan, 1993), 133–43; John R. W. Stott, *Basic Christianity* (Downers Grove, IL: InterVarsity, 1980), 61–80; Louis Berkhof, *Systematic Theology*, new ed. (originally published in two volumes, 1932 and 1938; Grand Rapids: Eerdmans, 1996), 74–79; Bruce Milne, *Know The Truth* (Downers Grove, IL: InterVarsity, 1982), 102–14; Wayne Grudem, *Systematic Theology* (Grand Rapids: Zondervan, 1994), 490–514; Robert L. Reymond, *A New Systematic Theology of the Christian Faith* (Nashville: Thomas Nelson, 1998), 440–58; and Millard J. Erickson, *Christian Theology*, 2nd ed. (Grand Rapids: Baker, 1998), 561–658.

2. Erickson, *Christian Theology*, 564–80.

3. Charles Caldwell Ryrie, *Ryrie Study Bible*, expanded ed. (Chicago: Moody, 1994), 2004–2005; Grudem, *Systematic Theology*, 490.

4. Erickson, *Christian Theology*, 781–823.

5. For a brief discussion of the view known as federalism, see Louis Berkhof, *Summary of Christian Doctrine* (Grand Rapids: Eerdmans, 1938), 75–76.

6. Reymond, *New Systematic Theology*, 430–36.

7. John Jefferson Davis, *Handbook of Basic Bible Texts* (Grand Rapids: Zondervan, 1984), 56.

8. Stott, *Basic Christianity*, 75.

9. Reymond, *New Systematic Theology*, 450–53.

10. The discussion of the atonement in this chapter was influenced by the following sources: John Murray, *Redemption: Accomplished and Applied* (1955; repr., Grand Rapids: Eerdmans, 1975); Leon Morris, *The Atonement: Its Meaning and Significance* (Downers Grove, IL: InterVarsity, 1983); Berkhof, *Systematic Theology*, 113–17; Milne, *Know The Truth*, 150–63; Erickson, *Christian Theology*, 761–841.

11. See discussions throughout Murray, *Redemption* and Morris, *Atonement*.

12. See Thomas C. Oden, *The Justification Reader* (Grand Rapids: Eerdmans, 2002).

Chapter 12: Don't All Religions Lead to God?

1. Peter Kreeft, *Fundamentals of the Faith* (San Francisco: Ignatius, 1988), 74–75; R. C. Sproul, *Reason to Believe* (Grand Rapids: Zondervan, 1982), 35.

2. William L. Rowe, *Philosophy of Religion*, 2nd ed. (Belmont, CA: Wadsworth, 1993), 174–75.

3. The most primitive form of Buddhism, "Theravada," is godless in belief.

4. I am referring here to the traditional adherents of Judaism. There are some Jewish groups (Messianic Jews) who retain their Jewish heritage and tradition but embrace Jesus Christ (Yeshua haMashiach) as their Messiah and Savior.

5. Richard L. Purtill, *Thinking about Religion* (Englewood Cliffs, NJ: Prentice Hall, 1978), 105–6.

6. Harold A. Netland, *Dissonant Voices* (Grand Rapids: Eerdmans, 1991), 37.

7. My contrast between Christianity and Hinduism was influenced in part by William Rowe's comparison of the two religions in Rowe, *Philosophy of Religion*, 175.

8. Alister E. McGrath, *Introduction to Christianity* (Cambridge, MA: Blackwell Publishers, 1997), 155.

9. Netland, *Dissonant Voices*, 160.

10. Huston Smith, *The Illustrated World's Religions* (New York: HarperCollins, 1994), 245.

11. Ronald H. Nash, *Is Jesus the Only Savior?* (Grand Rapids: Zondervan, 1994), 55. For a clear and insightful discussion of the formal laws of logic, see Ronald H. Nash, *The Word of God and the Mind of Man* (Grand Rapids: Zondervan, 1982), 103–12; and Ed L. Miller, *Questions That Matter: An Invitation to Philosophy*, 4th ed. (New York: McGraw-Hill, 1996), 31–54.

12. Harold Netland, "Exclusivism, Tolerance, and Truth," *Missiology* 15, no. 2 (April 1987), 84–85.

13. Hick's works on pluralism include John Hick, *God and the Universe of Faiths* (London: Macmillan, 1977); and John Hick, ed., *Problems of Religious Pluralism* (New York: St. Martin's Press, 1985).

14. Hick, *God and the Universe of Faiths*, 140.

15. John Hick, *Philosophy of Religion*, 4th ed. (Englewood Cliffs, NJ: Prentice Hall, 1990), 117–19.

16. Ibid., 119.

17. John Hick, "A Pluralist View," in *More Than One Way? Four Views on Salvation in a Pluralistic World*, ed. Dennis L. Okholm and Timothy R. Phillips (Grand Rapids: Zondervan, 1995), 39.

18. See C. Stephen Evans, *Philosophy of Religion: Thinking about Faith* (Downers Grove, IL: InterVarsity Press, 1985).

19. Nash, *Is Jesus the Only Savior?*, 36.

20. Michael Peterson, et al., *Reason and Religious Belief* (New York: Oxford University Press, 1991), 226.

21. Alister E. McGrath, *Intellectuals Don't Need God and Other Modern Myths* (Grand Rapids: Zondervan, 1993), 119.

22. John Hick, "A Pluralist View," in *More Than One Way?*, 29–59.

23. John Hick, ed., *The Myth of God Incarnate* (London: SCM, 1977). For a philosophical defense of the Christian doctrine of the incarnation, see Thomas V. Morris, *The Logic of God Incarnate* (Ithaca, NY: Cornell University Press, 1986).

24. C. Stephen Evans, *Why Believe? Reason and Mystery as Pointers to God* (Grand Rapids: Eerdmans, 1996), 141.

25. See Douglas Groothuis's critique of Joseph Campbell's book, *The Power of Myth*, in *Christian Research Journal* (Fall 1989): 28; see also Tom Snyder, *Myth Conceptions: Joseph Campbell and the New Age* (Grand Rapids: Baker, 1995).

26. Ibid.

Chapter 13: How Should Christians Respond to the World's Religions?

1. For good general information about these ten world religions, see Huston Smith, *The World's Religions* (New York: HarperCollins, 1991); John A. Hutchison, *Paths of Faith*, 4th ed. (New York: McGraw-Hill, 1991); David S. Noss, *A History of the World's Religions*, 11th ed. (New York: Macmillan, 2002); Lewis M. Hopfe, *Religions of the World*, 8th ed., ed. Mark R. Woodward (Englewood Cliffs, NJ: Prentice Hall, 2000); and Robert S. Ellwood, *Many Peoples, Many Faiths: Women and Men in the World Religions*, 7th ed. (Englewood Cliffs, NJ: Prentice Hall, 2001).

2. Hopfe's book, *Religons of the World*, has some good general information on some of the world's minor religions as well. For an introduction to the basic religions and many bygone religions, see Mircea Eliade, and Ioan P. Couliano, with Hillary S. Wiesner, *The HarperCollins Concise Guide to World Religions* (San Francisco: HarperSanFrancisco, 1991).

3. For a Christian assessment of the world's religions, see Winfried Corduan, *Neighboring Faiths: A Christian Introduction to World Religions* (Downers Grove, IL: InterVarsity, 1998); Dean C. Halverson, gen. ed., *The Compact Guide to World Religions* (Minneapolis: Bethany, 1996); Norman Anderson, ed., *The World's Religions* (Grand Rapids: Eerdmans, 1983); and Norman Anderson, *Christianity and World Religions* (Downers Grove, IL: InterVarsity, 1984). Corduan's book evaluates some of the world's basic or traditional religions as well. For an evaluation of some of the bygone religions (including mystery religions) that competed with primitive Christianity, see Jack Finegan, *Myth and Mystery* (Grand Rapids: Baker, 1989).

4. Karl Barth, *The Doctrine of the Word of God*, vol. 1, bk. 2 of *Church Dogmatics*, ed. G. W. Bromiley and T. F. Torrance (New York: Scribner's, 1956), 303.

5. See Millard J. Erickson, *Christian Theology* (Grand Rapids: Baker, 1998), 177–223.

6. Alister E. McGrath, *Intellectuals Don't Need God and Other Modern Myths* (Grand Rapids: Zondervan, 1993), 116.

7. See Hopfe, *Religions of the World*, 7th ed. (Upper Saddle River, NJ: Prentice Hall, 1998), 6.

8. Halverson, *Compact Guide to World Religions*, 16.

9. Augustine, *Confessions*, trans. R. S. Pine-Coffin (New York: Barnes & Noble, 1992), bk. 3, sec. 1, 21.

10. For a discussion of the proper relationship between general and special revelation, see chapter 3 on revelation in this book.

11. Clinton E. Arnold, *Powers of Darkness* (Downers Grove, IL: InterVarsity, 1992).

12. See the analysis of these passages by Douglas Geivett and W. Gary Phillips, "A Particularist View: An Evidentialist Approach," in *More Than One Way? Four Views on Salvation in a Pluralistic World*, ed. Dennis L. Okholm and Timothy R. Phillips (Grand Rapids: Zondervan, 1995), 230–37; and "Response to R. Douglas Geivett and W. Gary Phillips," by Clark H. Pinnock, 251–55.

13. McGrath, *Intellectuals Don't Need God*, 119.

14. This apologetic strategy is set forth in Curtis Chang, *Engaging Unbelief: A Captivating Strategy from Augustine and Aquinas* (Downers Grove, IL: InterVarsity Press, 2000).

15. See the positions of Alister McGrath, "A Particularist View: A Post-Enlightenment Approach," and R. Douglas Geivett and W. Gary Phillips, "A Particularist View: An Evidential Approach," in *More Than One Way?*, 151–80, 213–45, respectively.

16. Hick's works on pluralism include John Hick, *God and the Universe of Faiths* (London: Macmillan, 1977); John Hick, *Problems of Religious Pluralism*

(New York: St. Martin's, 1985); Paul F. Knitter and John Hick, eds., *The Myth of Christian Uniqueness: Toward a Pluralistic Theology of Religions* (Maryknoll, NY: Orbis, 1987).

17. See the treatment offered in the position by Clark H. Pinnock, "An Inclusivist View," in *More Than One Way?*, 95–123.

18. Ronald H. Nash, *Is Jesus the Only Savior?* (Grand Rapids: Zondervan, 1994), 11–12. Nash critiques both pluralism and inclusivism while defending exclusivism.

19. Karl Rahner, "Christianity and the Non-Christian Religions," *Theological Investigations*, vol. 5 (London: Darton, Longman & Todd, 1966).

20. *The Documents of Vatican II*, gen. ed. Walter M. Abbott, trans. Joseph Gallagher (New York: Guild, 1966), 35; Dogmatic Constitution on the Church, Article 16.

21. Clark H. Pinnock, *A Wideness in God's Mercy: The Finality of Jesus Christ in a World of Religions* (Grand Rapids: Zondervan, 1992).

22. McGrath, "Response to Clark H. Pinnock," in *More Than One Way?*, 131.

23. Robert L. Reymond, *A New Systematic Theology of the Christian Faith* (Nashville: Thomas Nelson, 1998), 1090.

24. Ibid.

25. Pinnock, "Response to John Hick," in *More Than One Way?*, 61–62.

26. See the interaction between McGrath, "Response to R. Douglas Geivett and W. Gary Phillips," and Geivett and Phillips, "Conclusion," in *More Than One Way?*, 256–58, 258–70, respectively; see also John Sanders, *No Other Name: An Investigation into the Destiny of the Unevangelized* (Grand Rapids: Eerdmans, 1992).

Chapter 14: Aren't Christianity and Science Enemies?

1. Bertrand Russell, *Why I Am Not a Christian* (New York: Simon & Schuster, 1957), vi.

2. Ibid., 22–26.

3. See Charles E. Hummel, *The Galileo Connection* (Downers Grove, IL: InterVarsity Press, 1986).

4. See Stanley L. Jaki, *Science and Creation: From Eternal Cycles to an Oscillating Universe* (Scottish Academic Press, 1974); R. Hooykaas, *Religion and the Rise of Modern Science* (Grand Rapids: Eerdmans, 1972); and Stanley L. Jaki, *The Savior of Science* (Grand Rapids: Eerdmans, 2000), 22–48.

5. Eric V. Snow, "Christianity: A Cause of Modern Science?" *Impact* No. 298, April 1998, available from http:www.icr.org/pubs/imp/imp-298.htm, (accessed January 7, 2003).

6. See Charles Van Doren, *A History of Knowledge* (New York: Ballantine, 1991).

7. Alister E. McGrath, *Science and Religion* (Oxford: Blackwell, 1999), 1–2.

8. Ibid., 2–3.

9. Ibid., 1–6; Michael Bumbulis, "Christianity and the Birth of Science," http://bex.nsstc.uah.edu/RbS/CLONE/jaki5.html (accessed January 7, 2003).

10. Nancy R. Pearcey and Charles B. Thaxton, *The Soul of Science* (Wheaton, IL: Crossway, 1994), 17–42; Hooykaas, *Religion and the Rise of Modern Science*, throughout.

11. While Newton was a serious student of the Bible, serious questions have been raised about whether his theological views were thoroughly orthodox. See Hummel, *The Galileo Connection*, 126–48.

12. Hugh Ross, *The Genesis Question*, 2nd ed. (Colorado Springs, CO: NavPress, 2001), 195–97; Hooykaas, *Religion and the Rise of Modern Science*, throughout.

13. Kenneth L Woodward, "How the Heavens Go," *Newsweek*, July 20, 1998, 52.

14. See Michael Peterson, et al., *Reason and Religious Belief* (New York: Oxford University Press, 1991), 210–14.

15. These points were influenced by Delvin Lee Ratzsch, *Science and Its Limits: The Natural Sciences in Christian Perspective* (Downers Grove, IL: InterVarsity, 2000), 36; and Pearcey and Thaxton, *The Soul of Science*.

16. Ratzsch, *Science and Its Limits*, 138.

17. John Polkinghorne, *Science and Creation* (Boston: Shambhala, New Science Library, 1988), 20.

18. Alister E. McGrath, *An Introduction to Christianity* (Cambridge, MA: Blackwell, 1997), 166.

19. Ratzsch, *Science and Its Limits*, 139.

20. For a thorough philosophical critique of naturalism, see *Naturalism: A Critical Analysis*, eds. William Lane Craig and J. P. Moreland (2000; repr., London: Routledge, 2002).

21. See Richard Taylor, *Metaphysics*, 4th ed. (Englewood Cliffs, NJ: Prentice Hall, 1992), 110–12.

22. Greg Bahnsen conveyed this to me in a private conversation in Irvine, California around 1992.

23. Paul Davies, "Physics and the Mind of God: The Templeton Prize Address," *First Things* 55 (August/September 1995): 31–35, http://www.firstthings.com/ftissues/ft9508/davies.html (accessed January 14, 2004).

24. Hugh Ross, *The Creator and the Cosmos*, 3rd ed. (Colorado Springs, CO: NavPress, 2001), 23–29.

25. Ibid., 92.

26. Ibid., 118–21.

27. Paul Davies, *God and the New Physics* (New York: Simon & Schuster, Touchstone, 1983), 189.

28. Hugh Ross, Kenneth Samples, and Mark Clark, *Lights in the Sky and Little Green Men* (Colorado Springs, CO: NavPress, 2002), 171–92.

29. Arno Penzias, "Creation Is Supported by All the Data So Far," in *Cosmos, Bios, Theos*, ed. Henry Margenau and Roy Abraham Varghese (Chicago: Open Court, 1992), 83.

Chapter 15: Doesn't Hypocrisy Invalidate Christianity?

1. T. Edward Damer, *Attacking Faulty Reasoning*, 3rd ed. (Belmont, CA: Wadsworth, 1995), 159–61.

2. Alister E. McGrath, *Introduction to Christianity* (Cambridge, MA: Blackwell, 1997), 75.

3. John Jefferson Davis, *Handbook of Basic Bible Texts* (Grand Rapids: Zondervan, 1984), 94.

4. McGrath, *Introduction to Christianity*, xix–xx.

5. Thomas V. Morris, *Making Sense of It All: Pascal and the Meaning of Life* (Grand Rapids: Eerdmans, 1992), 152.

6. Richard Purtill, *Thinking about Ethics* (Englewood Cliffs, NJ: Prentice Hall, 1976), 136.

7. Ibid.; see Matthew 7:12; Romans 15:1; James 2:14–26.

8. Ibid.

Chapter 16: Don't I Have a Right to Do What I Want with My Own Body?

1. Libertarianism takes various forms (political, economic, philosophical, ethical), but broadly defined it is the view that seeks to maximize individual freedom and liberty.

2. See Anthony A. Hoekema, *Created in God's Image* (Grand Rapids: Eerdmans, 1986), 5–10.

3. Original sin consists of the guilt, moral corruption, and susceptibility to death that were passed on to Adam's progeny after his fall into sin (Genesis 3; Ps. 51:5; 58:3; Rom. 5:12, 18–19; 1 Cor. 15:22).

4. Redemption refers to Jesus Christ's delivering human beings from divine judgment by paying the penalty for human sin himself upon the cross.

5. Thomas V. Morris, *Making Sense of It All: Pascal and the Meaning of Life* (Grand Rapids: Eerdmans, 1992), 25.

6. John Jefferson Davis, *Evangelical Ethics* (Phillipsburg, NJ: Presbyterian and Reformed, 1985), 191.

7. The sovereignty of God (Prov. 21:1; Rom. 9:21; Eph. 1:11) and human responsibility (Matt. 16:27; John 3:36; Rev. 22:12) are both taught in Scripture, sometimes even in the same verse (Luke 22:22; Acts 2:23). For a helpful discussion of this biblical and theological paradox, see Anthony A. Hoekema, *Saved by Grace* (Grand Rapids: Eerdmans, 1989), 3–10.

8. J. P. Moreland and Norman L. Geisler, *Life and Death Debate* (New York: Praeger, 1990), 27. Moreland and Geisler's chapter on abortion presents arguments and critiques on all sides of the abortion controversy (see 25–42).

9. Ibid., 28.

10. Francis J. Beckwith and Norman L. Geisler, *Matters of Life and Death* (Grand Rapids: Baker, 1991), 141.

11. Moreland and Geisler, *Life and Death Debate*, 65. Moreland and Geisler's chapter on euthanasia presents arguments and critiques for both the "Libertarian View" and the "Traditional View" (see 63–82).

12. Ibid., 76–78.

13. See Lynne Ann DeSpelder and Albert Lee Strickland, *The Last Dance: Encountering Death and Dying*, 4th ed. (Mountain View, CA: Mayfield, 1996), 151–60.

14. Question 1 of the Heidelberg Catechism, as cited in *Ecumenical Creeds and Reformed Confessions* (Grand Rapids: CRC Publications, 1988), 13.

Chapter 17: Doesn't Christianity Promote Intolerance?

1. Jewish rabbi, interview by Larry King, "Should Christians Stop Trying to Convert Jews?", *Larry King Live*, CNN, January 12, 2000.

2. Christian exclusivism affirms the following three tenets: (a) Christianity is the one and only true religion, (b) Jesus Christ is the only Savior, and (c) a person must have explicit (conscious) faith in Jesus Christ to be saved (see chap. 13 in this book). For a book-length defense of exclusivism, see Ronald H. Nash, *Is Jesus the Only Savior?* (Grand Rapids: Zondervan, 1994).

3. *American Heritage Dictionary of the English Language*, New College Edition, s.v. "tolerance."

4. Richard L. Purtill, *Thinking about Ethics* (Englewood Cliffs, NJ: Prentice Hall, 1976), 136.

5. See the critique of the political correctness movement in America in Francis J. Beckwith and Gregory Koukl, *Relativism: Feet Firmly Planted in Mid-Air* (Grand Rapids: Baker, 1998), 79–91.

6. These three points of clarification were influenced by Beckwith and Koukl, *Relativism*, 149–50.

7. Ibid., 150.

8. For clear and insightful discussions of the formal laws of logic, see Ronald H. Nash, *The Word of God and the Mind of Man* (Grand Rapids: Zondervan, 1982), 103–12; and Ed L. Miller, *Questions That Matter: An Invitation to Philosophy* (New York: McGraw-Hill, 1996), 31–54.

9. I am referring to the traditional adherents of Judaism with its major denominations being orthodox, conservative, and reformed. There are some Jewish

groups (Messianic Jews) who retain their Jewish heritage and tradition but embrace Jesus Christ (Yeshua haMashiach) as their Messiah and Savior.

10. "Contradictory" religious claims have opposite truth value, meaning that exactly one is true and the other false. Some religious claims could stand in a "contrary" relationship to each other. That is, while they cannot both be true, they could both be false.

11. See the critique of multiculturalism in America in Beckwith and Koukl, *Relativism*, 79–91.

12. Peter Kreeft and Ronald K. Tacelli *Handbook of Christian Apologetics* (Downers Grove, IL: InterVarsity, 1994), 361–83.

13. For a discussion of why denials of truth are self-defeating, see Ronald Nash, *Faith and Reason* (Grand Rapids: Zondervan, 1988), 161–67.

Chapter 18: Isn't Morality Simply in the Eye of the Beholder?

1. Moral relativism comes in at least four different forms; see J. P. Moreland and Norman L. Geisler, *The Life and Death Debate* (New York: Praeger, 1990), 3–6.

2. Ed L. Miller, *Questions That Matter: An Invitation to Philosophy*, 4th ed. (New York: McGraw-Hill, 1996), 403. This book (used as a text for the philosophy classes I teach) is an excellent introduction to the subject. It contains a brief but illuminating discussion of ethical relativism (see 402–6).

3. Richard L. Purtill, *Thinking about Ethics* (Englewood Cliffs, NJ: Prentice Hall, 1976), 3. This book contains a good introductory discussion of ethical subjectivism (see 1–15).

4. Moral philosopher Louis Pojman discusses five reasons why moral relativism is attractive to many today, in Louis P. Pojman, *Ethics: Discovering Right and Wrong* (Belmont, CA: Wadsworth, 1990), 34–37.

5. Miller, *Questions That Matter*, 405.

6. Ibid.

7. Louis P. Pojman, *Philosophy: The Pursuit of Wisdom*, 2nd ed. (Belmont, CA: Wadsworth, 1998), 271. This book (used as a text for the philosophy classes I teach) is an excellent introduction to the subject matter and contains a very good discussion of ethical relativism (see 270–76).

8. Pojman, *Ethics*, 22–23; Miller, *Questions That Matter*, 406.

9. Ronald H. Nash, *Life's Ultimate Questions* (Grand Rapids: Zondervan, 1999), 345–46; Miller, *Questions That Matter*, 406.

10. Nash, *Life's Ultimate Questions*, 345–46.

11. For an analysis of conventionalism, see Moreland and Geisler, *Life and Death Debate*, 3–6; Pojman, *Ethics*, 23–29.

12. Ed L. Miller, *God and Reason*, 2nd ed. (Upper Saddle River, NJ: Prentice Hall, 1995), 95–96.

13. Francis J. Beckwith, "Philosophical Problems with Moral Relativism," CRI Statement DA241 (Christian Research Institute, Rancho Santa Margarita, CA), http://www.equip.org/free/DA241.htm (accessed December 18, 2002). Online version is significantly revised from a chapter originally published in Francis J. Beckwith, *Politically Correct Death: Answering the Arguments for Abortion Rights* (Grand Rapids: Baker Book House, 1993), 19–25.

14. C. S. Lewis, *Mere Christianity* (New York: Macmillan, 1952), 17–21.

15. Pojman, *Philosophy*, 273.

16. Douglas Groothuis, "Confronting the Challenge of Ethical Relativism," CRI Statement DE195 (Christian Research Institute, Rancho Santa Margarita, CA), http://www.equip.org/free/DE195.htm (accessed December 18, 2002), originally published in *Christian Research Journal* 14, no. 1; also published in Douglas R. Groothuis, *Christianity That Counts: Being a Christian in a Non-Christian World* (Grand Rapids: Baker Book House, 1995), 93–96.

17. G. M. Gilbert, *Nuremberg Diary* (New York: Da Capo Press, 1995); Whitney R. Harris, *Tyranny on Trial* (Dallas: Southern Methodist University Press, 1999).

18. J. P. Moreland, *Scaling the Secular City* (Grand Rapids: Baker, 1987), 242–44.

19. As a philosopher, I have metaphysical reasons for preferring Coke over Pepsi: metaphysics is the study of reality, and Coke is, after all, "the real thing."

20. Pojman, *Ethics*, 30.

21. Miller, *Questions That Matter*, 406.

22. The four reasons for supporting moral absolutism listed here are taken from Moreland and Geisler, *Life and Death Debate*, 6–9.

23. See George Mavrodes, "Religion and the Queerness of Morality," in *Rationality, Religious Belief and Moral Commitment: New Essays in Philosophy of Religion*, ed. Robert R. Audi and William Wainwright (Ithaca, NY: Cornell University Press, 1986).

Chapter 19: How Can a Good and All-Powerful God Allow Evil?

1. For good general information about Hinduism, see Huston Smith, *The World's Religions* (San Francisco: HarperCollins, 1991); John A. Hutchison, *Paths of Faith*, 4th ed. (New York: McGraw-Hill, 1991); and David S. Noss and John B. Noss, *A History of the World's Religions*, 9th ed. (New York: Macmillan, 1990). For a Christian assessment of Hinduism, see Winfried Corduan, *Neighboring Faiths: A Christian Introduction to World Religions* (Downers Grove, IL: InterVarsity, 1998); and Dean C. Halverson, gen. ed., *The Compact Guide to World Religions* (Minneapolis: Bethany, 1996).

2. See Karl Menninger, *Whatever Became of Sin?* (New York: E. P. Dutton, 1973); and Kenneth L. Woodward, "What Ever Happened to Sin?", *Newsweek*, February 6, 1995, 23.

3. Richard L. Purtill, *Thinking about Religion* (Englewood Cliffs, NJ: Prentice Hall), 95–109.

4. Historian Stephen Ambrose calls World War II the greatest catastrophe in history in his introduction of the *American Heritage New History of World War II* (New York: Viking, 1997).

5. To see the full context of Hume's statement through his created philosophical dialogue (Philo), see David Hume, *Dialogues Concerning Natural Religion*, ed. Henry D. Aiken (New York: Hafner, 1948), 62–64.

6. For further analysis of the view known as finite godism, see Norman L. Geisler, "Finite Godism," in *Baker Encyclopedia of Christian Apologetics* (Grand Rapids: Baker, 1999), 246–49.

7. Richard Swinburne, "The Problem of Evil," in *Great Thinkers on Great Questions*, ed. Roy Abraham Varghese (Oxford: Oneworld, 1998), 191.

8. Alvin C. Plantinga, *God, Freedom, and Evil* (Grand Rapids: Eerdmans, 1974), 30.

9. Ibid., 12–29.

10. For various Christian responses to the problem of evil, see Norman L. Geisler, *The Roots of Evil* (Grand Rapids: Zondervan, 1978); Michael Peterson, *Evil and the Christian God* (Grand Rapids: Baker, 1982); Ronald H. Nash, *Faith and Reason: Searching for a Rational Faith* (Grand Rapids: Zondervan, 1988), chaps. 13–15; and John M. Frame, *Apologetics to the Glory of God* (Phillipsburg, NJ: Presbyterian and Reformed, 1994), chaps. 6–7.

11. William L. Rowe, "IX. The Problem of Evil and Some Varieties of Atheism," *American Philosophical Quarterly* 16, no. 4 (October 1979), 335

12. This is the form of the quotation that is most frequently used. Although not in the book in exactly this form, the idea is found throughout the book. See Fyodor Mikhailovich Dostoevsky, *The Brothers Karamazov*, trans. Constance Garnett, Great Books, vol. 52 (Chicago: University of Chicago and Encyclopedia Britannica, 1952), bk. 2, chap. 6, 33–34; bk. 2, chap. 7, 40; bk. 5, chap. 5, 136–37; bk. 11, chap. 4, 312; bk. 11, chap. 9, 345.

13. Gerard J. Hughes, "The Problem of Evil," in *Great Thinkers on Great Questions*, ed. Roy Abraham Varghese (Oxford: Oneworld, 1998), 194.

14. See Greg L. Bahnsen, *Always Ready: Directions For Defending the Faith*, ed. Robert R. Booth (Texarkana, AR: Covenant Media Foundation, 1996), 170.

15. Ibid.

16. For introductory articles on the life and thought of Augustine, see Kenneth Richard Sam-

ples, "Augustine of Hippo: From Pagan, to Cultist, to Skeptic, to Christian Sage," pt. 1, *Facts for Faith* no. 5 (Quarter 1 2001): 36–41; Kenneth Richard Samples, "Augustine of Hippo: Rightly Dividing the Truth," pt. 2, *Facts for Faith* no. 6 (Quarter 2 2001): 34–39. These articles can also be accessed on the internet at http://www.augustinefellowship.org.

17. Augustine, *Confessions*, trans. R. S. Pine-Coffin (New York: Barnes & Noble, 1992), bk. 7, sec. 5, 138–39.

18. For a helpful discussion of Augustine's view of evil, see Ed L. Miller, *God and Reason: An Invitation to Philosophical Theology*, 2nd ed. (Upper Saddle River, NJ: Prentice Hall, 1995), 163–70.

19. Augustine, *The Enchiridion on Faith, Hope, and Love*, chap. 11, in the *Basic Writings of Saint Augustine*, vol. 1, ed. Whitney J. Oates (Grand Rapids: Baker, 1992).

20. Frame, *Apologetics to the Glory of God*, 155–56.

21. Augustine, *Enchiridion*, chap. 11.

22. Augustine, *Enchiridion*, chap. 13.

23. See *Augustine through the Ages*, gen. ed. Allan D. Fitzgerald (Grand Rapids: Eerdmans, 1999), s.v. "Evil."

24. For a discussion of the paradoxical nature of God's sovereignty and human responsibility, see Anthony A. Hoekema, *Saved by Grace* (Grand Rapids: Eerdmans, 1989), 5–10.

25. For a helpful discussion of how evil relates to God's providence, see Wayne Grudem, *Systematic Theology* (Grand Rapids: Zondervan, 1994), 322–30.

26. Louis Berkhof, *Summary of Christian Doctrine* (Grand Rapids: Eerdmans, 1938), 46–47.

27. Bahnsen, *Always Ready*, 172.

28. Question 1 and Answer 1 in the Westminster Shorter Catechism, as cited in *Reformed Confessions Harmonized*, ed. Joel R. Beeke and Sinclair B. Ferguson (Grand Rapids: Baker, 1999), 3.

29. Premillennialists believe that evil will finally be removed only after the literal earthly millennium of Christ. For an amillennial interpretation of eschatological events, see Anthony A. Hoekema, *The Bible and the Future* (Grand Rapids: Eerdmans, 1979). For a premillennial interpretation, see George Eldon Ladd, *The Last Things: An Eschatology for Laymen* (Grand Rapids: Eerdmans, 1978).

30. Augustine, *Enchiridion*, chap. 11.

31. C. S. Lewis, *The Problem of Pain* (New York: Macmillan, 1962), 93.

32. Alister E. McGrath, *Intellectuals Don't Need God and Other Modern Myths* (Grand Rapids: Zondervan, 1993), 104–5.

Chapter 20: How Should a Christian Prepare to Give Reasons for Faith?

1. John M. Frame, *Apologetics to the Glory of God: An Introduction* (Phillipsburg, NJ: Presbyterian and Reformed, 1994), 1–3.

2. See Ronald H. Nash, *Worldviews in Conflict* (Grand Rapids: Zondervan, 1992), 16–33.

NAME INDEX

Abraham, 80, 106, 161, 249, 253

Adam, 29, 39, 68, 81, 150–53, 136, 182, 184, 194, 203, 213, 248, 271

Adler, Mortimer J., 161, 261

Adonis, 142

Allah, 176, 190

Ambrose, 93

Apollinarius, 131

apostle Matthew, 96, 100, 141

apostle Paul, 31, 46–47, 53–54, 78, 96–97, 99–100, 110, 127–29, 134, 137, 139–41, 168–69, 175, 177–78, 213, 216, 222, 252–53

apostle Peter, 69, 96–97, 99, 104, 137, 140, 168–69, 176, 257

Aristotle, 92, 188

Arius of Alexandria, 71, 131

Athanasius, 57, 93, 131

Attis, 142

Augustine of Hippo, 18, 25, 75, 174, 189, 239, 246–48, 251, 257, 261, 274

Augustus, Caesar, 169

Bahnsen, Greg L., 36, 195, 246, 262, 271

Barth, Karl, 43

Beckwith, Francis J., 272

Berkhof, Louis, 148, 249, 264

Blomberg, Craig, 40, 100

Bowman, Jr., Robert M., 13, 72, 261, 263–65

Boyle, 190

Bray, Gerald, 52, 63

Brightman, Edgar, 242

Bromiley, Geoffrey, 74

Bruce, F. F., 96, 101, 263

Buddha, 31, 114–15, 129, 176, 183

Burrows, Millar, 91

Bush, George W., 161

Caesar, 53, 92

Calvin, John, 48–49, 132, 263

Campbell, Joseph, 169–70, 269

Camus, Albert, 27

Chrysostom, 93

Clement of Alexandria, 96–97

Confucius, 31, 115, 129, 176

Copernicus, 79, 190

Copleston, Frederick, 80, 82–83

Craig, William Lane, 146, 261–62, 268, 271

Dalai Lama, 114–15, 183

Damer, T. Edward, 109

Davies, Paul, 196, 198

Davis, John Jefferson, 148, 150, 204, 215, 264, 267

Deissmann, Adolf, 93

Demarest, Bruce, 46

Donne, John, 215

Dostoevsky, Fyodor, 245, 273

Einstein, Albert, 202

Erickson, Millard J., 43, 48, 70, 264, 267–69

Eusebius, 96

Eutyches, 131

Evans, C. Stephen, 168, 262, 265

Father Divine, 114, 267

Fisher, J. T., 115

Galileo, 79, 190, 271

Gandhi, 183, 234–35

Göring, Hermann, 234

Green, Michael, 134

Habermas, Gary R., 262, 265

Henry, Carl F. H., 44

Herodotus, 92

Hick, John, 121, 165–70, 180, 269–70

Hippocrates, 211

Hitler, Adolf, 216, 230–31, 234, 241

275

SCRIPTURE INDEX

Subject Index

Kenneth Richard Samples serves as the vice president of theological and philosophical apologetics at Reasons To Believe, a nonprofit and interdenominational organization that provides research and teaching on the harmony of God's revelation in the words of the Bible and the facts of nature. He is also the founder and president of Augustine Fellowship Study Center (AFSC), a nonprofit educational center for philosophical and religious studies, located in southern California.

An experienced teacher and educator, Kenneth has taught courses in philosophy and religion at several colleges and is a lecturer for the master of arts program in Christian apologetics at Biola University in La Mirada, California. He has taught courses in philosophy and religion in adult education programs to employees of Pacific Bell, Chrysler Corporation, General Motors, and the Ford Motor Company. He also has delivered lectures and taught courses in various churches across the nation.

Kenneth worked as senior research consultant and correspondence editor at the Christian Research Institute (CRI) for nearly seven years, where he was a regular co-host of the popular call-in radio program *Bible Answer Man*. He also guest hosted the CRI *Perspective* radio program. An avid speaker and debater, Kenneth has appeared on numerous other radio programs across the country including *Religion On the Line, The White Horse Inn, Talk New York*, and *Issues Etc.* He has participated in debates and dialogues on many diverse topics relating to Christian apologetics, including the existence of God.

Kenneth is the co-author of several books and has published articles in *Christianity Today*, the *Christian Research Journal*, and *Facts for Faith*. He has held memberships in the American Philosophical Association, the Evangelical Philosophical Society, the Evangelical Theological Society, and the Evangelical Press Association. He holds an undergraduate degree in philosophy and social science and a master's degree in theological studies.

Kenneth lives in southern California with his wife, Joan, and their three children.